Journey of
Three Pure Hearts

Book One:
The Doonagore Theft Trilogy

Arthur Cola

Published in 2014 by FeedARead.com Publishing

Copyright © The author as named on the book cover.

First Edition

The author has asserted their moral right under the
Copyright, Designs and Patents Act, 1988, to be identified
as the author of this work.

A CIP catalogue record for this title is available from the British
Library.

Journey of Three Pure Hearts

Book One:
The Doonagore Theft Trilogy

By:
Arthur Cola

Graphics and Illustrations:
John Colaianni

Dedication:

To my wife, Donna, without whose constant love and support of my work this book, as well as my other works, would not have been possible. In particular, her retelling of a family legend inspired the concept for the creation of The Doonagore Theft Trilogy.

**The women who helped to inspire my legendary tales,
Anita, Marilyn, my mother-in-law Ruth Shields, Nancy
and
especially my wife, Donna.**

Table of Contents:

Prologue:

Standing on the coastline of County Clare in western Ireland is a 16th Century Round Tower House with surrounding enclosure walls. It is called Doonagore Castle and lies just above the Village of Doolin. The tower has served as a beacon of sorts for seafarers both legitimate and otherwise for centuries. In fact in 1588 a rather famous invasion took place. The Spanish Armada was headed for Britain proper to destroy its Queen, Elizabeth I of England. Philip II of Spain had his sights set on the British Isles but thanks to the forces of Britain, the Queen herself and the ever changing weather conditions along the British coastline the Armada of bulky ships was destroyed by the smaller and easily steered ships of England which found it far easier to navigate the churned up waters of the Irish Sea when storms brewed. It was the aftermath of that encounter in which Doonagore Castle was involved.

170 ragged survivors found themselves on the west coast of Ireland when they spotted the lone tower piercing the sky above Doolin. By the time they had reached landfall however, the Sheriff of Clare, Boetius Clancy, had also heard of their arrival and had them rounded up and imprisoned in the Tower of Doonagore Castle. All were later hanged and buried in a barrow in a mass grave, known as "Cnocan an Crochaire," as enemies of the Kingdom. Watching the proceedings from the tower was Sir Turlough O'Brien of Ennistsmon, the owner of the Castle and its surrounding lands.

Two and half centuries later Doonagore Castle still dominated the coastline over the Village of Doolin. Only now besides the enclosure walls around the Tower itself a series of short stone walls, often referred to as "famine walls," also broke up the land area around the castle. The walls were built by tenant farmers referred to as "cottier" who were driven from their small parcel of land, usually less than 3 acres, because they could no longer pay their rent nor support their families due to the "potato blight." The blight would become known as the Great Famine of Ireland or "an Gorta Mor." It lasted from 1845-1852 and devastated the staple crop on which these tenant farmers depended to survive. Many of these so called "famine walls" had no purpose other than to give work to the peasants who got a bowl of soup or piece of bread for their work. The people of County Clare were the most severely impacted by the famine with County Mayo coming in a close second in devastation and the resulting starvation and diseases related to malnourishment and exposure to the elements. The latter resulted when they lost their one room stone cottages with thatched roofs upon eviction due to either non-payment of rent to the often absentee landlord or a decision made by the landlord's "middleman" to use the land for sheep grazing rather than growing a grain crop. The potato crop was mainly used to sustain the tenant farmer's family and was often their only source of food. The "potato blight" ended that and their capability to pay the rent.

This "middleman system" which had evolved in the managing of the landlord's property was subject to exploitation of the tenants, who were 80% Catholic. The agent of the landlord was usually Protestant. And even though the Emancipation Act of 1829 was almost twenty years in force, the freedom to worship as one chose, that is openly, was still a relatively new right and not universally enjoyed. In addition to this animosity between the Catholic tenant farmer and the Protestant "agent of the landlord" that agent or middleman subdivided the land which he leased from the landlord into such small parcels so as to exploit as much rent as was possible from the holdings. This however resulted in eviction should a crop fail or the land be turned into grazing fields.

This practice of land use in Ireland was put under scrutiny in 1843 under the chairmanship of the Earl of Devon. In 1845, at the very beginning of the recorded "potato blight's" full impact, the report on how the laws were enforced with regard to the occupation of the land in Ireland was issued. The Earl reported that "It would be impossible to adequately describe the privations which they (the Irish labourer and his family) habitually and silently endure…in many districts their only food is the potato, their only beverage water…their cabins are seldom a protection against the weather…a bed or a blanket is a rare luxury…and nearly in all, their pig and a manure heap constitute their only property." Devon and his commission concluded that the Irish patiently endured suffering greater than any other country in Europe.

It is against this backdrop of privation and the "potato blight" that our story begins as three young people face the devastation of their land, their right to worship and their hope to seek a better life in a new land across the sea. This is a fictional account of life and love but one which reflects the 19th Century in Ireland and in the United States.

**Cromwell Fortress Ruin: Inishbofin Harbor
Ireland**

Chapter One: Victoria Regina

Queen Victoria was enjoying the relative isolation of what she called Osborne House on the Isle of Wight which was still under construction. Her husband, Prince Albert was busily overseeing each detail as its final façade was being constructed in the style of an Italian Palazzo. That relative informality, so unusual in London at Buckingham Palace or Windsor Castle, was to the Queen most welcome indeed.

She was seated in the lower garden of the estate next to an oval fountain when the news was brought to her as was custom in a black box. She removed the folder containing the reports she expected but found instead a request from the Corporation of Dublin. It was in fact a deputation of citizens of Dublin which included the Duke of Leinster, the Lord Mayor, Lord Cloncurry and Daniel O'Connell and was sent by the Lord Lieutenant of Ireland to Her Majesty, Victoria Regina, the Queen Empress. The Queen gave little notice to the construction workers milling about her as she opened what was then called a "memorial" or request. In this case it was one to recall Parliament into an early session for the purpose to recommend the requisition of some public money for public works, especially railways in Ireland. The request was dated 1845. Not long before receiving the request to convene Parliament she had discussed with Albert another communiqué in which her Royal Commission chaired by the Earl of Devon stated that the living conditions in Ireland were deplorable and the failure of crops and land use in Ireland needed revision.

Now she was reading that if "Ireland was indeed an integral part of the realm, the common exchequer of both islands should be used, not to give alms, but to provide employment on public works of general utility."

She folded the paper gently and looked up with an almost serene look and yet with a questioning glance. Prince Albert, upon whom she greatly relied for advice was summoned as was her Council of Advisors. The question was to address the issue of land use in Ireland and what seemed to be a growing "blight" on its farmers due to a potato crop failure. One thing she had already decided upon before consulting anyone. She wanted a firsthand look at Ireland for herself. That would take place but not until 1849 at the height of the "potato blight" caused by a crop disease which affected all of Europe called Phytophethora infestans. But nowhere was it felt so intensely as in Ireland. There because of the land use or misuse as the case may be Tenant farmers had come to depend on their potato crop for the sole support of their families. In the meantime the British Relief Association was formed to address the effects of the growing issue of famine in Ireland.

Across the Irish Sea and on the west coast of Ireland some two years later a slender youth clutched onto the rocky cliff overlooking a shallow harbor on Inishbofin, an island off the western coast of Ireland. As yet the relief efforts were in infantile formation and the blight itself was now a fact of life. Still the youth persevered despite his long thick black hair gathering in clumps and matting in his face causing his difficult climb to be even more perilous. The result of his hair and for that matter the rest of him being sopping wet was that a mist like spray was being forced upwards onto the cliff-side as the waves of the incoming tide were now nipping at his feet. Those almost bare feet were covered with a cloth like sandal for leather shoes were something only

14

people of means could afford for children. Most of the time children actually ran about barefoot. This foot issue made his precarious climb and route all the more dangerous as well as uncomfortable and unsteady. And yet the lad continued his climb up to a ledge which would serve as a pathway to his destination.

The wind continued to whip up the normally calm waters of the small harbor which this finger of rocky cliff seemed to embrace. The lad knew that once the high tide came in that the tip of the finger of rock would be cut off from the rest of the Inishbofin harbor area. Thus he plodded on, while grabbing onto the cliff-side's rock back wall, until he finally made it to that path like ledge. Leaning against the jagged wall to catch his breath, his already ragged shirt caught hold of a sharp edge of one of the rocks protruding along the pathway. Another tear resulted, another pathway for the chilly air to cause a shiver down his spine. He shook off the effects of the newly formed shredded gateway to his pale bare skin. The lad carefully lifted the faded material from the pointy rock and looked to his left.

There at the tip of the finger protecting the harbor entrance were the ruins of a 12th century fortress and Church. Its limestone walls with carved out windows were all that remained. Rising out of the Church like structure, given its peaked front and back walls and arched window areas in the Gothic style, a narrow ribbon of smoke made a steady upward movement into the clearing sky. The lad seeing the rising smoke began to chide himself for not having left for the ruins earlier, but that would have been most difficult as he had chores to perform and care to give his ailing mother while his father tried desperately to save a couple of the potato plants so that they might mature. Little did anyone realize that this blight which was now in its third season would go on for another three years.

So it was to backbreaking work that the lad's father went to try and save the garden set aside to support the family on the leased acre of land on which his father was a tenant farmer. That lease was created by the middleman or overseer of the property owned by what locals called the absentee landlord. In point of fact the lad had never seen the actual landlord in his twelve years of life. The leasing of the plot of land was an agreement between the farmers and the landlord but overseen by the landlord's representative. In that lease the farmer would raise a grain crop or sheep for export and the garden area was where they could grow potatoes which in Ireland had become the sole food supplement for the family of the tenant farmer. The lad had indeed seen the overseer many times when he came to collect the crop or announce that the grain crop would cease to be planted and the land would now be used to graze sheep. That latter alternative was the case in Inishbofin. With its rocky soil and rugged terrain it became financially more profitable for the overseer to use the land for sheep but that meant less money for the farmer as he usually had just a few sheep to raise and shared a common pasture which in itself was quite barren. And yet until the blight the family had managed to survive though in a most primitive state. Now going into a third year of crop failure the situation for the tenant farmers was becoming desperate indeed. Even the luxury of burning a candle was soon to be a fond memory. There was no money to buy new candles or supplies to make them. The exporting of the sheep for food or wool was profitable for the overseer and the landlord. What the farmer received for his toil was the use of the land and a plot to grow what he could to sustain his family. There was the cottage as well. The thatched roof edifice hardly kept out the elements and that is why the lad was running late for his rendezvous. His mother had taken ill.

The lad's stomach began to grumble as the digestive juices attempted to reduce the couple of slices of potato for absorption into the boy's scrawny body. That soup which was nothing more than hot water with a potato in it would serve as the family's only meal of the day. She cooked it over the hearth which was now their only source of heat and light. As for oil lamps, those would be found only in the homes of the land owners or the overseers.

The wind shifted causing that stream of smoke emitting from the ruin to waft toward the ledge on which the lad now stood under a small gush of water flowing down the rocky slope. The lad thought it provided an opportunity to wash off the mud splattered, hardened and crusted over his clothes and body after several days of chores in the field. He wanted to look his best for the arranged meeting in the ruin; so he scrubbed his tattered pants and shirt on a smooth rock and then rubbed his skin violently to remove the dirt which had become muddy. His rib cage clearly showed the ravages of lack of nourishment. The relief funding had yet to arrive on Inishbofin. Scrawny though he was he was better off than many of the children on the island. So many of his friends had taken ill or died that a special children's cemetery had been created. Would he soon join them? That was a question he didn't want to answer and that's why he made his way toward the ruin on the finger tip of the harbor.

As he ran his fingers through his long black hair so as to remove any clumps of mud which remained, the smoke floated toward the ledge on which he stood. His nostrils picked up the sweet smell of peat which was quite familiar to him and brought him thoughts of family gathered around the hearth in happier days sharing stories of the Island and folklore tales of how Inishbofin got its name of "White Cow." His grandfather would sit with the lad on his knee and tell the tale of how two fishermen were lost at sea and landed on the shore of the island. As they searched for signs of life they came upon an old woman carrying a stick and guiding a white cow along a path toward a lake. That lake was named Loch Bo Finne and from it the woman and the cow would come forth to warn of impending danger. The tale was told in the ancient language of course, one which the outsiders could not understand readily. The lad having stepped under the cascading stream, letting the cold water splash over him now wrung out his clothes as best as he could and slipped his pants over his boney legs and up to his waist. He tied the rope securely so that they would stay in place as there was little to hold them up otherwise. All the while he wondered why the old woman had not come to warn the people of Inishbofin of the landlord's overseers whose policies made it so difficult to support a family.

"And what about the crop failures?" he thought.

Certainly the impending disaster of the blight was worthy of a warning of some kind. He slipped his shirt over his narrow shoulders and rib cage. It hung like a wet rag on a clothes line but at least it was clean. More of the sweet smell reached him. It was from a peat fire for sure. He was acutely aware of that as peat was the source of heat and light in the family's stone cottage. He would help his father cut peat from the village bog and haul it home. He and his father as well as the other farmers were allowed to harvest peat as part of the lease agreement. And so it became a monthly chore which at least brought him into contact with other boys around his own age for there was, as yet, no formal school house on the island. The fragrance filled his nostrils again and he again felt that sense of family being about him. It was because of that love of family that he was about to do once again what was done before in the ruins on the fingertip of Inishbofin Harbor. What he was about to do was the last hope for him and his family.

The ledge on which the lad traveled was getting narrow as it approached a crevice which split the slope. On the other side the rocky surface was flatter. Soon that crevice and low lying area would be covered with the waters of the incoming tide. This would isolate the ruins from the rest of the island until morning when low tide set in and the waters would recess from the low lying surface leading to the ruins. He leapt across the crevice without much difficulty having followed this route in keeping this appointment on a regular basis since he was ten years old. He landed on the uneven surface of rock, slipped and found himself in a puddle of sea water. A curse from his young lips ensued, not a terribly horrific one. It was more of a "Saints preserve us" type of exclamation which was followed by a quick glance toward the source of the peat smoke rising in the center of the former chapel building. Picking himself up and checking for muddy residue which he had so laboriously sought to eliminate in the hasty cold shower under the waterfall stream, he shook his head and began the final leg of the journey. As he began he surveyed the entire landscape of the harbor from his vantage point.

Directly in his vision was a centuries old mast of a ship which had sunk in the harbor when it entered at low tide and struck a huge boulder. It was, according to his grandfather who had passed onto glory just over a year ago, a pirate ship.

"To be sure," granddad would say. "It belonged to the O'Malley clan which sailed along the western coast of Ireland searching for vessels to intercept and to loot seaside towns. Their claim to fame was none other than the pirate queen herself, Gracie O'Malley."

The lad smiled as he gazed upon the decaying mast worn by tides coming in and out for some two hundred years. *"Aye, but that was a great tale,"* the lad thought as he created the vision of the captured Pirate Queen being brought before Queen Elizabeth I of England. *"I wish I could have been there when the Queen and Gracie met face to face."* 'Twas at that meeting that one of his father's favorite terms was created when he was told the same tale. That happened when Her Majesty questioned Grace about her pirating ways and the conditions of western Ireland. She ended with the command that the Queen of Pirates should not feed the Queen of England any **Blarney**; that is exaggerated tales.

The lad laughed quietly and almost gave a skip as he turned to quickly reach his goal. How many times had his father given a similar directive when he returned home at a late hour after his scheduled rendezvous, the purpose of which his parents knew nothing at all. Then he became somber as he realized that after this day's meeting it may be too late for him to return home until morning.

"Oh, mi Ma will be upset and praying on the beads that I might not be dead," he spoke aloud but softly.

The lad began to fancy himself as a pirate of sorts as he approached the site for his clandestine meeting with someone who just a couple of decades ago, was in prison. He too would seek his fortune, save his family and buy that plot of land as poor as it was for them. And if that meant prison then he was willing to accept the consequences for his act of meeting with an ex-convict, who until the Act of Emancipation of 1829 sat in a prison cell waiting to be deported to Australia or Bermuda.

With the passage of that act by Parliament the convict was freed of the sentence of exile. After centuries of being forbidden to own land or even live within 5 kilometers of a town, he being a Catholic could once again sit in the British Parliament and practice the faith openly. However, Emancipation or not, most of the 80% of the Catholic population lived in abject poverty. And that state worsened with the onset of the blight as it took hold on the potato crop two decades later.

On the tiny island called Inishbofin that Act of Emancipation had hardly been understood let alone experienced. Within the 7th century ruins of a Church founded by St. Colman the Catholic population would gather in secret to worship. Rarely could a priest be concealed and sneaked onto the island. Even so on occasion through the efforts of the Pope and through Spain's help one was smuggled in now and then. The priest would arrive aboard a pirate ship which even in the 19th century still threatened those on the seas off western Ireland, celebrate the Mass and hastily be brought to other villages along the coastline.

It was with that sense of history and swashbuckling folklore that the lad came to an abrupt stop in the stone archway which served as the threshold of the Church ruin. At the opposite end of the ruin sat a man warming his hands over the peat fire which was the source of that smoky yet sweet fragrance which had brought on those family history lessons. The shadow of the back wall cast a pall over the black clad man. His flame red hair served to offer the only sense of vibrant color to the rather bleak scene of shadow and glowing embers. Next to the man, resting on a flat stone was a black leather sack. The man, having revived his hands over the glowing peat, turned slightly and opened the sack. He withdrew a black leather bound book. Its only ornamentation consisted of gold letters which read "Holy Bible" and an emblazoned gilded Cross below the words.

His now more nimble fingers began to page through the book of Scriptures until he came across the passage for which he was searching. Having found the verse he obviously sought he pulled a thin red ribbon attached to the binding and placed it across the page. Closing the Bible, he then looked up. The glow of the peat fire illuminated his stubbly facial hair which matched the flame red of his thick head of hair. The stubble somewhat concealed a scar across his right cheek. That he had received when arrested some twenty years ago when he was but a young man of twenty-two. It seems when arrested those who did so mocked his faith and struck him to test his knowledge of Scripture as to a disciple being required to turn the other cheek. The ring on the hand of his captor cut into his fair skin resulting in a garish bloody cut. His green eyes darted about the ruin until he noticed the slender figure pausing under the threshold. The lad smiled having recognized this face which was highlighted by the fading rays of daylight as well as that of the small fire contained in a ring of stones. It was indeed the man with whom the lad had been sneaking away to meet for two years. This was his teacher, friend and priest come to meet with him once again.

"Hi Father Thomas," the lad called out.

The priest smiled gently and waved to the lad to come to him. He pulled out a pocket watch and glanced at the time, knowing that it was well past the usual time for their meeting. He motioned to the lad for quiet as the term "Father" was still rather shocking to him after having been called so many things other than such a familiar term. Even after almost two decades of Emancipation for Catholics he was still nervous about being publicly recognized. His memory of being released from Lynch's Castle prison in Galway where he had been taken upon his capture on a small boat headed for the Aran Islands was still quite vivid. Back then he was a young man and newly ordained returning from Rome in 1828 as an Augustinian Priest in that year before Emancipation. The Prior had sent Father O'Malley back to his homeland to minister secretly. It wasn't long before he was hunted down for preaching and celebrating the Sacraments in another harbor village by the name of Doolin in County Clare. Authorities were dragging their feet regarding the release of priests who were considered to be undermining the authorities. The few remaining priests included he, Thomas O'Malley, of the very clan which had achieved fame for pirating and that was reason enough to continue to hold him.

It was decided to transfer those that remained to the Aran Islands just outside Galway Bay and isolated as to be able to keep a close watch on their activities. Upon arrival on Inishmor Thomas O'Malley built a small Church across from the ruins of the Seven Churches, so named as to recall the monastic community which for centuries had run not only a Holy place for worship but also a school which attracted young people from across Europe until Oliver Cromwell finally destroyed it during the English Civil War two hundred years earlier. Thomas O'Malley felt a connection to the ancient site founded by scholars sent from Rome as he had been. For almost twenty years he ministered to the struggling people of Inishmor, Inishmaan, and Inisheer who made their living by fishing in the coastal waters off Galway and the Atlantic Ocean itself. Some were also farmers trying to raise sheep and grow what crops they could on the soil originally created by bringing sand and sea plants out of the sea to be placed over the limestone surface covering the island. As it became more accepted to practice the faith O'Malley began to be an accepted figure on the three islands comprising the Aran Islands. He would travel from island to island each week-end to celebrate Mass for the farmers and fishermen, the latter being the main source of income and food for the residents of the islands. On one of those journeys, he hitched a ride on a fishing vessel and was caught in a storm. These quickly brew off the Atlantic Ocean. The fishing boat was blown off course up the coast of western Ireland. As the tiny fishing vessel was tossed on the open sea Father Thomas O'Malley prayed the Holy Rosary for the crew as they desperately brought in sail, so the wind would not rip them completely apart and thus prevent their use when the winds finally subsided. The Captain of the boat, one called Eoin O'Flaherty, shouted out orders as the waves came crashing over the side of the vessel threatening to capsize it. His crew was comprised of his two sons and a son-in-law. Each of them drenched to the skin despite their somewhat water resistant woolen sweaters knitted with a family pattern so as to identify them should they be drowned. At one time it was the O'Flaherty family who along with the O'Brien clan had held reign over the islands until the time of Queen Elizabeth I. During the English Civil War all their power was taken when Oliver Cromwell subdued the island. From then until the 1950's the islands would evolve very little from what could be seen on that tiny fishing vessel.

The O'Flaherty boys and the O'Brien lad were having a dickens of a time trying to bring in the sail. The boom shifted and knocked Adam O'Brien onto the praying priest huddled along the storage hold for the caught fish.

Apologizing fervently the lad added, "'Tis a wild storm it is Father, lost mi footing a bit. But she won't be getting the best of me." Then with a reddened face he turned into the wind and shouted, "Pog mo thon, ye beast."

The fact that the lad had just addressed the storm as a person so as to say that it should kiss his ass did not make the priest flinch in the least. In fact he slapped young Adam's back and helped the young man to his feet as he made it known that he did not build his Church nor endure prison to be drowned in the wilds of the ocean. And with that he pocketed the beads and went to help lash the sail into place. Once accomplished, the vessel, though still being tossed about, was no longer "leaning to" so far as to capsize.

The Captain held tightly to the tiller along with the eldest of his three sons, Aedan, a sturdy lad with arms which might well tow the boat onto a shore without help or so he would want you to think. They did however lend necessary steadiness to keep the tiller firm. After nearly the greater part of the day being spent righting the boat and fearing that their end was near the winds subsided as quickly as they appeared and the black clouds parted letting through rays of sunshine. The waves of the sea became such as to rock the vessel as one would a child in a cradle.

All save the Captain collapsed on the deck to breathe a sigh of relief and give thanks to God for their safety. 'Twas while the crew and priest lay on the deck that Captain O'Flaherty began to shout, "land ho." Scrambling to their feet the youngest of them, one called Aengus O'Flaherty parted his carrot red hair which lay matted across his face.

He was named after a prehistoric chieftain who had built a fortress on the Western Cliffside of Inishmor not far from the village of Kilmurvy. He thought himself to be a warrior more than a fisherman. But like any of those souls on the rocky islands there was little hope to ever leave what was home to them. This was especially true now that the blight had virtually devastated most of western Ireland. They at least could fish and sheep had been brought to the island to supplement the meager crops.

Aengus began to shout, "Dadai, I can see some kind of fort, a ruin of one. There's someone on the wall waving at us."

The youngest son was quite correct in his observation. There was indeed someone straddling the fortress's ruin of a wall facing the sea. It was a boy of around ten years in age, the very lad who would befriend the priest and be educated by him. He was doing more than offering a greeting, however. He was frantically motioning them to follow the watery passage away from the ruin so as to avoid partially and totally submerged rocks. The lad, who had rarely seen such a vessel even though it was quite modest in size to be sure, instinctively knew that it was too large to sail over the rocks surrounding the fingertip of the harbor of Inishbofin. And so he was directing them to steer to the left of the Cromwellian Promitory Fortress ruin, which had been built over the ruins of an even older church.

Thus did the thirteen year old Aengus found himself being the navigator and taking signals from a boy, even younger than him, from atop a rock pile which once was a fortress wall.

As the boat sailed closer the lad jumped up and followed along the wall all the while motioning and shouting to them as to where the safest entrance would be to the harbor. With hands on his hips the raggedly dressed lad with wind swept coal like hair then took both hands from his waist and gestured to an area just to the left of the sunken pirate ship the mast of which was quite evident to the fishermen as well as the priest. Captain O'Flaherty ordered that the anchor be dropped and signaled to the lad that all was well.

"'Tis grand," the lad shouted. "Welcome to Inishbofin."

The almost adult style of the language impressed O'Malley and the crew. They shouted back and began to untie the dingy, which was rather beaten up from the storm. This they used to row to the lad, who was now on the rocky ledge on which the fortress ruin stood. The boy in him was jumping up and down with excitement as the five men tied the dingy to a rock and began to climb up toward the lad. The storm had moved off to the east its line of dark clouds could still be seen in the distance. But over the harbor area there was bright sunshine and welcomed it was by the sopping wet men of the little fishing vessel named "Eoghanacht" after the village where the Ruin of the Na Seacht dTeampaill (Seven

Churches) is located as well as Father O'Malley's new church.

It was, however, the man in him (despite the rags covering those parts of his frail frame which needed to be clothed stating otherwise) that received the five burly men onto the ruin of what he identified to be his castle.

"Indeed mi lord, we are honored to be welcomed by such nobility," began Captain O'Flaherty.

"Aye, to be sure," chimed in the sons as they offered a slight bow.
"But most of all we owe ye a debt of gratitude," Father O'Malley started to say when he noticed an inquisitive look on the boy's face. He thought upon his words and corrected them. "That is, we give ye thanks for your help in getting our boat into the harbor safely."

The lad beamed his pleasure and understanding. Those words of **debt** and **gratitude** had been a bit over his head so to speak.

"If you would be so kind as to follow me, I have a fire ready," the lad said as the men looked at each other with surprise and followed obediently into the very church ruin where the lad would meet with Father O'Malley over the next two years.

As they huddled around the fire the lad made note of how wet they were and that a good fire was what they needed to warm themselves up after what appeared to be such a dangerous journey in a storm. It was then that the Captain had to admit that they were not on a journey but rather just blown off course from the Aran Islands fishing waters. The news that they were not on an adventure did not disappoint the boy. He inquired as to who they were and who their people were. The O'Flaherty and O'Brien names brought a smile to the lad's face for even on Inishbofin they had heard of the noble families from the old days. But when Thomas O'Malley introduced himself the boy could not be subdued within that fragile body any longer. He began to shout and jumped up to point back into the harbor and spew out the tale of the Pirate Queen Gracie O'Malley and how her people sailed the waters to bring vengeance on the ships which took away the goods grown and created in Ireland.

"And that is a mast of an O'Malley pirate ship, sir," the boy concluded. "Lost at sea they were just like you. Alas they had no one to tell them where the rocks are."

The lad was so excited now that he hadn't noticed the other men motioning to him, well more like pointing to Thomas O'Malley, who was blushing at the story being excitedly told. Captain O'Flaherty coughed loudly to gain the boy's attention.

"Mi lord, may I introduce you to Father Thomas O'Malley who is not a pirate but sent from the Holy Father in Rome to preach the Good News."

The lad made a sign of the Cross quickly from head to heart to each shoulder. "Father O'Malley, I had no idea that you were a priest. I mean you look like one of them." He pointed to the fishermen. "I just thought…."

Father O'Malley placed his hand on the boy's shoulder and smiled, while explaining that he was indeed a "fisher of men." He added how honored he was to be placed in such esteem as that of the Pirate Queen herself. Then he finally got to ask a question.

"And now young sir, would you honor all of us by telling us the name of the gentleman who knows of such tales and rescues seamen from the storm?"

"Aye, if you insist. It's just a common name on Inishbofin. Mi name is James Richard Shields."

Famine Era Cottage on Present Day Inishbofin

Chapter Two: "Mi Lord's" Education.

"'Tis not a common name Master James Shields," Father O'Malley began. "The bearer of the name is courageous and honorable and has saved these lads from peril the likes of which my ancestor's ship met in this very harbor."

The Captain and crew readily echoed the priest's remarks as they placed their knitted sweaters on flat rocks near the peat fire in an effort to dry them completely. The words of honor spoken of course made young James Shields most proud that he could assist them. The five men and the lad sat around the fire wondering in silence what would come next. The men were already internally plotting the course which would return them to the Aran Islands. The Priest felt the need to present himself and the crew to the townspeople and to the parents of James. It was clear from the lad's responses that they had no priest who visited on a regular basis. Other young ones like James had parents who sought to have them prepared to receive their Holy Communion. So many had already become ill from the lack of proper nourishment and others had passed on to "heaven" as the lad told them without ever having received the sacrament.

The men looked upon the skinny body of the lad and knew well how serious the blight had become. Only the fact that they had a fishing vessel had saved them from a similar fate. And so Aengus being moved by the stories had a thought.

"Dadai," he began. "Before the storm hit we already had some fish in the hold…."

He wasn't given time to finish his thought before his brothers caught hold of it and suggested that they bring their catch to the townspeople in recognition of James saving them from the rocks. The lad's eyes just about jumped from its sockets with joy.

The Captain sought to gain knowledge of the people's plight and soon realized that it was quite severe given that even the fishing was limited due to the lack of vessels and those being owned by the landlord thus requiring that most of the catch had to go for payment of the vessels. It was decided to row back to their fishing boat, gather their catch and bring it to shore. The decision having been made, the sweaters were once again put on and the fire put out.

James watched in awe as if he were seeing the heroes of Celtic legends come alive as the sweaters were pulled over their muscular bodies and broad shoulders. Not since he was a wee lad had he ever seen such physiques on full grown men. The heroes of the tales like Dagda and Lugh came to mind as the fishermen noticing the awe struck lad further dramatized their strength with flexing of muscles and a bit of combative jabs at each other. While all this took place the lad asked himself a question.

"Could it be possible that one day I too might grow into such a man whose strength and skill would make my family proud?"

As if they could read the gapping lad's mind the Captain pounded a beat with rock on stone. The fishermen and Priest began to sing a song which had been newly written. It talked about justice and starvation, saving the lives of children and having hope instead of despair. It was more like a poem which spoke of the effects of the famine and leaders such as Daniel O'Connell.

> The blight did come
> As if in the stealth of night.
> It ravaged the land,
> So no man's hand held even
> A loaf nor spud.
> The Wee ones perished before our eyes.
> Hope vanished.
> Hearts grew in despair.
> Then a voice cried out
> To save the land called Erin.
> Danny Boy claimed the Tenants' rights.
> Keep the crops for the homeland was his plea.
> For Ireland did he bring back the visionary sea.
> So raise a glass to Danny Boy.
> Ahoy there lads hoist them high.
> 'Tis O'Connell himself who
> Brought back the hope.

The bugged out eyes of the lad, James Shields, glistened with joy. For nearly three years the singing had not been heard, save perhaps at Christmas time. His smile grew as the son with the arms of steel, Aedan, took hold of him raising him up in one swoop to sit upon his shoulders. James laughed as he hadn't for such a very long time. That hope, of which the fishermen sang, filled his heart though he barely understood the feeling.

"Aedan, sir, I can walk. I'm no wee one," James protested, though in truth he rather was enjoying the perch upon which he sat.

"Mi Lord," Aedan responded. "The Lord of this castle deserves to be carried before his subjects whom he has saved."

The wide grin gave notice that the wee lord of the castle was quite ready to accept the honor. Amidst shouts and cheers for James' good health the lad was brought outside the Cromwellian Fortress walls down the rocky slope to the waiting dingy. The little rowboat stood waiting though a bit battered from the storm and rocked slightly upon gentle waves. Now James had never been on a boat before and was filled with a bit of apprehension. He shuddered as he was lowered onto the arms of Father O'Malley who stood somewhat wobbly upon the boat's leaky bottom. In point of fact its entire bottom surface was now water covered.

As Aedan handed the lad down to Father Michael he could sense the lad's body becoming tense. Staying in good form and acting out his role, Aedan spoke.

"Fear not mi Lord, the craft is sea worthy for our purpose." Then addressing the priest he added. "'Tis a bit of work we need to be doing while here, I think."

All agreed that some modest attention was needed as they boarded. O'Malley held unto the lad keeping him steady as he placed him at the bow of the dingy. Aengus shoved the boat off and jumped aboard as the Captain stood at the bow holding onto James' shoulder.

"For the offering of a good measure to ye lad...I mean mi Lord."

The lad smiled up to the Captain and Priest alongside him with oar in hand with Aedan holding the other.

"To the ship," the Captain ordered most authoritatively for the pleasure of James.

For his part, the lad "put on a brave face" as his mother taught him to do in the face of danger, uncertainty and when his stomach hurt for lack of nourishment. It helped to conceal the effects of his queasy stomach and that happening with only a few strokes of the oar to move them along.

In a matter of a few minutes, the priest was lifting James up to the starboard side of the fishing vessel and Aedan was pulling the lad aboard, thus avoiding a rope ladder slung over the side for the others to use. As for the weathered vessel itself, it was a tiny boat even by 19th century standards. And yet to the lad, it was a grand vessel, a pirate ship like the one sunk in the Inishbofin Harbor from his grandfather's tales.

Captain O'Flaherty went about giving the orders to gather the fish caught before their almost disastrous demise. It was his intent to bring the fish over in sacks using the dingy for transportation. James however had a plan which would save doubling up on short trips to the shore.

"Captain, sir," James began. "There is a pier which you could reach if ye knew the way to avoid rocks and silt piled high beneath the water."

The Captain became most attentive. "And would you be up to guiding us once again to the pier and save us from the same fate as the O'Malley Pirates?"

"Aye sir, that I can do easily," the lad replied like a sailor in training.

"Then you've had much time spent on vessels. Is that so?"

The lad became ill at ease. He knew full well that he had spent no time aboard a ship of any kind but he had watched from his perch in the ruins many a fishing vessel and even several delivering goods and supplies enter and leave the harbor. He began to shift his weight from foot to foot. This did not go unnoticed by the Captain nor by the sons who were his crew. Casting his glance to his sons then to the priest, the Captain was perplexed as to what path to take so as to not imply that he did not trust the boy's capabilities to guide the vessel safely to the pier. James gave no answer as these glances were exchanged. It was then that Father O'Malley intervened. Placing his hand on the lad's shoulder then brushing his hand across his hair so as to remove strands of hair from covering his eyes he spoke with trust in his voice.

"Captain, did not the lad guide us safely from certain doom at the mouth of the harbor. Did not this Lord of the Castle ruin show knowledge beyond his tender years?"

"Aye Father, 'tis the truth ye be speaking." And with that Captain O'Flaherty gave orders to place the lad at the bow of the vessel from where he would point the passageway to the pier.

What James hadn't realized was that his vantage point on the bow was not elevated like that perch of his on the ruins of the fortress wall from which he could easily see the submerged rocks or sand bars which discolored the water. And yet he was confident that he could guide the vessel safely. Aedan took the tiller while his brothers hoisted, just slightly, the sail so as not to create speed but a gliding across the harbor waters. The Captain and priest stood behind James.

Word had been spreading through the village and now had brought several of them to the pier area. Seeing the vessel approaching the pier several men ran onto it and shouted for the O'Flaherty lads to throw them a rope as they got closer to the pier. In short order the vessel was tied to the pier and James was once again hoisted upon Aedan's shoulders and carried into the village as a hero. The fish brought ashore was not a full load but abundant enough to make the villagers marvel. The few loaves of bread kept aboard were an added delight for this population experiencing encroaching severe malnourishment.

A parade of sorts began when a couple of donkeys (one attached to a cart) were brought to the fishermen. The beasts of burden would bring the harvest of the sea to the village proper. What constituted the village was nothing more than a few cottages lining a street from which the one or two acre plots radiated. Most of these cottages were family dwellings. Any similarity to a comfortable home a la 1849 style was accomplished only through the charity and warmth of the family who dwelled within it. Other buildings consisted of a general goods store, which was owned by the Landlord's representative, a warehouse for sheep's wool and a grain house. The latter was not being used for that purpose since the land simply did not produce enough grain to make it profitable and so grazing of sheep had become the major industry of the island. It had been turned into a pub where talk of the blight, rebellion and local gossip took place. At the end of the street was a two story house, whose stones were plastered and white washed. This was the home of the Landlord's representative.

Now this middleman or overseer collected the rents in the form of crops or sheep. He actually was a native of Inishbofin who had gone to the mainland. It was to the mainland he went seeking the opportunity to break the chains of eking out a meager living by back breaking efforts to make something grow amongst the rocks which constituted most of the land mass. The overseer was a young man then, only in his teens. Though poorly educated he could read and write English with some accomplishment. This skill made him an attractive prospect to work for the landlords of County Mayo as he could also communicate with those who held onto the ancient Gaelic language. In no time Kiernan O'More found himself serving as a clerk in Castlebar of County Mayo for a firm which handled the landlords' property. He showed no sign of allegiance except to that of his work. In those days before the Act of Emancipation, it seemed the prudent thing to do; that is to keep one's faith closeted. It was his understanding that his lot would be much better served should he throw his allegiance to the Church which was controlled by the British since the Act of Union. Ireland, by this act, had been united to England, Scotland and Wales.

Back on Inishbofin little note was given to this Act of Union. Life went on as it had for centuries on the rocky tiny island. Its people just lived day by day off a few sheep and a potato crop which fed the people. All that came before the blight, of course.

Reaching manhood while on the job in Castlebar, Kiernan at the same time stuck to learning the accounts and soon found himself becoming a favorite amongst the landlords who on occasion met with the firm's leaders. His charm and wit served him well as he knew his accounts and used a touch of blarney to beguile his superiors. Thus when it was deemed necessary to have a personal representative for the landlords who owned most of the good land on Inishbofin, Kiernan was the one chosen. When he returned, he was quite different from the innocent lad who had left to seek his fortune. He was educated and his bearing took on a superior nature to those of his native island. It was into that two story Tudor style house with its white washed exterior that he moved. Its stone work and shingled roof served to further accentuate this separation between he and his fellow Inishbofin citizens who lived in those thatched roofed often one or two room cottages which dotted the island. He went on to serve the landlords well through upholding the agreements made between them and the tenants of the land. At the same time he turned the other way when a priest was secreted onto the island to celebrate the sacraments before the Act of Emancipation. And so the struggle to live and raise a family went on as it had for centuries until the blight began to affect the island as well. Kiernan was powerless to change the agreements and that was why it was so important that in England, Queen Victoria received the commission to address the plight of the Irish people.

Kiernan sat at his desk next to a window overlooking what could be called the main street of the village off the harbor. He had just received a newspaper which had an article written about Daniel O'Connell being part of a commission to address the needs of the people of Ireland. He was in mid-article when the parade with all its commotion jarred his senses. Looking up, he saw people flooding onto the streets. They were escorting strangers and a lad riding a donkey.

The strangers were singing a song about the very person of whom he was reading, Daniel O'Connell. Placing a paper weight at the spot where he had reached in the article, he rose and walked into the entrance hall of his house. Slipping on his frock coat he opened his front door and went out onto the portico attached to its façade as he placed a British style hat upon his head. That is not a tweed cap of wool but a high hat of silk.

The caravan marched directly in front of him. The lad James Shields, who Kiernan knew well, waved. The overseer smiled confused as to how to respond for again the O'Flaherty's were singing that song which could hardly go unnoticed. Kiernan was well aware of who Daniel O'Connell was even before that recent news came to him. The overseer knew of Daniel's reputation as a fighter for the rights of tenant farmers. Yet he, unlike many of the middleman who represented landowners, was a native of Inishbofin. Thus, he was, more or less one of the people even in his high hat and frock coat and despite his line of work and public display for the Church of Ireland rather than his Catholic roots. It was this latter fact which probably was the only bone of contention as the Island kept its Catholic faith even in the dark days of religious persecution going back to Olivier Cromwell.

The parade marched along a route, which in the present day is called the Inishbofin Cloonamore Loop. The little band of fishermen and priest strode the dirt path with a strength not seen on the island for two years. They passed the bogs where the peat was cut to burn in the cottage hearths and came to St. Colman's 14th Century Church ruins. It was there that Father O'Malley suggested that they pause to celebrate Mass and distribute the fish to the villagers. It didn't take long for the ruins to be filled with singing people and the celebration to follow.

It was onto this jubilation that the ailing Kathleen Shields aided by her husband, James Sr. entered. The father of the lad had kept his wife unaware that their son had been out all night in the ruins. He did so with a series of excuses from running chores for Kiernan O'More to looking for stray sheep. He, seeing the smoke coming from the ruins, knew full well that the lad James was once again camping in the fortress. Now what they saw could hardly be comprehended. There was James Jr. helping to set up an altar comprised of stones piled into two pillars and a flat stone slab resting upon them. Kiernan had arrived carrying a basket containing a loaf of brown bread and a bottle of wine. This he was handing to young James and Father O'Malley. This middleman of the landlord knew how important it was to the people of Inishbofin to have a priest amongst them once again.

Clare Morgan arrived with a table cloth fashioned from the remnants of her wedding gown for just such an occasion and a local farmer, Colman O'Connor, came with a pewter cup to serve as a chalice. The altar table was set and ready when Kathleen Shields took from under her shawl two partially used candles. Kissing her son on his forehead, much to his dismay, she called to Seamus Dougherty to loan her the use of his lantern from which to light the candles. She smiled at Father O'Malley, gave him a slight bow and took a few steps back to her husband's waiting arms.

All was ready, that is except for Father O'Malley himself. He was now rummaging through his bag and pulled out his Missal and a green stole which he placed around his neck. Sunlight shone upon the congregation within the ruin as if the blessing of God Himself was being received. A murmur to that feeling was spreading amongst the people when Father O'Malley, now ready to begin Mass announced that the celebration of the Holy Eucharist, which he was about to begin, would be one in which young James and any child who has reached the age of ten shall embark on a journey of learning to prepare to receive their First Holy Communion.

Parents rejoiced as they brushed their children's hair with their fingers and adjusted the lads,' and lasses,' clothing. For Kathleen Shields only tears came as she looked at her young James dressed in rags and a rope tying his pants. James however was thrilled and oblivious to his mother's sadness over his appearance. Rather he took the pewter cup from the elderly Mr. O'Connor and placed it on the stone altar. Father O'Malley placed the basket with the loaf of bread and bottle of wine next to the cup. Then taking the bottle out of the basket he gave it to James to hold until such time as its contents would be needed. The boy bowed his head and stood like a soldier ready for duty. His uncertainty however could be seen in his eyes as he looked toward his parents who knew full well that he had no training in serving at mass as one had not been celebrated on Inishbofin but once in a year's time.

The priest smiled at James. "Take heart lad, I shall motion to you when the wine will be needed."

The relieved boy nodded his understanding.

All was ready as those gathered broke into an ancient hymn in a language which the Celts would be quite familiar; that is the Breastplate of St. Patrick. They sang in the old language. As they did so the children watched as their elders with tears streaming down their faces began to worship as the sun's rays continued to bathe the ruin in holy light.

"I bind myself today, the virtues of the star lit heaven.
The glorious sun's life giving ray,
The whiteness of the moon at even,
The flashing of the lightning free,
The whirling wind's tempestuous shocks,
The stable earth, the deep salt sea
Around the old eternal rocks."

The lyrics took on a special meaning for those gathered amongst the ancient rocks of the Church ruins as the wind picked up and the pages of Father O'Malley's missal fluttered so that he had to motion to James to hold the pages steady.

Then as the hymn ended, the priest intoned in the language of the Church the words of greeting and blessing.

"In nomine Patris, et Fillii et Spiritu Sancti."

All made the sign of the cross as he did so. And Kiernan stood silently and joined them in that gesture of blessing grateful that none of his superiors were present to witness his act.

Father O'Malley chose for one of the readings a passage from Jeremiah 6:16 and used that verse to speak to his flock. To him the prophet's words hit at the heart of what they who lived on the tiny island off the west coast of Ireland believed.

"Thus says the Lord: stand by the earliest roads, ask the pathways of old
which is the way to good, and walk it; thus you will find rest for your souls."

Twenty years after the Act of Emancipation those who listened knew what the priest meant as he read that passage to them. When he preached there was no doubt as to why he chose that particular reading as he concluded his sermon.

"And so good people of Inishbofin, stand firm on the path, be loyal to your history, abide by ancient lessons and walk with faith."

A sudden gust of wind swept through the ruins lifting the former wedding dress now altar cloth so as to require small stones to be placed on each corner of the altar stone to keep it in place. It was as if the breath of God filled the sacred space. The air began to chill and a mist formed beyond them across the harbor area. The O'Flaherty's fishing vessel rocked ever so slightly and tiny waves formed. The mist rolled onto the land and clouds began to gather over the ruins and yet all of it was oblivious to those who worshiped. That is until Fr. Thomas elevated the consecrated bread and wine. At that moment the gathering clouds split thus allowing a sunray to pierce through and illuminate the pewter cup and bread with such brilliance that James had to rub his eyes. The gesture however allowed the pages of the missal to flutter and turn one after the other. The lad felt negligent and clumsily sought to return the missal pages to where they had been before the gust swept through. The

45

difficulty for the lad was that he could not read English let alone Latin. Thus his attempt was doomed to failure.

Young James looked up to the priest and cast an eye toward his parents whom he was convinced that he embarrassed. The priest lowered the Bread and Cup and without losing a beat flipped the pages to their rightful place while at the same time intoning the Lord's Prayer.

"Pater Noster…"

Kathleen and James Shields gave a nod to their son that all was well. In her heart the lad's mother knew that the ray of light which reflected off the cup and onto her son was a sign from heaven that her son should serve God as a priest. She began to formulate her thought as she approached the altar to receive Holy Communion. It was her intent to present this interpretation of the event to the priest after mass.

The hymn being sung was one written by St. Thomas Aquinas and though sung in Latin was understood since childhood to speak of the Bread of Angels being made bread for mankind, gifted bread from heaven.

"Panis angelicus, fit panis hominum, dat panis coelicus figuris terminum."

Kathleen Shields thought of those better days when her father-in-law would teach them the ancient hymns in secret including the very one being sung. The ending line of the first verse came to her mind: "Oh, thing miraculous! This body of God will nourish the poor, the servile, and the humble."

"O res mirabilis! Manducat Dominum, pauper, servus et humilis."

She was not alone in thinking of the poverty of Inishbofin. One only needed to look around the ruin. Nor would one be hard pressed to see those who lived to serve others. There was Mr. O'Connor feeble now but never stopping to ask if a neighbor needed his help. And then there stood Mrs. Morgan, the one who had fashioned her wedding dress into a table covering. To each villager she would offer its use on a special day in the life of their family, be it a wedding, a baptism or an anniversary. She did so with selflessness never wishing to be honored or recognized. Kathleen Shields' heart skipped a beat. She held her folded hands next to her breast and tapped slightly upon it. 'Twas the sign of asking forgiveness that she made. She never felt that she was truly humble as the hymn extolled. She would have to work on that virtue to be sure. And yet not a person on Inishbofin would ever be found to say that Kathleen Shields was unduly proud; be it her husband or the light of her life, young James.

With her shawl covering her head and hands clasped she took a step up to Father O'Malley and received a morsel of the bread of angels given to all mankind.

As for that husband of Kathleen, sure he could see that something was afoot behind those glittering eyes fixed on their son. He watched her return to stand at his side, she with bowed head not so much from attempting to be humble as to prevent James Sr. from looking into those green eyes that spoke volumes. They had not been married for almost fifteen years and not have developed a sense of being able to read each other's souls.

The final blessing having been given the assembled began to sing another verse from the Breastplate of St. Patrick.

"Christ be with me. Christ within me.
Christ behind me. Christ before me.
Christ beside me. Christ to win me.
Christ to comfort and restore me.
Christ beneath me. Christ above me.
Christ in quiet. Christ in danger.
Christ in hearts of all that love me.
Christ in mouth of friend and stranger."

The words took on new meaning for Kathleen Shields as she saw her son who had come riding into the village upon a donkey and being hailed a hero for saving the fishing vessel with its crew and the very priest brought to them that day. No sooner had that last line pertaining to friend and stranger been sung as the very image of its sung words came into view for Kathleen. The O'Flaherty clan and various men of the village had walked to the far end of the ruin to build a fire. Mrs. O'Connor and others had gathered the fish from Captain O'Flaherty and were already preparing them for cooking.

It would be a feast to be enjoyed by all gathered including Kiernan. The planned feast would be a simple one of fish and bread but one which would, by Inishbofin standards, be grand indeed. Grand or simple, it would be at that feast that Kathleen planned to present her interpretation of events thus far on that day. Thus she positioned herself so as to be seated next to Father O'Malley. After some reflective conversation about the conditions on Inishbofin, the quality of the priest's sermon and so forth, she managed to come to that point in the mass when the light of the sun reflected off the pewter chalice.

Father O'Malley not wishing to make more of a natural event than what it was made note of how it indeed shined into the eyes of young James. He bent over to look down the rocky wall which was being used as a table and smiled at the lad. He was in deep conversation with the lads of the village informing them of what it felt like to ride upon the harbor waters in such a vessel that he himself had saved from destruction. Kathleen would have none of it and went on to present her interpretation that it was a sign from heaven that her son should serve the Lord.

"Madam," the flabbergasted priest had replied. "James is indeed a bright lad and a clever one as well, given what he did this day. But in truth he is but ten years old. Perhaps we should prepare him for his First Communion before launching him into a vocation for the priesthood of which he knows nothing at such a tender age."

The priest turned slightly to seek agreement from the lad's father.

"Aye Father, he is our only son after all. Who would take over the sheep and our wee parcel of land?"

Kathleen would have none of it. "Sheep, land; is that all you can think about my love? 'Tis not the value of one's soul, the souls of all here gathered more important?"

Her eyes flashed her conviction but she smiled ever so slightly to try and cover up her feelings. It didn't work. James Sr. knew what was behind those eyes filled with wonder and awe as to what the future could hold for their son. Then she began to cough and that made both her husband and the priest concerned for her well-being. Father O'Malley ran to the make-shift altar to retrieve what was left of the bottle of wine while James Sr. began to comfort Kathleen with words like; "love, don't get yourself upset."

She in turn knew that he meant well. "I'm not upset love. I just have a little cough, that's all." James Sr. smiled knowing that she didn't want to get him worried.

"Mrs. Shields," Father O'Malley began holding the bottle of wine and the pewter cup. "Perhaps a sip of wine would help."

"Father, I couldn't possibly…"

She was interrupted by her husband. "Now my love, listen to His Reverence. It's to help that slight cough."

She took the cup and sipped the fruit of the vine which she couldn't remember ever having partaken in many a year. After a few sips then gulps she returned to the original conversation.

"Now Father, as far as my son's tender age and his preparation for Holy Communion; I think that is a fine first step in fostering a vocation. Now just when do you intend to return to begin the instruction?"

Father O'Malley looked over Kathleen toward James Sr. Her husband just shrugged. As for the priest; he had never given a thought to returning on a regular basis. There would be the need for transportation to the Island. He was also concerned that he was still being watched by the authorities as a dissident. Then, of course, there was the congregation over which he was Pastor on the Aran Islands. All of these thoughts flashed through his stunned brain.

Kathleen lifted the cup to take another sip of wine almost as if she were toasting the priest. She smiled and waited for a response.

Smiling absentmindedly as a courtesy, into the mind of the fugitive priest there began a flashback of all that happened to bring him to Inishbofin. *"Perhaps,"* he surmised to himself, *"that these events were indeed a sign that he is needed elsewhere. Just maybe this lad who saved him and the O'Flaherty fishermen was meant to be more than one trying to farm someone else's land and an early death which was sure to come if the blight did not subside."*

Kathleen Shields was now tapping her foot. Luckily, her long black skirt hid her building impatience as she waited for the pensive priest to respond to her. She lifted the woolen shawl over her head as the wind began to kick up again which also caused another group of clouds to form thus subduing the fading sunlight. In fact torches had been lighted from the cooking fire and placed around the ruins.

Young James himself interrupted the apparent stand off as he ran up to his parents and stood between them and the priest. The excited lad announced that Captain O'Flaherty and his sons had taken out a flute and fiddle.

"James dear, hush yourself," his mother scolded gently. "'Tis important business that his Reverence and I would be discussing."

The lad glanced at his father, who just rolled his eyes. As for the priest, the announcement served to bring his focus back to the flame red hair and ruddy complexion of Kathleen Shields. This time he was looking right into the eyes of the woman, who was a good foot shorter than he. She had managed to balance herself upon a rock to make sure that she could make her point once again.

Father O'Malley chose to address his next comment to the lad in the hope that the news might end the discussion of a vocation for the ten year old lad.

"Aye lad, the O'Flaherty clan is not only made up of good fishermen. They also have musical talent as well. Perhaps ye might wish to inquire as to be a help to them."

"Yes Father," the lad replied then paused once again looking at his father with gleaming eyes. "Da," he began taking hold of his dad's hand. "Ye need to get out granddad's pipes. You can be a help too."

The elder James gestured no but that didn't stop the urging. The priest found this to be a way to distract and create a new focus.

"Mr. Shields, sure it would be grand to have the song of the pipes to play with the O'Flaherty clan."

"Aye, Father if it is your wish," James Sr. answered. "But I haven't played them in a long time."

"You indeed show how the virtue of humility is a gift to you." The priest glanced back to the still impatient mother of the boy.

She smiled, taking on the meaning of the priest's statement as to address her lack of such a virtue. She was not detoured however. She just used a different approach which supported her son's wish and still gave her time to finish her thought about her son's future.

"Love, do play," she began. "The lad has not heard the pipes since your father went to heaven on that 20th of May day over a year ago."

The husband gave up his humble protests and went off toward their cottage with James Jr. beside him.

As they left, Kathleen Shields called out. "I'll just stay here with the Father and finish our conversation."

The hope which seemed to prevail was lost with her statement. The priest knew that this was one mother who would not give up. "And now madam, you were saying?"

The exhilarated woman now took a deep breath and let him have it. "Priest or not, your Reverence, 'tis mi son of whom we had been speaking and of his future."

The priest's cheeks turned pink as he looked over the ruin wall and down the road hoping to see the lad and his father coming with the pipes. The street was empty. Oblivious of his desire, she continued.

"Now then, despite his tender age 'tis a special lad that mi James would be. Just ask any in the village. Each would tell you that he is a special lad indeed."

"So I've been told along the procession route before I had the honor of meeting you."

"'Tis no blarney that you'll be handing over to me, Father O'Malley."

"Trust me madam. I speak the truth. There seems to be great admiration for the lad. And I concur, that he is indeed a bright and courageous lad. But again I say to you that he is but ten years old."

Kathleen Shields began to soften, not in her conviction, but in her demonstrative body language. Not saying a word she stepped down from the rocks. Then looking up at the priest and seeing sincerity and honesty, she felt that he did listen to her and was just protecting the boy's childhood or what was left of it.

She quietly spoke. "Aye, 'tis true that mi James is but a lad but he may never reach manhood let alone seeing the graying of hair unless you do something."

Her sudden quieting and yet increased seriousness of her tone cut into the priest's heart. He felt her anguish and knew her meaning. He began to ask himself a series of questions. *"What if the blight did not end soon? What if, in fact, it got worse and the crops don't recover?"*

This pondering came to an abrupt end when a sudden gust of wind blew through the windowless stone frames of the

Church ruin. Kathleen seemed to be caught in it and began to falter as if about to faint. Father Thomas gave her his hand.

"Perhaps Madam, you'd be better served if you sit for a moment."

And with that he helped her back to the stone which she had stepped from. It stood on the sparsely covered ground save for a clump of shamrocks peeking out from behind it. A Holly bush provided a lovely backdrop for the setting. He placed his coat over it and asked her to be seated.

In turn she gave a slight curtsy taking hold of the worn apron tied about the waist of her full skirt of faded black wool and took a seat. After an awkward pause of unbearable silence, she whispered.

"So then do we have an understanding?"

The exasperated priest surrendered. "Aye madam that we have... somehow I shall return to Inishbofin on a monthly basis, perhaps two, depending on the availability of a vessel heading this way up the coast."

The lovely though frail woman smiled broadly. She informed him that she would do her part and begin instructing her son and other wee ones so as to prepare them for the priest's visit and First Holy Communion. Then her smile vanished and tears welled up in her eyes. She had begun to realize what she had done. Should the young James excel in his lessons 'tis to another land that he may have to travel so that he may be ordained to the priesthood.

Father O'Malley virtually read her thoughts. He placed his hand on her shoulder and in an effort to uplift her waning spirits turned her so she may see that her husband and son had returned and joined the O'Flaherty clan in the playing of the music and dancing of the jig.

"We seem to be missing the festiveness madam. Look there, is that not your son dancing a jig?"

She beamed with joy. "Aye, he has an ear for music as well. That might be quite useful wouldn't you say, when he sings the mass?"

The priest rolled his eyes once again and escorted her to the celebration.

And so Father O'Malley was true to his words and had been making the promised visits for almost three years. He prepared the lad for First Communion to be sure, but also in lessons of math, reading, of English, and writing as well. James in turn taught him to play the pipes and dance a jig.

Harbor Path: Inishbofin, Ireland

Chapter Three: The Announcement

The months had turned into years of hitching a ride on a fishing or trade vessel for Father O'Malley as he remained true to his word and brought the Gospel to Inishbofin and lessons to young James. Now as the lad's day for receiving First Holy Communion was at hand, so too was his progress in his studies which had created a literate person of the boy who sought higher education and perhaps service to the Church.

Those days of their first meeting when the O'Flaherty fishing boat was saved from the rocks to his subsequent visits flashed through the priest's mind as he heard young James call out his name. He looked up from the fire which he poked with a long stick causing it to sparkle and crackle.

"God be with you, lad."

"And also with you, Father."

Both had spoken in Latin. The priest was more than pleased with the progress James made in his studies, particularly how well he took to Latin, the language of the Church. Now when he looked upon the boy, he saw a lad of thirteen. No longer a simple boy who helped tend flocks and yet he was still frail as the source of food had not improved as the blight had gotten worse in Western Ireland. And yet it was obvious that the lad was passing through the threshold into a young man. The darkened color above his upper lip and the crack in his voice as he shouted his greeting made that apparent. After all, as James himself pointed out, he was indeed soon to be a man and capable of working and going out on his own. And that prospect looked fairly good as he had survived his deprived youth thanks to the provisions Father O'Malley brought with him on his visits.

The priest gestured for the lad to come closer to the fire. Despite his outward appearance still clothed in raggedy garments which were patched as best as was possible and almost skeletal thin frame, the lad virtually skipped to the fire. Then in a surprise move he threw his arms around the priest's neck and pulled him down to his level. The lad was now looking into the shocked eyes of the priest and realized that he may have been too demonstrative to his tutor. He jumped back.

"Sorry Father, I'm just excited about tomorrow."

The wide eyes of shock had subsided on the priest and a smile formed under the trimmed beard. "Don't fret. I understand that receiving Holy Communion is a time for joy."

"Oh, that too Father."

James lowered his head contritely, knowing that he had overstepped in his enthusiasm or so he thought.

Now a look of puzzlement crossed the priest's face. His big green eyes bugged out. His concern was not over the hug. Rather it was the response James made to his statement about receiving the Eucharist for the first time. He cocked his head and wondered what was going on in the lad's head which caused him to say, 'that too.' He poked the peat fire and stirred up the embers once again. A flame shot up while sparks flew about. This startled the lad who had seated himself on a boulder of the same type of brownish limestone which made up the fortress ruin. He was so surprised that he fell off his stool of stone onto his backside. Given that he didn't have much padding anywhere it was more than an ouch which he yelled out like a sheep herder yelling to his flock when they wandered off.

The red faced lad looked up from his perch on the rocky ground to see the priest laughing. The holy man, in his mind, appeared like a gigantic black clothed shadow. At first, he was taken aback but then began to giggle and rub his rump.

"I don't have much padding Father."

"Is that so? Well then it would be grand that I have brought a bit of fish and bread to fatten you up."

The shadowy figure stretched out his hand to lift the boy up. The lad's eyes sparkled as he gently took a seat on his perch of stone. He watched quite intently every move of the priest as he skewered the fish and handed the stick to James. The fish sizzled as it was held over the glowing embers and small flame. Father O'Malley then went about cutting the bread with a knife he removed from a leather sheath hanging from his black leather belt. All the while he was telling the story of the Gospel in which Jesus used fish and bread to feed his flock of people who had come to hear him preach.

Concluding the story of the miracle of the loaves and fishes, he moved on to probe the lad about his statement regarding Communion. From the tone of the questioning it was not a reach for James to realize that his priest, friend and teacher, wasn't quite accepting of his lack of enthusiasm regarding the reception of the Sacrament. And so young James began to tell a story which he hoped would convince the priest that he was indeed quite excited about First Communion Day. He went on and on as to how his Mom was preparing for the big day to be celebrated. That is, what she could do with the limited means which was now affecting the entire island as well as the mainland.

"Now James, you needn't hand me any more blarney. Just tell me honestly as to what you meant by saying, 'Oh, that too.'"

The lad grinned from under his black locks hanging in his face. That position he deliberately chose for holding his head over the peat fire for it made sure that his hair would fall into his face and conceal his reddened expression. For it was the blarney he'd be telling the priest to be sure, at least the embellished part of the preparation story. He was caught and he knew it. Taking a deep breath, he brushed aside the long black locks from his almost turquoise blue eyes and cast up a meek glance with the slightest of grins. A look of a puppy being caught at being naughty as he chewed on the family furniture came to mind. But the priest said nothing. He just took the skewer from the lad and removed the fish onto a metal plate. Having done so, he handed the fish back to the boy, who graciously received it. A pall of silence ensued as the priest waited for a comment from James which wasn't forthcoming as he was far too interested in the steaming fish on the plate than anything else at the moment. This did not go unnoticed by Father O'Malley.

"First the stomach James, then your thoughts."

The relieved lad smiled. Grace was prayed and the fish devoured. Now as the last morsel was consumed the priest who was sitting pensively across from the lad became concerned when James told him about his mother not improving but rather having a bad time of it with her health. The priest at first worried that cholera may have crossed onto the island of Inishbofin. The dreaded disease was spreading from village to town across Ireland. But as yet, he hadn't heard of cases on the islands off western Ireland. Such a development was a grave concern to the priest who understood how close James was to his mother.

He decided not to probe James about the comment. Rather he rummaged through his leather sack and removed a Bible. Two ribbons, one red and one gold, stuck out from it and he used the gold ribboon to open the Scriptures to the Gospel of Mark, thinking that a tale of Jesus and his holy mother and guardian father might just be what James needed to hear. He read the story to the wide eyed boy. No sooner had he shared the story of the twelve-year-old Jesus being lost in the temple of Jerusalem teaching the elders and then being found by his distraught parents, than James shouted out excitedly.

"Father, that's exactly what I meant."

The priest looked at the passage once again trying to garner from it the meaning it might hold for James. He of course was thinking of the mother Mary's love for Jesus and the joy of having found him in the temple.

The lad saw the bewildered expression upon the priest's face and began to explain. He talked about how he was about the same age as Jesus was when he decided to go out into the world and make his mark. Father O'Malley was beginning to understand the lad's interpretation of the passage, not that he avoided telling the lad that Jesus was obedient to his mother and foster father and returned home. James however glowed with the thought of going out into the world and continued to speak of it as they made their way down the rocky cliffside back to the harbor's dock area.

The lad continued to draw upon the analogy of he and the Lord when at last, he came to his actual meaning.

"Father, you asked why I said 'that too' in telling you how I felt about receiving our Lord in the Eucharist."

The priest nodded affirmatively and paused looking back at the ruins. He was now thinking that those ruins represented the Temple of Solomon in Jerusalem and his returning the lost boy to his home.

They were now standing along the rocky shoreline of the harbor and heading toward the very road on which James was triumphantly brought into town upon the back of the donkey some three years prior. A slight thin line of smoke still rose from the fortress ruins even though James had dosed the fire with dirt before they left. They looked at it for a moment and then it vanished. They turned to face each other and continue their journey as young James brought up the needed courage to continue.

"Well, I am joyful about receiving Holy Communion. Actually I never thought it possible so soon until you entered our harbor on that stormy day almost three years ago."

Father O'Malley took the lad by his shoulders and looked into his eyes. What he saw was a deep faith and a sincere message about to be delivered.

"James mi messy lad, I never doubted that joy. But there is more isn't there?"

They walked up the road and were now by Kiernan, the overseer's home. There was no activity at the house as he was about collecting the month's rents. They turned left at the fork in the road and strode toward the Shields cottage as James finished his thought.

"You're right, there is more. Like our Lord, I must leave my family and follow a different path. I want to be a priest but one just like you Father. And to do that, I must leave home."

Stopping dead in his tracks, the priest stumbled over a rock in the road as he became overwhelmed by the adulation of the youth. He had never thought of himself as an example to follow, especially since his confinement in prison as a dissident. Tears welled up in his eyes and were about to flow out when he lost his balance and began to fall. The lad reacted quickly and held out his hand to steady the tall lean priest. To add to the scene the sunny day had become overcast and a soft rain began to fall, all the better for the emotional priest as the rain drops could not be discerned from the tear drops. Hardened as he may have become from his time in prison, the sudden and unsolicited remark from the youth touched his heart in a manner which he thought had long vanished within the Lynch Castle prison in Galway.

Still holding onto the lad's shoulder to regain his balance, the priest gathered himself and quipped that the announcement may have been a bit unexpected. "It seems that you are just full of surprises this day James. But you place too much on a call to serve the Church if it's based on my calling."

Father O'Malley dropped his intent of saying more about his background as he thought better of telling the lad of his prison days as that too might become a sign of heroism of some sort, so he just smiled and suggested that they move on as the soft day was now becoming a rather intense one as to be creating a muddy road beneath their feet. James smiled and promised to speak no more of it, "for the time being," he added.

With that, they picked up their pace and were soon sprinting through mud puddles which splashed their soggy mess onto their legs as the Shields cottage appeared about a stone's throw ahead of them. In the doorway stood Kathleen Shields; her woolen shawl drawn up over her auburn hair. Saying not a word she watched the two as they became more and more splattered with the mud of the road. As they approached she waved.

The priest with his leather sack thrown over his shoulder noticed the frail woman in the doorway coughing into her shawl and thinking that such a day would not be in her best interest. He waved back as James shouted a greeting. The priest urged him to run to his mother.

The lad obediently ran off leaving the priest in a puddle. She hugged him as if he had been lost at sea and had found his way home. James, now taller than she, looked at her, a bit of confusion on his face as to why the emotional embrace of welcome. At the same time he was bursting with news of his final lesson as tomorrow Father O'Malley would be celebrating the mass for the First Communicants of Inishbofin.

"Momai wait 'til you hear." The lad paused. "Where's dadai?"

Stroking his cheek she answered. "He'll be home shortly. 'Tis in the pasture he is with the sheep." Then calling out to the priest, still standing in that puddle watching the heart-warming scene of mother and son, she invited him to come into the cottage for a bit of tea to warm his bones.

Meanwhile young James went on with an explanation of the scripture lesson about Jesus leaving his parents to go to the temple to teach.

Though only forty-two years old, Kathleen Shields looked weathered and worn out. And yet within those saddened eyes a spirit of joy still danced. Her sadness came from an instinctive understanding of where James was going with his telling of the Bible story. That knowledge stirred her heart. She lowered the shawl to her shoulders and went directly to the hearth and the kettle of water hanging within it. She of course knew the story of Jesus in the Temple as a boy, having had heard the story from her father-in-law reading the Scriptures from their family Bible up to the time of his passing. Nevertheless, she encouraged her son to tell her all about the lesson. Motioning to the priest to come near the hearth, she did comment on the cleric's wet condition and that the flames might help to dry him a bit.

James, oblivious as to the heart of his mother being stirred as Mary's must have been when Jesus told her that he must be about his Father's business, sputtered on and on until he came to the very idea which she knew was coming.

Father O'Malley sat quietly next to them having received the cup of tea she had been brewing. Such a delightful drink would have been unheard of given that it was just an ordinary day and how limited their tea supply was. He smiled his thanks, knowing how precious the drink was and remained silent. He chose not to interject his thought on James' story so as not to create even more trauma which he saw in those sad eyes. He sipped away and listened to the conclusion of the lad's retelling of the Gospel story.

"And so Momai, you see don't you," the lad glanced toward the priest who just took another sip of tea. "I mean you do understand that I want to be just like Father O'Malley, a priest in God's Church."

The sip became a gulp and caused the priest to choke. Kathleen Shields tended to the kettle over the fire and pulled it toward her. She gazed at her son sitting on the cottage floor next to her. The fire glowed on the lad and cast a light about him so as to give him a radiant appearance. She tenderly brushed his hair to the side and placed her hand under his chin, lifting it ever so slightly. The light of the flames also radiated off her continence which caused the priest to gasp at that moment as he saw in them the Blessed Mother Mary looking into her Son's eyes after he spoke similar words.

Tears began to streak down her cheeks as she turned away from the lad and with kettle in hand offered another cup of tea to the Father. In his eyes, those tears which had been forming since James first announced his intent spilled out. But Kathleen Shields said nothing and poured more tea into his cup, though he motioned not to do so. Finally, he spoke.

"Mrs. Shields, your son is a fine lad and a bright one to be sure besides. I am honored that he thinks of me as one to model a vocation in him in the future."

She poured herself just a touch of the tea, smiled and responded. "So then Father, you still believe that mi son is still too young for the making of such a decision, is that it?"

Before the priest had a chance to answer, the door of the cottage swung open. A gust of wind and rain followed behind the drenched James Shields Sr. He stood for a moment taken aback by the scene at the hearth and the cups of tea being shared. Nodding to the priest he then noticed the tears in his wife's eyes, which she was quickly dabbing with the corner of her apron.

"The blasted wind got some rain on you my love. Here let me dry you off." And without further comment he took the apron's hem and patted her face, placing a peck on her cheek as he did so. Then placing his arm around her he could feel that swelling of emotion within her. The source of that emotional state along with the priest being in the house, gave to him an understanding of the root of its rising.

James Jr. for his part looked upon the scene of tenderness with admiration while Father O'Malley looked upon it as Joseph comforting Mary in the Temple after Jesus announced His decision.

"Now there, all's well," James Sr. continued. Then with an effort to refocus what was sure to be an emotional revelation, he went on with his own news.

"I have news for ye." He turned toward the priest. "And Father, perhaps it's also news to you."

"Indeed, well then do share it with us Mr. Shields," the priest replied.

"Well then, Kiernan came to collect this month's rent right on time as usual."

He paused as Kathleen shuddered and gasped as she knew that it would be difficult to meet the sum. Her husband resumed.

"Now my love, be still, it's not what you think. All's well."

A look of disbelief crossed Kathleen's face as her eyes crinkled up and those eyes told a story of blarney being shared. He in turn knew full well what her thoughts were.

"Now love, 'tis not blarney I'd be sharing this day. The Queen herself is coming to Ireland to see for herself the plight of our people."

Despite the priest's presence, Kathleen could not remain silent any longer and spoke to the remark.

"And how James Shields does that affect the rent due?"

The lad was rather enjoying the story being told despite the tension it was causing. The priest wondered, like herself, as to how such a visit would help the family as well. But James Sr. just went on for he knew he had them in the palm of his hand. Sitting himself next to the lad on the floor, he asked for a cup of that newly brewed tea which was being saved for the boy's First Communion celebration. Kathleen dutifully poured him a cup and handed it to him with that glance of disbelief still written across her haggard face.

With dramatic flair he spoke in a whisper as if sharing a secret that he alone knew of and then built up to a crescendo. The priest, wife and son sat with steady eyes, as if they were glued to his every word.

"Well it seems that Her Majesty has contributed a rather large sum to a fund established to relieve the suffering of the Irish people. Kiernan O'More felt that the least he could do was to reduce the rent of these next few months following the example of the compassion of Queen Victoria."

Rising from the stool upon which she now sat to hear the news, Kathleen took hold of the kettle and added just a touch of tea to the cup of her husband, Father O'Malley and also gave a cup to the lad. And without further ado she commented that they should warm themselves as a storm seemed to be brewing. This she said without further comment on the rent.

"Now then love, it's quite beautiful that the Queen will be visiting Ireland. High time I'd say. Perhaps the good Father might include her in the prayers of the Mass tomorrow."

"Woman, what on earth is going on?" He rose from the floor leaning on his son to do so and rustling his fingers through the lad's hair.

"Now James mi love, 'tis other news ye should be hearing this night. Sit yourself down and be calm."

She then pulled over the only other chair in the cottage and placed it next to the lad. Her husband obediently sat upon it. Completely deflated he crossed his legs and folded his hands across his chest glancing at the priest, quizzically looking at his wife and once again rustling the lad's hair. It was then that he noticed his son wringing his fingers so as not to fidget.

"Pray tell, what could be so newsworthy as to best the visit of the Queen?" James Sr. asked with a touch of annoyance. "And may I add worthy to be received with the last of our tea. And don't ye be telling me about storms and such. For that which brews is no better nor worse than any other day on this God forsaken island."

"James Shields, the Father would be visiting us this day," the now embarrassed Kathleen chided.

"'Tis begging your pardon Father, but the truth is the truth no matter who should be hearing it."

"Well said Mr. Shields," responded the priest.

Now as an awkward silence ensued during which James Sr. gave a glance as if asking forgiveness to his wife for his rudeness, the lad took hold of the moment.

"Dadai's right," he shouted as he jumped up and onto his father.

"Son, what on earth…"

"Sorry momai but 'tis true what dadai said. This island is forsaken and the blight has made it worse."

The elder James grabbed hold of his son and squeezed him tightly while a broad smile crossed his face. Kathleen wiped her hands on the apron tied about her waist and turned toward the priest.

"Father O'Malley, ye must forgive the men of this house. They are an outspoken lot to be sure." This she said as if she herself had never commented that the Queen's visit was long overdue.

"Now Mrs. Shields do not worry, for I have sailed these many months with fishermen all along the coast. 'Tis much worse that I have heard on those journeys, speaking of which, I have some fish for your family."

"I thank ye for your understanding." She then received the fish graciously and went about preparing them.

As a silence fell across the room, the sound of the crackling peat bricks was all that could be heard. James Sr. didn't quite know how to insert himself into the exchange without raising the ire of his wife once again. So he playfully jostled his son resulting in the lad sliding back down to the floor as the man rose to speak his piece. Instead Kathleen handed him the plate of fish to skewer and place over the fire. The man did his duty without a further word being spoken. The lad jumped up to help his mother prepare the table and returning his father's chair to its usual place.

"Father, if you'd be so kind as to move I'll take your chair to the table."

This, the priest did but lifted the chair and took it the couple of feet to the table himself as the lad directed him as to where to place it. He in turn brought out two stools upon which he and his mother would sit as the chair the priest had been given was hers. Father O'Malley refused to use the chair and told them the other seat would be quite fine with him. He then sat himself on the stool next to the lad. Kathleen lighted the single partially burned candle having set the table with her mother's rustic pottery china depicting the shape of the shamrock around its edges. These would be used only for special occasions and Father O'Malley's visit was just such a time in her mind. And so it was a second meal the lad and priest would have that day, unheard of in all the boy's days of memory.

James Sr. finally spoke but it was the asking that the priest give the blessing over the meal. With bowed heads they crossed themselves and the priest prayed.

Praise God from whom all blessings flow.
May this food restore our strength, giving new energy to tired limbs, new thoughts to weary minds. May this drink restore our souls, giving new vision to dry spirits, new warmth to cold hearts. And once refreshed, may we give new pleasure to You, who gives all. And in that giving may You bless the Shields family for their kindness and faithfulness.

All responded, "Amen."

No sooner than that Amen left their lips than young James blurted out another petition of his own.

"And bless my journey Lord with success."

His mother's hand began to shake. The spoon she held clinked hard against the bowl onto which it dropped. Her husband reached over and grabbed her shaking hands as she gathered herself to speak, knowing full well what her son was asking as it indeed paralleled her own wishes for him. But the hearing of such words struck her heart nonetheless.

Her green eyes glowed with firelight as she asked, "And why, pray tell, would ye be needing such a blessing?"

She rose and stood next to her husband who continued to hold onto her. A silence pervaded the room with the sounds of three distinct gulps; one from her husband, another from the priest and the last from a confused lad who had no idea that such a reaction would take place.

"After all," he thought. *"Isn't that for which he prayed exactly what momai desired to be in mi future?"*

As his mother and father waited for a further explanation as to why such a blessing was requested, in County Clare a small village named Doolin was coping with the potato blight as well. In that village other events were stirring which would eventually set the stage for two lives to meet.

Present Day Doonagore Castle: Doolin, Ireland

Chapter Four: Doonagore Castle

On a bluff overlooking the Atlantic Ocean, a cylinder shaped castle tower served as a visual lighthouse sign for fishermen and trade ships working their way up and down the west coast of Ireland. On a clear day one could actually see those very islands which Father O'Malley had his Church built. That is the Aran Islands. At the base of this round castle keep an enclosure wall stood some three feet in height. It surrounded the tower as well as several outer buildings used for storage of crops and feed in good times. They stood virtually empty. The sheep grazed outside the wall on what pasture growth that was available to them on the rocky slope.

The castle itself had a long history and its name, Doonagore is often translated as "the fort of the rounded hills" given its location hugging the coast of County Clare. Below this unusually shaped castle tower, so thought because of its round shape (as opposed to the usual rectangular shaped castle keep towers scattered throughout 19th century Ireland and to the present day), stood the village of Doolin. It was a tiny port of sorts which received fishing vessels. On the main street of the village trade shops and a pub stood to serve crew and villager alike prior to the blight. County Clare was one of the most hard hit of the Irish counties as the potato famine grew worse with each passing harvest season.

As for Doonagore Castle itself, it was in a state of decay and its current owners didn't even live in it any longer as they had little to repair it or keep it up to any reasonable degree due to the devastating effects of what was now being recognized throughout Europe as a famine. It was made of stone in the 16th Century and built near the site where Tadgh MacTurlough Macon O'Connor taking stone from the Tra'Leachain quarry had built a more traditional 14th century castle. That one was made up of a rectangular tower house or what is called "the keep" around which a protective wall was built. Little of it remained when Doonagore was built some two hundred years later.

Doonagore itself was an elegant smooth stone round tower crowned at the top with a peaked roof circled by pointed stone as traditionally seen on a royal crown of the period. The protective wall surrounded it and the outer buildings. The wall itself was being restored by a work force made up of village men simply to give them work for a bowl of soup for their efforts. Such famine walls would eventually be seen across Ireland. The storage buildings were rather barren save for some grain which was scheduled to be shipped out despite the severe state of starving people around Doolin. Shipments of grain out of Ireland continued in 1849 despite the efforts of people such as Daniel O'Connell and the Duke of Leinster who called upon the government to feed the population first before shipments were made. And so the exports continued to the detriment of the Irish people.

Radiating from the Castle tower were pastures cordoned off by other "famine walls." Current construction was under way for new walls to connect the radiating ones thus enclosing the pasture. Each rock was carefully stacked and fitted with others usually with no mortar being used. The plan was to create a circular pattern. It was that wall which was currently under way as men from the village received some type of relief payment for its construction. The practice was to provide some type of work for the payment.

This was based on the theory that some sense of accomplishment would be derived from the work and thus they were being paid for their service and not being given a hand out for doing nothing.

The setting sun cast the tower's shadow across the pastures. Beyond it one could still see the turquoise blue sea water of the Atlantic Ocean. A painter's sky of oranges and reds crossed the sparse clouds hanging over the shoreline. Indeed today, artists such as Phillip Gray would have his easel out, catching the scene in oils. However on this evening in the summer of 1849 the only person about to view the scene had his head cast down and a sack thrown over his shoulder which swayed back and forth as he slowly strode into the shadow of the tower which cast its pall across him. His slow walking gait gave evidence of a tired man who was quite lean. His bushy black hair streaked with gray became even more unruly as a sudden gust caught hold of it. The wind made him blink and pause for a moment. He looked up and cast an eye toward the tower.

What he momentarily saw was a portrait of serene beauty. The Doonagore Castle Tower's light gray stones looked like dark shale from the side he was viewing. At its curves the sunrays still illuminated the stone and brought the reds and orange colors to dance upon them. Thus a golden halo effect was created as if the sun itself had taken up residence within its stones. Dropping the sack from his shoulder, Sean O'Grady rubbed his dark blue eyes which matched that of the darkening sky behind the Tower. He sighed heavily not at all enthralled by the serene scene. He only saw that which was once his family's ancestral home and now housed the Nagle family. Quinn Nagle was the new overseer for the landlords of Clare County. Even he had limited resources to keep up the medieval castle. Thus its roof, the wooden trim around the windows and doors, some of the stone work as well as the tiled pointed roof were in a state of disrepair. Its outer buildings barely stood on their own and were even in greater structural distress.

Back in 1829 when the Emancipation Act was proclaimed Sean's father had hope that they would be able to restore and increase their flocks and field crop now that the Irish Catholic families could own their own land. That hope gave way to despair as the potato crop failure began to destroy the entire economy of Ireland especially in County Clare. The O'Grady family could not pay their taxes on such a grand building and its land. They had no choice but to allow the landlords who lived in Britain and Dublin to increase their holdings at their expense. An agreement was struck which allowed the O'Grady family to live in what was once the farm hands' cottage. The overseer's family would have use of the Castle and thus the taxes for it were paid by the landlords of the area from the profits of the exports of sheep wool and crops of wheat and corn. Those exports had to continue despite the growing effects of the famine which each season devastated more and more families especially the children who now were buried in children's cemeteries created by the Church so great were their numbers.

It was to that century old stone cottage with its blackened thatched roof which gave evidence of it being weathered away to which Sean O'Grady made his way. He stooped down and with a twinge of pain in his back lifted the burlap sack which contained a few puny potatoes and a bag of grain. It was his pay for working on the famine walls being created around the castle pastures for the week. He began his walk once again just as a young lad ran out the door of the round tower. It was the thirteen-year-old son of Quinn and Bridget Nagle. The lad's mother was active in the Church of Ireland and the lad was soon to be sent to Galway as there were no secondary schools in the Doolin area. Only children of landowners and their middlemen could afford such an educational opportunity. But that would be months away thus Michael Nagle would still be a summer time playmate to the thirteen-year-old daughter of Sean and Colleen O'Grady. Not that Sean particularly appreciated the lad's attention toward his precious Meghan. Yet he had little to concern him as she was a headstrong lass, whose disposition matched her fiery crimson hair and flashing green eyes. She could hold her own with any of the lads of the village. In point of fact the lad, Michael, was a nice enough boy but there was just something about his overly polite manner which rubbed Sean O'Grady the wrong way.

The lad was now violently waving to Sean and calling out to him. His thoughts of his daughter's future and relationship with such a boy was placed on hold as he waved back but kept up his pace toward the cottage. In short order however, Michael had caught up with him and engaged him in a conversation which he had hoped to avoid at all costs.

"Good evening Mr. O'Grady," said the polite lad. "Coming home from work?"

"Good evening Michael," came the courteous reply. "Aye, you speak the truth."

"May I hold the sack for you sir. You look…" the lad paused not wanting to insult the man whose family once lived in the castle.

Sean saved him from finishing his sentence. "No lad, I am quite fine and looking forward to getting home."

"Oh, I see. I just thought I could be of help, sir."

"Indeed, you were kind to offer. But I must be on my way lad."

"May I walk with you, sir. I thought should your daughter be home that we might be able to talk…I mean, you know I'll be off to Galway come September for school."

"So I've heard. Now as for Meghan…"

Sean's words were interrupted when Meghan herself came running across the pastures radiating from the Castle tower complex. Her voice carried quite far as she seemed most excited and being full of news.

"Dadai, dadai," Meghan called out.

Sean and the lad stopped in their tracks and waited for her to reach them. A bit out of breath was she so that her words were full of deep gasps at first.
"It's grand news…" she took a breath. "Mommie brought home post from the village."

Sean placed his arm around her as she stooped to catch her breath. It was in that bent position that she saw Michael Nagle standing slightly behind her father.

"Oh, by the Saints!" She quickly stood upright and adjusted her ankle long skirt of brown cotton and knitted head scarf, the latter she lowered to her shoulders creating a neck scarf of sorts. "Good evening Michael. I didn't see you at first."

"Good evening to ye as well Meghan. I was just…"

The pleasantries having been observed Meghan refocused on her father and cut off Michael in mid-sentence. Not that she meant to ignore him but the news was bursting to be presented. Her father turned to the lad and suggested that Meghan should present the glad tidings so that they could get in a word of their own. The lad smiled and nodded affirmatively.

"Now mi sweet lass, just what is this grand news all about?"

"Oh nothing at all," she stated coyly so that their interest might grow. Then without a blink of the eye she couldn't play the game any longer. "In the post was a letter from Dublin."

"Indeed, all the way from Dublin."

"Dadai, did ye not hear me? It came from Dublin itself."

Meghan flipped her long fiery red hair behind her shoulders. She expected a bit more emotion or at least surprise that they would receive a letter from Dublin or for that matter most anywhere given they had limited communication beyond the Doolin area. She squinted her eyes and held her lips tightly closed as if she was biting them. Then she cast a glance, which only her wild green eyes could cast, toward her father to show her frustration. Her nose crinkled causing the freckles across it to seem to dance across her face. This in turn amused her father and gave Michael a bit of a chuckle.

She stamped her foot in outrage, well moderately so as she couldn't appear unladylike given Michael's presence.

"Yes my darling daughter, I indeed heard every word. Now do tell us all about it."

A grin formed and Meghan licked her lips. Her eyes widened and she crossed her hands across her hardly developed breast. Then she commented, turned and walked back toward the family cottage.

"Mommie said that I couldn't say another word until we were all together."

Her pace became a full out run as Sean stood speechless for a moment. He was about to shout after her when Michael came into view. Placing his hands on his hips as the sack had been dropped as soon as the sarcastic message was delivered.

"Well lad, it would seem that ye will not be conversing with Meghan this evening. I'd suggest that you call upon her tomorrow."

"Certainly sir, tomorrow then." And off Michael ran toward the castle tower stumbling as he did so on one of the many rocks protruding from the pasture soil.

Meghan was but a speck in the distance by the time he stopped smiling while picking up the sack once again. He observed Michael's dramatic "almost tumble" and wondered if the lad had any future at all. For already he had to be thinking of his daughter and what could possibly lie ahead for a lass with no dowry to speak of. The lad, it seemed simply didn't take to the land. Then as he made his way over the last of the radiating famine walls, his thoughts wandered to his own family's future as he gazed upon the weather beaten cottage, which by the standards of those on Inishbofin would have been a grand one indeed, but to him it served as an ugly reminder of what was once the O'Grady inheritance and now gone.

He placed his free hand on the door latch attached to an oak door long devoid of its paint save for a few blotches of red here and there. He turned and once again saw that golden halo surrounding the Doonagore Castle tower and offered an oath of sorts.

"One day, our family shall return to the castle."

How that would be possible depended on his ability to pay the taxes on the land upon which the Castle stood. And the sack he held was a symbol of why such a pledge may never be fulfilled. He lifted the latch and entered the cottage.

The outside of the O'Grady home may have needed a bit of attention but the interior was spotless and appeared in good condition given its contents being made up of Colleen O'Grady's family furniture. Her people were the McMahon family. Those furnishings were mixed with those allowed to be taken from the Castle-keep by Sean when they could no longer meet the taxes and had to move into what was once the farm hands' cottage. A similar fate was being experienced across the barren rocky surface of the interior area of the county (called the Burren). Cottages were springing up wherever one looked despite that nothing of value could grow and grazing was minimally possible. Such tenant cottages sprung up along the coastal area of County

Clare as well. All due to the overseas landlords taking control of any good land. Unlike those on the Burren, the O'Grady cottage had three rooms. To the left was a doorway which opened to Sean and Colleen O'Grady's bedroom. At the rear of the room was another door which led to a smaller bedroom which was where Meghan held court with her wooden dolls with corn husk hair made by her grandfather before he passed on, to join his wife in heaven as her mother would put it, just as the potato blight began to raise its horrendous head across Ireland.

To his right was the hearth over which a kettle was hanging. He placed the sack on the rough oak table and called out.

"Would the woman of the house be at home this day?"

There was no answer forthcoming, so he tried another tactic.

"And where's mi sweet daughter who left the lad standing with reddened face?"

Only silence continued. With a shrug, he removed his faded jacket with mismatched buttons and walked into his bedroom. It was empty of people. After he placed his jacket and cap on a hook across from the double bed covered with a white cotton bedspread which in recent years had seen a patch or two sewn onto worn out areas, he thought about sitting on the bed to remove his shoes. That thought he quickly pushed out of his thinking process as his wife would never stand for anyone to sit upon her meticulously made bed. Instead he walked back into the main room with the hearth and dining area. Never gave a bit of notice to the cupboard in which his wife's special china which once belonged to her mother was kept. He pulled one of the four chairs which surrounded the dining table to the hearth and placed his feet on one of the rocks at its base. Stretching out his arms which seemed to take in all the cottage, he leaned back and enjoyed the warmth of the fire entering his shoes as they dried from the walk across the damp soil and grassy areas of the pastures.

The last rays of the sun pierced the window next to the front door through which he entered. Still no wife or daughter was to be seen or heard. In a semi-sleep stupor his mind wandered back to thoughts about Meghan's future. He and Colleen had discussed her education in Galway as she got older, that was until the blight changed all thoughts of future years as they struggled just to survive. Still he never gave up the hope of one day improving their daughter's lot and seeing her grow into an educated woman. As he mused about how he might bring that hope into reality, he noticed an envelope sitting on the mantle. It wasn't very big and was propped up against one of the twin candlesticks. These in turn stood guard over the Holy Picture of the Blessed Mother of Jesus.

His stare grew more intense. His feet slipped off the rock before the hearth fire. He rose ever so slowly looking about for his wife or daughter. He stood looking directly at the envelope inscribed with the name of Colleen O'Grady of Doonagore. *"How on earth,"* he wondered, *"could this post get to this cottage all the way from…"* He stopped his own thought as a chill made him shudder as if a gust of wind caught his back. And indeed it had.

"Sean love," his wife called in greeting as she stood in the doorway with Meghan directly behind her. "the kettle should be ready. Let me pour you some tea."

The rather surprised husband turned to respond just as Meghan closed the door cutting off the breeze which followed them into the cottage. Colleen never missing a beat regarding her suggestion for a warm drink, walked directly to him, gave him a peck on the cheek then tended to the kettle hanging over the hearth fire. Meghan, as her mother went about the business of preparing tea, brought the chair back to the table. Sean was beside himself. He wanted to grab the letter and shove it in their faces and demand to know what it contained that their daughter could not speak of it. But he couldn't muster the fervor to do so. He just repeated what Meghan had told them about the post.

"I don't want tea and besides save it for a special time. There's not much left."

"Nonsense, you've been working on that wall all week and it's been many a soft day these last few days." Colleen dipped the tea holder into the kettle. She dwelled on the subject of rain rather than the slightest hint of the letter.

"Dadai, come sit by the table. You look tired."

"What I am daughter is curious as to what is going on in mi house and who would be sending a letter to your mother."

Taking his daughter's suggestion however, he did take a seat at the table. Colleen came over with the kettle as Meghan took three cups down from the cupboard. She had set the McMahon china cups and not the usual pewter ones used on a daily basis. This did not go unnoticed and Sean inquired as to why such a grand tea was being served. It was apparent that he was in no mood for teasing or playing games, so

Colleen took the letter which she had slipped into the pocket of her apron after she poured her husband a cup of tea.

"I suppose you saw the letter on the mantle, have you read it?"

"Woman it's addressed to you."

Colleen smiled just ever so slightly having stood at that doorway watching her husband wrestle with himself over what he should do regarding the post on the mantle.

"Sean mi love, 'tis a letter from Dublin."

"I gathered that much from what Meghan told me out on the pastures. By the way Meghan I sent that Michael lad back home. He should be here tomorrow to offer his greetings and the news about his going to school in Galway come this fall."

"And why, pray tell, would I care what Michael Nagle had to say to me?"

Sean just smiled and went back to addressing the news within the letter from Dublin.

"So who would be writing you from Dublin?"

"It's from my sister, Margaret."

"Maggie!" Sean said. "What's she doing in Dublin. Nothing's happened to your family in Enniskillen has it?"

Colleen's eyes widened. Within them Sean saw an excitement long absent since their forced moved from Doonagore Castle to the cottage. She took a sip of tea purposely holding the cup so that the design of a spray of shamrocks and roses could be seen in the firelight. She lowered the cup and slipped the letter out of the envelope; carefully she flattened the paper placing her cup on one corner of the letter.

"No love, all's well in Enniskillen. 'Tis what has taken place near the Village of Belleek that she has news."

"Belleek!" now Sean was totally confused. "What's in that place? And where is it anyway?"

"Tis but a small village on the northern end of Lough Erne a wee bit in distance from Enniskillen itself. But it's of no importance at this point. Mi father, Margaret and I would go fishing in the good days along the Lough. Once we hit upon a storm and were blown far from Enniskillen. Lost our bearings on the Lough we hit upon a land area on which we came upon a Castle."

"So that's how you ended up in Belleek, is that it?"

"Not at all, not at all. We landed on the estate lands of Castle Caldwell. Meghan, fetch your geography book and find a map of Ireland."

Meghan went off to find the book while Sean sat gulping his tea confused as ever. Colleen patted Sean's hand as he traced each line of the letter with his finger as he began to read it. Looking up from the letter he questioned as to what her and Maggie's landing on Castle Caldwell grounds as children had to do with Maggie being in Dublin in 1849.

"Well I'm trying to give you background."

"Oh, I see."

Meghan quickly returned with book in hand and placed it on the bare table in front of her mother.

Colleen then went on about how their small boat was swept uncontrollably to the top end of Lower Lough Erne. Fearing for their very lives the girls held onto each other as their father managed to lower the single sail and take hold of the tiller firmly. In a sweeping motion following the flow of what seemed to be enormous waves and pounding rain the craft danced across the water as if being turned from one partner to another. Suddenly the storm ended as quickly as it had appeared, and the burly Dennis McMahon, father of the girls managed to hold the tiller so that they floated into a tributary to the lake. It was there that they washed ashore on the shoreline of the Caldwell Castle estate. Dennis lifted the drenched twelve-year-old Colleen up and swung her over the side of the boat onto land. Then instructing her to take hold of her younger sister, he did the same to Margaret, though he always called her Maggie much to their mother's protest as it being an undignified term for such a lovely little lass, scrawny that she was at the time. Looking like two rag dolls the girls stood holding onto each other waiting for their father to steady the vessel so that he might jump off it without it washing out into the river. The sun was breaking through the clouds as the drama unfolded and sitting not far from the scene was a lad of around 14 years old. He had taken refuge under a rocky crevice during the rain and was just then emerging as the storm passed.

Seeing the vessel rocking rather unsteadily he ran to Dennis to offer a hand. Dennis threw the lad a rope and in short order the boat was pulled ashore. The grateful Dennis was thanking the lad profusely as the girls shivered and held back tears as they knew not how they could possibly get back to Enniskillen from such a distance. Despite the lad having taken a form of shelter he was a bit damp himself and his bushy black hair was matted down around his round rose colored cheeks. A tall lad he already reached the height of Dennis and would surely pass him up as he matured further. By the cut of the cloth of his clothes it was also evident that he was a lad who came from a propertied family as no other could afford actual leather shoes, a button down shirt with jacket and pants that matched. The girls ogled him as a god come down from Olympus.

Having secured the boat, the lad noticed the shivering girls and suggested that they come up to the house and sit by the fire and discuss how they might sail their boat back to wherever they came. When he heard that it was Enniskillen, the lad stood amazed that they had survived such a horrific time on the lake.

"Maggie, of course, told him that our father was the best fisherman in Enniskillen. But that was how we were saved on that frightful day."

"And grateful I am that you were my love; for I may never have met you and we would not be sitting here with our darling Meghan." Sean grabbed their hands and kissed the

91

hand of his wife. "But how does that bring Maggie to Dublin?"

"Sean O'Grady, stop that and in front of our daughter. I'm getting to that point if you weren't so distracting."

Sean winked at Meghan and then folded his hands on the table like a schoolboy in Church.

"That's better. Now it turned out the lad's name was John Caldwell Bloomfield and the house he referred to was none other than Caldwell Castle of which he was heir. He was home for the summer holidays but on this day his parents were also impacted by the sudden storm and hadn't gotten home from Ballyshannon where they went to inspect their fishery business."

The excitement in Colleen's voice as she shared her tale was infectious and Meghan became caught up in it and begged for more of the story. And more was told and with the drama of theatrical flair as well.

"And so there we were two raggedy waifs and a soaked dadai, who nevertheless kept his posture rigid and bearing noble, so that the lad would not appear as tall as he was. Into this great room we strolled as if this was the type of living that we enjoyed on a daily basis. John called for some help. Margaret and I stood in front of the fireplace pulling our fingers through our hair trying in vain to untangle the mess. Dadai placed his fishing sack with a few things we brought for lunch should we catch some fish next to us to dry off as well and began to speak with the lad as if he were of his station in life."

"Was he handsome Momai?" asked Meghan.

Colleen grinned. "And how should I remember such a thing at my tender age at the time?"

Meghan's facial expression soured in disappointment as she had already had a picture in her mind of a Knight of the Round Table who had come to save her mother and aunt.

Colleen noted the frown. "Aye lass he was indeed." Then she quickly added. "But not nearly as dashing as your dadai."

Sean smiled with satisfaction. His role as hero of the family was not tarnished.

The lass' green eyes bugged out of her head as it were as she waited for more of the tale to be shared. Her mother went on with the story.

"Well there was your grandfather drinking a toast with the lad and saluting him for his good manners and helping hand. Your Auntie and I stood watching and wondering what such a liquid was as it had a strong scent which when consumed made our dadai shudder with delight. 'Now that will warm mi bones to be sure Johnny mi boy." Imagine calling the heir to a grand castle 'Johnny boy.' But that was your grandfather. No one was better than he, nor his family."

"But momai, dadai inherited a castle too, so aren't we grand as well? I mean Doonagore really belongs to us doesn't it dadai?"

Sean couldn't take this talk of castle and station in life any longer. "Aye lass it does indeed." And with that he went to the cupboard which held the McMahon china and opened a drawer below the display case. Taking out a thick book, which turned out to be a missal for prayers at mass he then removed a thick envelope. Mother and daughter watched and wondered though Colleen knew full well what that envelope contained but hadn't looked at it since their days of having to leave Doonagore Castle and move to the cottage.

"And here mi girl is proof of that ownership." Sean spread out the title bearing his family's name and his own name as heir to the castle itself. "And one day lass, when these days of blight end we shall be able to pay the taxes and return to our real home." He then turned quite solemn. "But should these dark days be longer than my life, now mind you they won't be, but should that come to pass, then you will know where you and your mommie may find this title and claim that which is rightfully yours."

Colleen and Meghan sat somberly not wanting to address such a future without him. Sean folded the title, replaced it into the missal and took it back to the cupboard. He turned with a wide smile to break up what had become a rather gloomy scene.

"Now then we were in Castle Caldwell with this young Lord who wasn't as dashing as me."

It worked and a laugh was had by all as Colleen picked up the story from where she had left off.

"Now as they consumed the last drop of that bone warming drink, a maid entered. She looked at John Bloomfield and

94

then with a nod from him came right up to us in her long black silk dress with a white apron so starched that it could stand alone should she choose to take it off. Asking for our hands she guided us out of the great room as the heads of stuffed beasts watched our departure. Up gigantic wooden stairs she took us, all the while telling us how wet we were and they not wanting us to catch a chill and fall ill."

Colleen went on to explain how they entered a bedroom which the maid informed them was used for guests. Naturally the two young girls were thrilled to be called guests of the castle. Within that room was a bed so big that should the girls choose to lie upon it they could very well be lost in it. There were two armed chairs one of which was situated in front of a dressing table on which were various combs and brushes. Each girl took turns on the chair as the maid dried their hair with a large cotton towel and then brushed their hair. As for their clothes, that created more of a challenge as there were no young girls in the household. But the maid made do by giving them a shirt and pants which once belonged to John at a younger age. As for dresses more suited for the rubbish heap than wearing she hung those to dry before another fireplace within the guest bedroom.

Having been washed, combed out and clothed the girls were returned to the great room with the heads of beasts hanging upon its walls. There under the glass eyes of Irish Red Deer and boars they found their father and the lad sitting at a round table enjoying yet another type of drink, this one poured from a crystal container. They heard John calling it brandy. The lad himself did not partake of that drink. Despite the dress of a boy the girls, Colleen with wild fluffy auburn hair and Maggie with long black as coal straight hair looked very much like girls. John immediately rose making no mention as to the clothes they wore were his very own and offered the girls a seat at the table where a meal was to be served shortly. Even in those days before the great famine, such a meal was unheard of in their young lives. For not only did they have fish and bread, but also potatoes, a vegetable soup and cake, a delight that the girls only experienced at Christmastime.

"So there we were taking the last crumb of cake from the plate when the lad asked our father as to what his plans were to get back to Enniskillen. The storm having passed, dadai told the lad that we'd be asking if an Inn were nearby so that they could get an early start the next day as he had his business to tend to. And that's when the talk began which flourished to this day."

Now Sean's eyes were about as wide as Meghan's as they heard the tale of how John Bloomfield took an interest in this McMahon business venture. Now Sean was quite aware that his father-in-law was a fisherman who created pottery on the side. In fact, the very china on their cupboard shelves was created by him. What he wasn't aware of was that the side business was being noticed, grew and now brought in extra income all these years. Thus they had been able to keep their modest cottage home and meet their taxes even when the blight spread north.

"'There is an Inn nearby. It's located in a small village called Belleek, which is on this Caldwell Estate land,' John Bloomfield informed mi dadai."

"'Then with your gracious permission we should be on our way,' mi dadai said."

"And this lad told mi dadai that it was getting dark already and there was plenty of room in the castle to put us up for the night. 'Besides' said John, 'my parents would never forgive me for not offering our hospitality.' And there you have it. A friendship had been formed between this young man and mi very own father."

The heads of the red deer and boars seemed to appear about them as Colleen brought them back to those days around the time of the Emancipation. They could see Dennis McMahon not wanting to insult his host, and yet being a proud man, insist on giving a gift to the lad. Within the traveling sack sitting by the hearth besides a few knives and hooks his wife had packed some of his own made dishes so that they may have a proper dinner time with the caught fish. Instead of the roughly hewn pottery ware she had actually put in a few pieces of the fine china he crafted, wrapped in cloths. Dennis presented the three dishes of fine white dishes with a rose pattern to the lad. At first John hesitated to receive such a fine gift knowing that such work took many hours of the skilled craftmanship of an artisan to create.

"In the end he accepted them with delight and the conversation went into the wee hours as to how such fine pieces were created and so forth. As for Margaret and me, we wearied of such talk and were soon led up to that room with the enormous bed which was to be ours for the night. I think it was that very night when Margaret decided that she would one day go to the city and make her way in the world."

Colleen opened the faded pages of the book to the map of Ireland. On it she searched for and found Enniskillen, traced

97

her finger up the Lower Lough Erne and into the river to Belleek and where the Castle stood.

"There as you can see, we were quite a distance from home. Getting back would be no easy task to be sure."

"But you did get back," Sean said as Colleen gave him that look which stated 'watch yourself' and quickly he added. "And as I said, we thank God for that. But what about this chap Bloomfield and Maggie's being in Dublin?"

He and Meghan soon learned that about a year or two after that chance meeting John went off to Trinity College in Dublin to study. There he met two chums by the name of Robert William Armstrong and David McBirney. Robert was from County Lonsford and David from a merchant family in Dublin itself. After college Robert went to London as an architect and David took over the family business. They remained friends over the years.

"Grand just grand," said Sean. "And that's why Maggie's in Dublin, right?"

"Sean O'Grady…" Colleen stopped and glanced at her daughter. She held her tongue and went on. "That's exactly why. Last year David was sent a sample of Margaret's weaving by John Bloomfield and was then offered a job at his Dublin store in charge of the Linen Department."

"Damn good fortune love. I'm happy for her. But she being alone in Dublin that is not like Enniskillen love."

"'Tis the truth you'd be speaking Sean," Colleen replied. "But her loneliness won't be much longer."

With that she turned the page of the letter over and pointed to a passage which Sean began to read.

...and so dear sister I have met a fine gentleman by the name of Colin Logan. His duties include overseeing the Export Department for the McBirney Mercantile Co. That dear one means that he meets with me on a regular basis. We have fallen in love and he has asked me to marry him. This is why I am writing to you. He belongs to the Anglican Church. What will father say of a match between a Protestant and his Catholic daughter?

Sean stopped reading. "Good God Colleen, your father will never condone such a match. Not now that we have some religious freedom."

"And that my dear husband is why she is coming to Doolin."

"I'm confused again. Meghan, does this make sense to you?"

The lass woefully shook her head negatively to and fro, then positively up and down.

"You're no help at all."

His confusion was soon to be illuminated. Maggie was to stay with them while Colin went on to Galway to make arrangements for their marriage. The ceremony would take place in St. Nicholas Collegiate Cathedral before his departure for America to open trade talks. Colin went to school with the Cathedral's current Rector who would overlook the mixed marriage issue.

Sean bolted from his chair and began to pace.

"By all the saints! Colleen don't you understand. Maggie will be excommunicated from Holy Mother Church which we have fought all these years to preserve."

"Momai, what does excommunicate mean?" asked Meghan.

Her mother and father suddenly became distressed. Not wanting to cause the lass grief they simply told her that because of who their families were, one in Enniskillen and the other in Dublin that there was a problem to arrange such a marriage. It wasn't a complete lie but it made do.

Colleen pulled Sean to the side of the hearth hoping that the young ears of their daughter would not hear her whispered plea.

"Sean, they're in love. Are we to shun them for being in love? What if you were Anglican and I Catholic, would you not have married me?"

"That's different."

"No, love, it's not. Will you allow Meghan and me to go to Galway and witness their union?"

He looked into her tear filled eyes. Such a decision belonged to her, he told her. After all Maggie was her sister. He went on to make an observation concerning the cost of such a trip all the way to Galway. It was pleasant news to hear that the

McBirney family was covering the cost of the trip to Galway for Maggie's family due to the hastiness of needing to send Colin off to America.

The two walked hand in hand back to the table. Meghan watched, looking for a sign of some kind as to what was really taking place. What she saw were two smiles.

"Well now," Sean began. "It seems that there is little to do save wait for Aunt Maggie to arrive."

"Isn't this all too grand," Meghan responded. "And we're all going to Galway too."

Inishbofin Harbor

Chapter Five: An Inishbofin First Communion

Now a letter was hastily sent off to Maggie in Dublin. It expressed the O'Grady family's joy on the news of her impending marriage to Colin Logan and her being welcome to come to visit them. It would take over a week for it to cross Ireland from Doolin to Dublin, though it was May and the weather was improving.

At the precise moment of that letter being sent off to Dublin, on the Isle of Inishbofin the Shields family and Father O'Malley ate their meal of fish and bread silently. Their eating of the meal was quick as they continued to absorb what young James had told them concerning his offering of a petition for God to bless his journey during the Blessing before the meal.

Kathleen Shields, the mother of the lad, rose from the table to begin the cleaning after the meal. She took the plates and placed them into a bucket of water. Father O'Malley rose to assist her but she had refused his help, despite her frail condition. 'Twas her husband James Sr. who then took the bucket outside for the washing.

"It would appear my love that your long time desire for our son is about to be if not fulfilled certainly addressed openly."

"Aye my love," began Kathleen. "And yet I don't feel pleased. He's our babe. I can't live without him about."

Sinking her head into her husband's shoulder she wept. In her heart she wanted a better future for their son. In her mind she was acutely aware of the famine as she herself would be a prime example of it. All around them the tragic stories of children dying reached them from all corners of not only their island but across on the mainland as well. And so she wept in the caressing arms of her husband. That weeping was being observed by Father O'Malley as he stood by the window at the backside of the room. He quietly turned toward young James and was about to question him as to what was on his mind. Instead he paused and watched the lad carefully remove the single brass candlestick with its half burned candle from the table and placed it on the mantle. On the flat stone ledge there was a family Bible propped up against the stones of the hearth's chimney. On the blackened stones of the chimney hung a Crucifix in the Celtic style made of stone. The lad made the sign of the cross, touched the Bible and sighed heavily.

For almost three years Father O'Malley had been training the lad in the core teachings of the faith and in secular studies as well. He saw potential in him and yet he was just a boy soon to be but fourteen years old. In the inside pocket of his black frock coat a document stood ready to be enacted should the time arrive when the priest could verify a true vocation within the lad. It was at the boy's own mother's urging that he had pursued the idea of young James being sent to a preparatory seminary for training. For her such a future would mean salvation from the curse of the blight and the making of a fine servant of God. And yet she wept and this touched the priest's heart.

"Perhaps this is not the time for the lad to discuss his future," he mused to himself. *"And yet he has brought the subject up and his First Communion is at hand. What better time than now when the spirit moves within him?"*

"James lad, do come here," Father O'Malley began.

The lad obediently came to the priest and stood next to him at the window. Then taking the lad's shoulders into his hands, he turned him toward the window so that his parents were clearly in view. What he saw was his father wrapping the shawl of his mother about her tightly and dabbing her eyes with its edge. She looked up to him with a faint smile, took a breath and tucked her arm into his as they moved to the doorway. The boy turned as they entered. He and the priest took a few steps forward so as not to give notice that the scene outside was seen by them.

Kathleen walked directly to the lad and took his face between her damp hands. He gave her a smile as he ignored the cold hands on his skin.

"So my darling boy, tell us more about being like Jesus in the Temple." Then wrapping a part of her shawl about him she guided him to the table. The two men followed, each casting an eye to the other but not speaking a word.

James enjoying the warm wool about him snuggled for a moment, then sat upright and as if coming out of a cocoon slipped from its warmth onto the chair next to his mother. With a sudden shudder as his ragged shirt hit the cool air and spread that coolness across his chest the lad began to explain his intent. With the fervor of honest conviction and a strong faith he reiterated that he wanted to be a priest just like Father O'Malley. The priest bowed his head humbly once again not seeing himself as such a role model. The elder James patted him on the back as he did so. It was a sign that he was indeed such a model of service for the Lord.

"And so momai, dadai, it's plain to see that to become a priest I must improve my Latin, my knowledge of the faith and of the world. To do that I must leave for a time."

There was a collective gasp from his parents. The words of Simeon in scripture came to life for them: "And a sword shall pierce your own heart."

The lad took his mother's hand, stretched his arm across the table to grab onto the hand of his father. "But don't worry, Father O'Malley will be with me, won't you father? And he'll make sure that I get home to you."

Now it was the priest going through scripture in his mind as he was feeling what Joseph must have felt when given charge over Jesus and his mother. He however, had never given it that kind of thought. And yet within that coat pocket was the directive of the Prior General of the Augustinian Order. In it were two tickets for passage on a ship to America. He was being assigned to St. Augustine Church in Philadelphia, Pennsylvania. There had been trouble, exactly what kind he didn't know. What he did know was that a new school was being founded and he was to help establish it. And that school would be a fine place for the young James to be educated, so thought the Prior. However with the emotions running fairly high at dinner it seemed imprudent to address the issue. Thus he tried to change the subject to the First Communion Mass scheduled for the next day.

"Mr. and Mrs. Shields," he began as if young James hadn't set off a wave of heart rending thoughts. "Have you given any thought as to how we should arrange the children who will be receiving their First Communion at mass tomorrow?"

The elder James just looked at the priest with an expression of furrowed lines on his forehead and disbelief in his asking such a question after what his son had just announced. Father O'Malley returned a slight smile and a wink which eased his thinking of the priest as being a bit daft. Kathleen however took the bait not wanting to insult the man of the cloth. There would be plenty of time to address the real issue, that being the future for the young teen James Shields Jr.

"Well Father, you needn't worry yourself about the mass. We mothers have it all under control. Those receiving Holy Communion for the first time shall stand in front of the altar and form an arc as in a doorway of the ancient Church before its destruction."

"That sounds quite grand Mrs. Shields. The children will be able to see everything and during my sermon I'll be able to speak to them directly."

Now during this exchange the father and son sat dumbfounded and had nothing to contribute to the issue which really was a non-issue as everything was planned and if the elder James knew anything about the women of the island, as he did, then all was set in stone and whatever they might suggest would fall on deaf ears anyway. And so they sat, one knowing that the discussion would go nowhere and the other wanting to talk about his vocation to the priesthood.

"That will be lovely to be sure," Kathleen said.

Then she fell silent as did the priest. The four now sat around the table each desiring to find a word which might express the joy of the occasion rather than the issue of a vocation for the lad. Darkness shrouded the island. Neither stars nor the moon were making their presence felt due to a cloud cover. A hazy golden light did its best to light up the interior of the Shields cottage but for all at that table the pall of darkness only brought attention to the unnamed and unspoken issue of young James leaving home to pursue a vocation to the priesthood.

After several minutes of sitting without a word being spoken, the elder James rose, went to the mantle and relit the candle which the lad had returned there. Bringing it to the table was a mistake for it gave illumination to the faces which were the windows into the hearts of those seated around it. And what was seen through that human window was anxiousness for the lad who was bursting to talk of his intent, despair of a mother who sought this very moment but knew too well that despite promises to the contrary her son would never return home, and an uncomfortable priest with furrowed brow who patted his breast pocket in which a certain letter he didn't wish to share rested.

As for the father of the lad, he had purposely swept the candle cross the table to illuminate the faces and then set in dead center between the four of them.

"So then Father, 'tis unusual for a lad to leave home at thirteen wouldn't you say? I mean shouldn't he be given a chance to become a full grown man first?"

There, it had been said and his heart revealed to all.

"But dadai, our Lord was twelve," chimed in young James.

"Aye, that being the truth," the elder James paused deliberately adding a bit of drama to the scene. He stretched his arm around the boy's shoulders and leaned into him. "But, he went home with his parents until he became a full grown man. Is that not right Father?"

The priest didn't know how to respond. Certainly the bible story did say that Jesus returned home to grow in wisdom and grace. At the same time in the 19th century world to become a priest especially in Ireland was most difficult which was why those who sought to serve the Church often went to Europe's mainland to study. Instead he fumbled with the letter which he removed from his coat pocket hoping that it would address the issue better than he could.

Kathleen, who had said nothing and just looked at her son being held by his father, sat motionless. Her eyes, however, began to follow the movement of the priest as he placed the letter onto the table. And yet she remained quiet allowing the priest to speak the first words in what had become an unbearably long period of silence.

"Mr. Shields, before I address your question, let me just say that I know how you must feel about your only child wishing to leave home. So too must have Mary and Joseph in the Gospel story. It is true that they had the enjoyment of Jesus at home for many more years. On the other hand here we sit over eighteen hundred years later in a land which is being devastated by the worse blight in history. On your own island a children's cemetery has been created to receive the children who have died from lack of nourishment and decent living conditions."

"Father please, we are painfully aware of the loss of Inishbofin children."

"I am sorry Mr. Shields. I only mention this horror to give example to what is happening not only on this island but throughout Ireland from what I have heard in Galway and on the Aran Islands."

Another period of silence was about to commence as Father O'Malley felt that he had just insulted the lad's father. Young James looked first at his father who mumbled something inaudible and waved his free hand to indicate that the priest should not feel badly. Then he looked toward the priest, who with cast down eyes was turning the envelope over and over in his hands as he pondered how to approach the subject.

Kathleen had continued to say nothing. She just watched the priest turning that letter in his smooth pale hands… hands which never tilled a field, built a wall of stones or pulled a fish from the sea. What she didn't see were the scourge scars across his back. These he had received during his time of imprisonment for nothing more than being a Catholic priest who sought religious freedom for his flock. She dwelled on those hands because for her they symbolized a future for her son. For her, it would be a future which would see him as a "fisher of men." It would be a future in which he wouldn't be forced to till another man's lands; a future in which he would be clothed and fed through the writings he would create now that he had learned to read and write with a flair which would be the envy of members of Parliament.

With all of these visions flooding her brain she decided that she couldn't allow silence to destroy her dream of a bright future for her son, even if it meant that, for a time, he would have to leave her.

Before the priest could respond or her husband offer an apology she continued.

"Now 'tis only out of love for our son did mi husband speak so, Father."

The priest nodded understanding and smiled at the elder James. Kathleen watched the wordless exchange of contrition and forgiveness. That is the Augustinian priest being sorry for his graphic description of children dying and her husband being sorry for using the Gospel against whatever the priest intended to say. Then both forgave the other with a smile and nod of the head.

The air now being cleared, it was time to make her move. She chose to do so with a statement so casual and innocent that one would never have felt the tension which pervaded the room just seconds ago.

"Now then, could it be true that the men of this house have no curiosity at all?"

She paused and waited for a response. None came as her husband and son just looked at each other in bewilderment. And as for the priest, he was clueless as he let the envelope slip through his fingers and fall onto the table while he too looked at her with wide eyed confusion.

"Well for all the saints!" she virtually shouted. "Do none of you see the envelope which just fell from the Father's hands?"

Kathleen grabbed the envelope before the priest could react and waved it in front of the face of her husband.

The lad and his father sat with mouths open. The former not wanting to push the issue in order to spare his parents' feelings and the latter not wanting to face the issue at all. Now however, it was at the urging of one's wife and the other's mother which forced them to speak to the issue. Though her heart was already aching regarding that which may be in that envelope, it was also at her insistence that Father O'Malley initiated the contact.

As quickly as she moved to get a reaction so too did she stop the waving and just stared at the worn envelope on which the seal of the Augustinian Order was evident in the red wax holding it closed. Then she placed it gently back on the table in front of the priest.

It was the lad who spoke and softly did he do so. At the same time he tried to act curious and unknowing of its possible contents. As he spoke he made his way around the table to stand between the priest and his mother.

"So Father, is this about the First Communion?" he began.

The elder James rested his rough hands on the table but remained stoic in expression save for glistening eyes revealing his inner turmoil. Kathleen held onto the lad's arm. The moment she had wanted so badly had arrived and now she wasn't quite sure that she wanted to hear the results of her request. She began to cough nervously. James urged her to sip a little of the tea still steaming in her cup. That steam created a fog of vision as she looked through it toward the priest who was breaking the seal on the envelope.

The crack of the breaking wax seemed like the sound of an ax splitting wood to them and yet it was but an almost gentle sound barely audible beyond the table. The slivers of wax fell to the rough oak table top as the priest lifted from the envelope a cream colored parchment paper. The single candle flickered and reflected its light through the paper. A dark cursive hand written ink was visible in the not so steady hands of the priest.

"This letter would not be in reference to the Mass for those receiving Frist Communion tomorrow," he said softly. "Perhaps it would be best if I just read its contents and then address its meaning afterwards as I have no idea as to what it contains."

Young James took a seat on his mother's lap. The elder James sat back and tried to show interest and a relaxed posture leaning back into the chair so as to ease the building tension. Kathleen held onto her son as the priest read the letter emblazoned with the crest of the Order of St. Augustine in gold and black depicting a flaming heart pierced by an arrow overlaying the open pages of the Gospel.

"Dear Father O'Malley:
May the grace of our Lord Jesus Christ be with you and to those with whom you are sharing this response to your inquiry regarding a possible vocation to the priesthood.

*Upon prayerful consideration with our Council and Vicar
General it has been determined that despite the young age of
the possible candidate, James Shields, the weight of your
argument on his behalf and the desire of his mother should
be addressed."*

The lad squirmed upon hearing his name. Kathleen gave him
a hug and James broke a slight smile with a nod of his head.
Father O'Malley continued.

*"It has been determined that given the current conditions in
Ireland, a history of persecution of Catholic priests which
has required us to train our Friars in Europe and therefore
resulting in Ireland as not having a preparatory seminary
all candidates for the priesthood should ordinarily be sent to
our House in Rome..."*

The priest was cut off in mid-sentence as the lad exclaimed,
"Rome! Mommie, Dadai 'tis to Rome they want me to go."
He jumped from his mother's lap and ran to his father who
took him onto his lap and embraced his boney frame.

"Aye lad, ordinarily that would be the case. But if I may
continue..."

"Oh sure Father, what else does it say?"

Making no further comment as to the lad's enthusiasm, the
priest continued.

*"however, since the candidate has had few educational
experiences it has been determined that he would need
further studies at one of our schools for younger students.*

Therefore, should the parents grant permission for such relocation, we recommend that you take the candidate with you to the City of Philadelphia in the United States of America to the parish of St. Augustine. A new school is being prepared for operation and while you are to be assigned to assist in that formation it is with our blessing that the candidate accompany you and take his preparatory studies at St. Augustine School."

"That's about all the Prior General writes, except for a closing reflection from the works of St. Augustine, which he specifically writes for young James to consider," Father O'Malley noted as he continued.

"So that we believe in Christ, dwell in his words. By dwelling there, we will truly be his disciples. For he doesn't have only twelve apostles as his disciples. He also has those who dwell in his word."

With the reverence of closing the Missal at Mass, the priest gently folded the letter and replaced it into the envelope. Then he held it up to the lad's father. But with a nod of permission it was the boy who took hold of the letter and held it over his heart, which was then pounding away with excitement he tried to control. His teary eyed parents sat silently just looking at each other, all the while thinking, *"America, that's across the ocean. Even if he should survive such a voyage it would still mean that we would never see our son again."*

Excited though he was, young James also felt a twinge of regret. He had of course heard of America. In fact his father and the men of the village would often speak about the many from the mainland; those who were leaving Ireland to seek a new life there. But the City of Philadelphia was quite another quandary for the lad. So once again it was he who broke the silence.

"So then 'tis not to Rome that I'd be going." He caressed the letter held next to his chest as if by rubbing it the Prior General himself might appear and answer his questions. "That being the case, where is this place called Philadelphia?"

"Now lad," Father O'Malley said kindly. "All your questions will be answered in due time. However it's the questions of your parents which I must address first."

The lad rose from his father's lap and took a chair, placing it between he and his mother. Then he waited with letter in hand for them to speak. Turning his head from left to right and back again so as to look them in the eyes he waited for one of them to speak. And speak they did in a bombardment of questions which spilled out so rapidly that the priest was hard pressed to address them as he may have wished.

By the time the barrage of questions had ceased the lad had heard that he indeed had been accepted as a candidate but one which needed further training before entering the seminary itself.

He heard the quivering voice of his mother who hadn't considered the lad being sent across the ocean to America. She had asked about a time frame and how long would her son have to study in America. Where would he enter the seminary and of course, where was this City of Philadelphia located. She, her husband and the lad pondered on the priest's answers.

These included an explanation of the usual time frame for studying for the priesthood- that is finishing secondary school, going on to college and then the study of Theology in preparation for Ordination. In all, they heard that such preparation may well last up to ten years given that James was only on his way to turning 14 years of age and had little formal education except that from the priest himself. However, he noted that the college years may very well be back in Europe but not Ireland given that it had no formal Catholic institutions for such studies as yet.

Throughout this exchange of time lines, study opportunities and geography lessons, the young James remained prudently quiet. He just watched the soft rain end from his position at the table which allowed him to peer through the window opposite him. His parents and the priest were now in such serious discussion of his future that only the lad noticed the faint reds and oranges bouncing off clouds over the harbor area. He propped his head up on his fisted hands and wondered if America also had such a sight at sunset. He never noticed that all conversation had ceased and that all eyes were now fixed on him.

"So mi lovely boy," began his mother. "'Tis a great moment in your life that we'd be discussing."

"Aye son, what is your feeling on going to America?" asked his father who in his most inner being hoped that the lad would refuse to go.

There was no answer forthcoming from the daydreaming lad. The adults interpreted this silence to be the result of the enormity of such a move. And so they waited. Still the lad peered out the window for now there was a shadowy figure approaching the cottage and this caught his interest. Finally Father O'Malley stepped in.

"James are ye with us on this or not?"

The question was asked forcefully so as to jar the lad from his distraction.

"Oh, sorry Father, I was just watching the sky."

"James mi boy, show some respect for the Father," chided the lad's mother.

Now the lad felt remorseful as he hadn't meant to offend. His demeanor of watching the last rays of the sun however, seemed to indicate to his parents a disinterest in the conversation.

"Momai, Dadai, I meant no disrespect. It's just that I was wondering what a sunset in America would be like."

The comment struck his parents in the heart. His father pulled at the collar of his flannel shirt. Suddenly despite the dampness of night setting in and the hearth fire but a flicker he still felt warm under the collar. This was not at all what he wanted to hear. A teardrop was wiped away by the lad's mother with the corner of her apron.

Father O'Malley, for his part, could hardly avoid taking in these emotional responses though unspoken they were. Yet he felt compelled to have his question answered.

"So lad, does such wondering, about sunsets in America mean that ye are with us on the Prior's recommendation for your studies?"

With a wiggle to set himself upright in the chair, young James with those now widened sea blue eyes, which looked to his parents with love and then to the priest with excitement for what his future may hold, responded. With a politeness which under normal circumstances his parents would find most praiseworthy answered.

"'Tis an honor for me to be sure Father but..."

'Twas that last word, "but," which clanged in the ears of the adults when they expected a smooth symphonic note of affirmation to the plan sent by the Prior General.

"But?" the adults asked with one voice.

Before the lad had chance to elaborate further there was a knocking at the door. The startled adults bolted in their seats as the senior James jumped up wondering aloud as to who would call at such an hour. The lad pressed his face against the window but only saw a shadowy figure. His father approached the door while speaking to the others.

"Now who could be calling at such an hour?"

"I did see someone outside our window, dadai," called out the lad.

His father swung open the top half of the door. The last of the flickering peat fire in the hearth barely illuminated the slender figure in frock coat and woolen cap which being of

119

dark color blended with the night which had fallen as that conditional word, "but" was spoken.

"Mr. Shields," the voice was that of Kiernan O'More, the landlord's representative. "Blessings on this house. 'Tis with regrets that I disturb you this evening, however I have news which may be of interest to you."

"Mr. O'More is it? And welcome you are to be sure. Peace be with you."

Mrs. Shields was at her husband's side so quickly that the priest hardly realized that she had left the table.

"Do let me take your coat sir," she began.

Now their welcome was quite genuine as the young man was of their island, and though he espoused the Anglican Communion he none-the-less supported freedom of religion and all in the village knew it. Now the taking of his coat was not without a challenge as he held in his arms several bricks of peat newly cut from the village bog. He made it known that the thin streak of smoke from their chimney indicated that their allotment might be depleted. Thus he handed the bricks to the elder James who in turn motioned for the lad to come to him. Into his arms he placed the bricks of peat. Young James hastened to the hearth to place one of those bricks into the now smoldering fire. A few pokes with an iron rod kept for such purposes and soon it began to glow with newly formed flames.

"That's most kind of you Mrs. Shields." He removed his coat and handed it to her while Mr. Shields took his cap. "I see that you have a guest. Could that be the priest who has been visiting you these many months?"

Mr. and Mrs. Shields stood motionless and speechless as they knew that at one time the young priest had been imprisoned in Galway before the emancipation act became law some twenty years prior. And yet despite that some priests were still under suspicion as malcontents. The quiet tension filled the cottage. The lad stood frozen at the hearth then took a breath to answer the landlord's representative.

With a step toward the priest, the lad prepared to make introductions as his parents obviously had given up taking such an initiative.

"Mr. O'More, may I present Father Thomas O'Malley of the Order of St. Augustine."

With genuine courtesy Kiernan approached the priest with an outstretched hand.

"Thank you young James, I am most pleased to meet you Reverend O'Malley. The villagers have talked so much about your visits that I feel that I already know you."

A sudden sigh of relief broke the frozen tension among the parents. They immediately invited the representative to have a seat at the table where he stood shaking the priest's hand vigorously. For his part, the priest responded cordially as well though it was only a veneer of courteousness which he offered. Within him there still was an apprehensiveness as to why this government official would be making a call on the Shields family under the cover of night.

"My visits have indeed been pleasurable sir. The people of Inishbofin are most welcoming."

Kiernan agreed. This was followed by silence again so once again the lad took the lead.

"We were just discussing my education Mr. O'More. It's to America that I'd be going with Father O'Malley."

Kiernan stroked his short scruff of a beard but offered no sign of shock.

"Indeed, and it was upon seeing the light in the window of your cottage that prompted me to share with you the news of education for our young people of Inishbofin. It is that very subject which I have come to discuss."

With a clumping sound of chairs being slightly lifted and dragged closer to the landlord's representative so as to take in every word, the adults virtually surrounded him. What they heard was the news that the owner of the Isle of Inishbofin, the Second Marquis of Sligo Howe Browne had a son named George Browne and he was interested in the plight of the people in their landholdings particularly of its children. Throughout Ireland the local schools, which were religiously affiliated were being replaced by government schools called the Kildare Schools. It would be the son of the Marquis' hope that Inishbofin would soon have such a school.

The reaction to the news was dramatic as the Shields elders cheered. The lad however said nothing and this didn't go unnoticed by Kiernan O'More, nor the priest, nor the lad's parents.

"Now young James, doesn't this news please you. All of Inishbofin knows of your desire to be educated and how well your studies with the good Reverend here have progressed. They also have heard your parents speak of your desire to become a priest."

The lad's parents urged him to speak and speak did he with courage and determination in the face of his better who spoke for the Marquis himself.

"Mr. O'More, it is true that I wish to serve the Lord," began the young teen. "I am pleased that my friends may learn to read and write as have I thanks to Father O'Malley. But..."

There it was again, that word which caused pause in the conversation of his parents and priest. Perhaps now they would have his conditional term explained.

"But what?" asked Kiernan O'More.

"But will that Kildare School be one in which I may advance to Ordination?"

Kiernan was hard pressed to answer such a question in that he was no longer a practicing Catholic. He did however know that the government run schools were to have no religious affiliation other than having the Bible read as part of the classes. Thus the "but" was answered in his mind as he responded.

"Lad ye shall have the Bible study as part of your schooling when the school is established here. Imagine Catholic,

Anglican, Presbyterian children all studying together! Isn't that grand? We may have peace amongst us yet."

Now young James nodded, offered a meek smile and contemplated the remark. "Whose Bible would be used?"

Now the question was received with astonishment coming from such a young person. For it was quite clear that what was being asked was whether or not the St. Jerome Vulgate Bible (the Catholic version) or the King James Version (the one used by the Anglican Church) of the Bible was to be used. No one had to answer for all knew that it would be the King James Version of Scripture which would be studied. And so the lad nodded again.

"I understand and the Word of God is for all to be sure. However for me, there is more to be learned. So I must look to mi momai and dadai and their wish for mi future."

Father O'Malley now understood what that first "but" meant. The lad would indeed desire to go to America but only with his parents blessing or not at all. He placed his hand on the boney shoulder of the lad and both looked toward the parents as did Kiernan as he noted that he had indeed heard of the Kildare Schools and their success with children.

None of what the priest nor Mr. O'More's enthusiasm for the prospective school mattered to James and Kathleen Shields. Both were now thinking of their son's future. Perhaps he wouldn't have to leave for America after all. As for the priest, he was still dwelling on the lad's question of which version of the Bible would be used in the school. He wondered whether such a possibility of all religious

124

denominations coming together in one school could be possible. Then he dismissed the thought as an impossible dream as long as Ireland was an occupied country. In his opinion, despite the Act of Emancipation, the Irish people were being forced into the ever expanding British Empire.

Despite this silent turmoil tearing at the lad's parents and the priest as well, they all regarded Kiernan O'More as a sincere fellow despite his role as the landlord's representative.

"Aye 'tis the hope of peace which we must never lose," commented the elder James, thus breaking the awkward silence following the question about the Bible.

And so the conversation swerved from the topic of Bible version to the concerns of what the potato blight was inflicting upon Ireland as the "Great Hunger" spread across the land. The hearing of the news, that thousands on the mainland were departing for the Americas and Australia to seek a better life, overwhelmed the simple folk in the Shields cottage. It also brought the conversation back to the lad's future. And once again it was the lad who would refocus their dialogue on that dream.

With his brilliant eyes peeking through his coal like wavy hair, once again hanging in his face, he spoke with conviction and also with a twinge of regret that what he was about to say may hurt Mr. O'More's feelings while also causing grief in his parents. He rose from his position on the floor in front of the hearth. His ragged clothes gave evidence once again of the poverty and deprivation in which his family survived, for one could hardly call it "living." Such a term as that would indicate some degree of comfort and joy outside their family life.

He shifted his weight from foot to foot as he scanned the room as if to take in a sight to which he would soon bid farewell. His heart thumped rapidly. It seemed that all present could hear its rhythmic beat as if a drum were being pounded. And yet the adults were still caught up in the news of schools, the "Great Hunger" and the Queen's upcoming visit. So he cleared his throat and gulped hard. All heads turned toward him and on their faces he could see the thoughts they held. They in turn readily saw each torn piece of shirt and holes in his pants as the orange-red glow of the flames peeked through the holes and emphasized the ragged cloth in eerie shreds of material through which the flames' light sought to travel. The boy spoke and all listened with awe and heartbreak.

"In America everyone is equal. Everyone is happy and everyone has money enough to eat and wear shoes even if it's not Sunday. And their clothes are fine woven frocks and coats with no patches I'd say as well. I shall send Momai a new bonnet and shawl and dadai a bright flannel shirt and wool cap to keep him warm."

The lad paused to take a breath. His eyes glistened and yet he stood firmly in place. His heart wanted him to hug his parents and yet he knew what he had to do if they should have a chance to survive and hold onto the hope his mother placed in his service to the Church. What he saw were four adults with gapping wide mouth expressions which not only spoke of the lad's outlandish speech of freedom but also the dashing of all hopes that the Kildare School might be an alternative for his education.

Father O'Malley remained silent so as to allow time for the lad's parents to respond. But it was Kiernan O'More who broke that silence after the lad's declaration of independence of sorts.

"So, it would seem that young James has grand plans in mind."

The thirteen-year-old heart pounded a loud "thump, thump, thump." The boy wanted to speak his mind but once again chose to be prudent and say nothing for the moment.

"Our son has been prepared for this moment for almost three years Mr. O'More. 'Tis unlikely that the news which ye have brought would likely change that which his mother and I have sought for him thanks to the good Father here."

Such words coming from the lad's father who had never outrightly encouraged either the lad's vocation to the priesthood and certainly not his leaving the island let alone Ireland startled the boy. It would seem impossible for his pounding heart to increase its beat and yet it did.

"What next," he thought. He waited and watched the faces of each adult.

With a broken heart in the knowledge that her dream for her son was actually about to become a reality, Kathleen Shields tugged her shawl about her shoulders quite tightly as if to give her the courage she needed. No tears, just glistening eyes looked back at her son, while the men watched and waited to hear those as yet unspoken words to be uttered. She turned her head so as to peer directly into the eyes of Mr. O'More, who himself shifted on the wooden chair

127

handed down to Kathleen as part of her dowry. It creaked as he did so.

"Mi husband has said all that is needed for this night Mr. O'More. Tomorrow we shall celebrate Holy Mass and our James shall receive our Lord in Holy Communion. For now that shall be what needs to be discussed at this time."

The young overseer of the Marquis of Sligo's lands didn't know how to respond to the boy nor to his parents. The talking of freedom and equality aside, the thought of speaking of Mass and Eucharist openly despite the Act of Emancipation was still a rarity.

 In what can best be described as a hoarseness in his voice he said, "I understand."

Then he was rescued by Father O'Malley's intervention.

"Aye, we should be finalizing our plans for the celebration to be sure, Mrs. Shields. And in that vein I have a surprise for you and the lad as well."

Now the prudently patient lad could no longer hold his tongue for a second longer. He ran to the priest and plopped himself onto his lap so as to look directly into the man's clear green eyes which widened with shock at the emotional plop on his lap.

"Is it what ye promised Father? Is it? Is it?"

The priest's hand swept through the lad's thick and unruly hair not unlike his very own. He smiled.

"Aye lad, it's that very thing."

Now save for the lad and the priest not a soul knew what the meaning of this exchange meant. What was this promise, one could only guess. All froze in anticipation of what would come next. The lad jumped from the priest's lap and ran to hug his mother and father. Then he stood before the overseer with a wide grin.

"'Tis Captain O'Flaherty and his sons who shall be returning to Inishbofin for the celebration," he excitedly stated. "Is that not so Father O'Malley?"

"That's the truth that you'd be speaking lad. It was to be a surprise but this night being so full of the unexpected, I thought it best to confirm the visit now. They are anchored just beyond the harbor entrance for they will need your guidance once again lad as they enter the harbor on the morrow."

The lad's joy soon became infectious. Soon they were speaking about the O'Flaherty's first visit when the young James had guided them safely into the harbor. There was talk of the great feast they provided at that time and of the parade right past Mr. O'More's house. And wasn't he so pleased to remember the lad upon the donkey's back, he reminded them.

"'Tis welcome they shall be Reverend O'Malley. In fact should they wish, they may enjoy the hospitality of my home should they be able to enter the harbor this night, as you too are welcome in my home."

"That is most gracious of you Mr. O'More, but given the time and the tide perhaps it's best that they stay anchored at sea. And as for me, it would appear that I am too long in this Shields home full of hospitality. For the tide has surely come in and cut my path off to the fortress ruins."

"That would be true, Father," confirmed Mr. Shields.

"Then 'tis here that ye shall stay Father," offered Mrs. Shields. "Humble that it may be."

"Such an invitation is most appreciated dear lady and most kind are you to make the offer. However on this last night with your son, I shall remove myself to the harbor area bluff."

Now all that had transpired in the talking of the O'Flaherty Clan's arrival really sank into their consciousness. For the Captain, and his brood, were coming to take not only the good Father back to the Aran Islands, but also the lad. It would be the beginning of the young James' journey to America. Tears did form as this realization of why the Captain had come entered their hearts as well as their brain.

Kathleen opened her shawl and wrapped it around her son as she embraced him. The elder James rose to join them taking hold of the two in what were once strong arms which removed rocks from fields so that potatoes could be planted.

Moved by this sight as if the Gospel had come to life the priest rose and outstretched his arms over the three Shields and blessed them.

"This night may the Grace of our Lord Jesus fill your hearts and give you comfort. May the joy of knowing that young James is about to become a disciple in the Lord's service fill this house and all of Inishbofin. In the name of the Father and of the Son and of the Holy Spirit."

There was no more that could be added. The elder James looked up from the huddle and smiled at the priest and overseer. With that, Father O'Malley placed his hand on Kiernan's shoulder and suggested that it was indeed time to depart. Turning once again at the door thus facing the trio at the hearth, he spoke to the lad.

"We shall meet at the harbor entrance lad, at daybreak."

With that being said, he opened the weathered door and walked into a moonlit night with Kiernan at his side.

At the hearth the family took a seat on the floor. There their eyes were lifted to the mantle on which the family Bible, which had belonged to the lad's grandfather, rested.

Outside the moon peeked through wispy clouds floating about as the soft night turned cool and promising a clear day in the morrow. Priest and Overseer walked along the still soggy dirt of the road with only the moon and stars to illuminate their way so as to avoid a puddle scattered here and there.

"Reverend O'Malley, this island will not be the same without that boy scampering about talking of the Pirate Queen. 'Tis a hero we shall be losing tomorrow given how he saved Captain O'Flaherty and his ship on that first visit."

"Good sir, you have spoken with truthfulness. Yet there is more which shall be taking place in the morrow. I shall leave with you a sum of coins which I hope shall be enough to pay rent on Mr. Shields' land for the next several months so that he may tend to his wife's needs. Their grief shall be as if young James had succumbed to the blight and buried in the children's cemetery. This I assure you shall be their mood."

Kiernan agreed to hold the sum in Mr. Shields' name as the priest knew the man would never have accepted such charity without working for it. The coins of the Realm having been given their talk then focused on the location for the Mass given that no Catholic Church had as yet been completed since the Emancipation Act. The one started had come to a halt given the plummeting economic condition brought on by the "Great Hunger" having arisen in Ireland. Thus it was to be held once again in the ruins of St. Colman's.

"'Tis a good night to ye that I'd be offering Mr. O'More. You are an honest man and in these troubling days that is a rarity."

Father O'Malley stopped from saying anything further so as not to offend the Overseer and raise up the political issue of land ownership and true freedom of worship.

"God Bless ye Mr. O'More," the priest concluded as they stood before Kiernan's house. "I thank you for the invitation but shall part for the bluff at harbor's edge so that I may welcome the Captain at first light."

They shook hands and in that moment Catholic and Protestant parted as equals to be sure but also with an understanding of why Father O'Malley would rather sleep on the rocky bluff than in the home of the Overseer of the Landlord's land.

With his sack thrown over his shoulder Father Thomas O'Malley OSA made his way up a rock strewn path to a bluff overlooking the harbor, much like fellow Friars had done since the days of St. Augustine himself. Moonlight reflected off the mast of the sunken pirate ship, as legend would hold. Its tip rose out of the water some two feet given the tide being in. He grinned while thinking of young James' excitement upon learning of his relationship to the Pirate Queen herself.

He continued his trek up the path and met several stray sheep who like him sought a safe haven for the night. He spoke to them as a shepherd might do or so he thought. Though all he could do was offer them consolation in the knowledge that the Good Shepherd watches over all and will seek his own. They having been so comforted made their way to a grassy patch and the once renegade priest continued on his way up to the ridge ahead.

Looming across the harbor on a pointed finger of rock jutting to its mouth were the ruins of the Cromwellian fortress in which he had hoped to spend this last night on Inishbofin. Within those walls he had first met the adventurous lad. Later, on each subsequent visit, he would spend his nights within its confines not unlike hundreds of captured priests had done two centuries prior and even to his lifetime. Father O'Malley felt a kinship to these priests who were held prisoners awaiting deportation to the Americas, Australia or the Bahamas simply because they were Catholic priests. And by Oliver Cromwell's orders none would be allowed in Ireland even in the hell he referred to as Connaught.

Often he would sit upon the now submerged rock called "Bishop's Rock." In point of fact it was the very one on which he first met the boy as he guided the ship into the harbor. It was also one onto which a 17th century Irish Bishop was chained so that the captured priests might see their leader struggle as the tide came in and he perished beneath the water. It was over zealous captors who would set this example that allegiance to Rome would not be tolerated. It would be two centuries more before such threats of imprisonment would cease and still animosity existed between the privileged circles of government and landowners and the people who worked the land and grazed the sheep.

Having found a large crevice within the rocky wall behind the ridge path he trod, he dropped his sack. Collecting good sized rocks which filled the palm of his hand, he created a circle of them and placed a peat brick within its center. The stars were sparkling across the night sky and the full moon reflected off the still waters of the harbor.

"There would be no soft rain this night," he thought again as he rolled out a red plaid woolen blanket inside the small cavern. He knelt upon it and offered his evening prayer for the family of young James and what they were about to face on the morrow.

Back in the cottage of James Shields a sleeping lad stretched out before the hearth as his parents held each other with tear filled eyes and the unspoken words that "this night would be their final time alone with their only child." And yet they felt comforted in their hopes and dreams of an America where their son shall thrive with proper nourishment, grow in faith and knowledge under the tutelage of Father O'Malley and the Augustinian Order. Then one day he shall preach the Word of God and administer the Sacraments of Holy Mother Church without fear of reprisal or even worse, imprisonment in a place like the Cromwellian Fortress.

DOOLIN, IRELAND

Chapter Six: Aunt Maggie's Surprise

Father O'Malley, having prayed the "Holy Office," settled down for the night. The camp fire still provided some light as he watched the flames dance as if in the starlit sky from within the tiny one-man cave looking beyond the crevice which served as its entrance. This he did while tossing about the events which would take place the next day in his mind. First there would be he and the lad guiding Captain O'Flaherty and his ship into the harbor. Secondly would be the celebration of the Mass for the First Communicants. Finally, the dreaded final farewell to the Village and for young James to his parents caused him to second guess himself.

"Perhaps I shouldn't have shared the Prior's letter at all," he reflected. *"After all the lad is their only child."*

And yet he was quite aware that not only the "Great Hunger" was a threat to the very life of young James and children like him but also the growing scourge of Cholera which was spreading across Ireland. Both would end the lad's chances to reach maturity. He took solace in that thought that he may very well be saving the very life of the lad. And then there was the plan of Mrs. Shields, who herself concealed her frailty quite well except when she had those coughing fits.

"Maybe young James is destined to serve the People of God in His Church."

Taking comfort in that possibility, he turned, pulled a rock out from under the blanket, which was causing him some discomfort in his lower back, tossed it aside and settled in for a rest.

Seconds later the bleating of the two wandering sheep, the very ones he had met earlier on the pathway, disrupted his being drifted off to sleep. They too had found a haven for the night. The fact that it would be shared with a human didn't seem to bother them at all. Perhaps he had bonded with them too well in their earlier meeting. In any case the two wooly creatures nestled into each other, gave a glance to the human and then lowered their heads as did the priest. The latter human thinking of a story often told of St. Francis of Assisi, who though the founder of the Franciscan Order, had a reputation familiar to all Christians within and outside of religious life. It was, of course, about his love for all of nature, which he strived to keep unspoiled, for the good of all. He ended with a little prayer that the Saint would be joined by the founder of his order, St. Augustine, to watch over him and his two new friends.

While all of this was unfolding on the ridge above Inishbofin Harbor, just outside of Doolin at the cottage of the O'Grady family a pounding was heard at their door.

Colleen and Sean O'Grady had sent Meghan off to bed not long after the reading of the letter from Dublin from Aunt Maggie. It, having caused quite a stir, that all three were exhausted by nightfall. Much had to be accomplished to prepare for the visit of Colleen's sister and the trip to Galway for the wedding between she and Colin Logan. Exactly who this Protestant merchant was had yet to be determined. But Maggie loved him and that was all Colleen needed to accept him when they met at the wedding in Galway.

The pounding on the door continued. "Thump, thump, thump…"

"For God's sake, who would be out this way?" a testy Sean muttered as he threw off the cover and rolled out of bed in his nightshirt, which hung just at his knees. Grabbing his pants he pulled them on so quickly that they caught his genitals and bound them in a combination of pants and nightshirt quite tightly. Not since he was a mere lad had such a predicament present itself.

"Owe," he yelped as he adjusted himself quickly.

"Sean, what on earth?" the wakening Colleen inquired, not referring to the door knocking but as to what he had done to himself with those precious things which helped to bring about their beautiful daughter.

Knowing full well her train of thought, Sean grinned as he spoke.

"Not to worry love, all is well. Did ye not hear the ruffian at the door?"

"I thought it was the wind; then of course there you were….ahem."

Without so much as a blush, which in the 19th century was virtually unheard of, they were interrupted with more thumping sounds at their front door.

"Wind indeed," Sean replied as he searched for his father's Shillelagh.

Taking it up, he went to the door of their bedroom while lifting it up so as to confront any intruder lurking about.

"Be careful…"

"Shhh…maybe it's just a stray sheep but just in case…" He raised the shillelagh above his head.

Pulling the door toward him quickly so as to surprise whoever or whatever, he stepped into the main room of the cottage. The white nightshirt hanging over his pants half tucked in and his bare feet on the stone floor made quite the sight. Hardly one which may have intimidated a would-be evil doer.

"It's all clear. Not a soul about," Sean called back to Colleen in a hushed tone.

"Praised be the saints. Maybe… 'tis only the wind after all."

Another thumping at the cottage door alerted them that "it," whatever "it" was, still remained outside their door. Then all went silent. Sean crept toward that front door. The sudden quiet was not comforting.

"Sean, be careful." The nervous Colleen advised as she peeked her head outside the bedroom door.

He in turn, waved at her to stay back. Just then Meghan came out of her room rubbing the sleep from her eyes.

"Da, is that you?"

"Yes Meghan, get back into your room. Someone's at the door."

Creeping along the short distance from bedroom door to front door, Sean made his way in a threatening manner with wooden stick in hand. Meghan, now becoming fearful, ran to her mother and held onto her tightly. They watched intently as Sean lightly touched the latch holding the upper half of the door shut and lifted it up. Then with a sudden shove, he swung it open, hearing a profanity as he did so and a woman's scream. The half door had just missed the person's head but did knock his silk hat off his head. It was the hat that Sean first noticed. It being a tall silk type gave him relief in that no thug would be wearing such a hat, at least in his mind.

Looking up from the hat, now in a puddle outside the front door, Sean saw a man and woman arm in arm. The clatter of a wagon could be heard in the distance but no other sound save that of heavy breathing from the couple was audible. In the bright moonlight it became evident that they were people of some accomplishment as their clothing would be termed as refined in comparison to the O'Grady clothing since their days of expulsion from Doonagore Castle up the hill.

Watching from a window high up that castle tower was a young lad. Michael Nagle hearing the clatter of a wagon sought to see who might be approaching the castle only to see that it was traveling to the cottage of Meghan's family beyond the round towered castle. It was a single horse drawn cart which held a driver and a man and woman in formal apparel obvious to him as the man wore a silk high hat and the woman wore a bonnet and a coat rather than a shawl. Other than that Michael could not distinguish who the occupants were.

"Good grief sir, is this how you would greet your sister?"

"Colin, love, I'm his sister-in-law."

"Margaret, is that you?" The excited voice was that of Colleen O'Grady as she pushed Sean from the doorway, opened the bottom half of the door and ran out with open arms. Maggie identified herself as she did so.

Colin jumping away from the outstretched arms intent on embracing Maggie, tried to shield his eyes from the nightgown clad Colleen. She not even wearing a shawl to cover her partially exposed breasts had no thought of another man viewing the sight. Swinging their arms around each other Colleen spoke first.

"But we just sent the post this very day, having read your letter."

Maggie looked into her sisters eyes. They were of almost identical height. Both wore their hair long. Maggie with straight auburn and Colleen having ginger colored wavy hair. Both were about four inches shorter than the men.

"I know, this is without notice but the business of business waits for no man, right?" Maggie turned to Colin as she quoted him and winked.

With his back turned to the two sisters he muttered, "Quite so." And that was that.

Meghan, now next to her father in the doorway, called out.

"Aunt Maggie, we're so happy for you."

Her aunt turned toward the doorway and could hardly believe what her eyes saw. She hadn't seen her niece, nor her sister for that matter, since she left for Dublin to weave in a factory; the very one in which she met Colin. And the rest, as her letter had described, was a match made in heaven.

Meghan, wrapped in a shawl, smiled and curtsied.

"Come to me, love; you too Sean."

With a smile of fright rather than that of hospitality, he hastily began to tuck his nightshirt fully into his pants. Then he followed Meghan, who had run to her aunt.

The lass was already being embraced by her aunt as he took steps toward the gentleman not yet known to any of them.

"Meghan my love, you're a young lady. I can hardly believe my eyes."

The niece smiled meekly and nestled into the fine silk dress covered with an actual coat made of wool. Meghan laid her head on her aunt's shoulder for she at age 13 was almost as tall as her aunt.

Maggie flipped that long auburn hair behind her shoulder. Her slight figure was augmented by a firm bosom covered in the silk and lace of the bodice of her dress. The full skirt was floor length and appeared quite dark. It was of midnight blue in color, which was popular amongst the social classes in Dublin and London.

Opening their arms to receive Colleen into their embrace, the three made their way to the doorway. Colleen was already talking in a fashion so quickly stated that one would think she would pass out from lack of breath. The men stood an arm's length away from each other watching the scene. Three pieces of luggage stood behind Colin. Neither however made a move to pick them up, nor follow the women.

As this stand-off of sorts took place, Aunt Maggie suddenly stopped the
progress of the three and their chatter. With a tug on their arms, she brought them to a halt.

"Heavens, where are my manners?" Maggie turned, tugged on her sister and niece to accompany her and made her way to her fiancé.

Standing rather rigidly and offering only a side glance at Sean, Colin had been keeping his eyes focused on the environment about him. His urban experience in Dublin hardly prepared him for this scene in Doolin. The scene of women in nightgowns out in the open, that of such emotional interaction and those eyes watching in the tower toward which he faced made him uneasy to say the least. Should he embrace his fiancé's sister even though she was in a nightgown? Or should he simply keep his eyes averted in an effort to show some degree of respect?

He never got to answer his own questions as Maggie had grabbed his arm and wrapped it about her now coatless body as she had given her coat to her sister Colleen. She knew full well how awkward her Colin was feeling at that moment and tried to help ease him into the first meeting of her family.

"Now my love, what was I thinking. Here you are all aflutter and left alone on this barren land," Maggie began as her family lined up like soldiers to meet her beau. "Now then, this lovely woman…oh my that coat certainly looks better on you Colleen than it did on me."

Colleen smiled meekly as she finished tying her somewhat fly away crimson hair behind her with the ribbon taken from her nightgown sash.

Maggie continued unabashedly. "Now then as I was saying love…this is my darling sister Colleen."

Colleen curtsied rather neatly given that such a gesture had not been used probably since she and Maggie first met Colin's friend John Caldwell Bloomfield when they were stormed tossed lasses on the Caldwell Castle estate lands.

"'Tis my pleasure Mr. Logan to be sure."

"It's Colin, ma'am, if you please. It is my honor to meet you," he said with a bow.

"Good now then this lovely lass is my niece, Meghan. It is she that I have been telling you about."

Colin extended his hand. Meghan looked to her mother and then her father who gave a nod to do the same. She took his hand and curtsied at the same time.

Maggie wrapped her arms around Meghan and whispered how proper her etiquette was performed. "And finally this is my brother-in-law, Sean. Sean this is Colin Logan the man I love."

"Welcome to our home Colin. We only wish that we would have known about your arrival so that we could be better prepared."

Though Sean's statement of welcome was warmly given, his words referring to being better prepared was hardly accurate. For since the days of losing possession of the castle and then the blight spreading, their ability to present themselves and their home in a more elegant fashion wasn't really possible no matter how much notice they would have been given.

"Oh Lord! It is rather late but Maggie my love was just so excited about seeing all of you that as soon as we arrived in Doolin she sought out a driver and cart."

"And that would explain the sound of clatter all right. But now you're here so do come in and we shall give you some tea, right Colleen?" Sean stepped to the side and motioned to Meghan to lead her Aunt to the door. Colleen joined them while the men waited for them to enter.

"Sean, if I may call you by name…"

"Sure 'tis fine to do so. We're going to be family."

"And a pleasure it will be for us even though we'll be moving on soon. But let Maggie tell you all about that. For me now however, I had the strangest feeling that we were being watched from the castle tower beyond."

146

Sean turned his head slightly and spotted a light in the window high up the tower. He knew immediately that a certain young lad who had eyes for his Meghan had been watching the scene below.

"Not to worry Colin, it's but a young lad, Michael Nagle, who was surely the one watching. He has eyes for mi lovely daughter."

"And if I may say that's a good eye the lad has to be sure."

With a hearty laugh and another tuck of the nightshirt, Sean threw his arm around Colin's shoulder and led him toward the cottage. Then noticing the silk hat still sitting in the puddle, he stooped to pick it up, wiped it off with his nightshirt tail and offered his apology for its condition.

"Not to worry Sean, 'tis better that it was the hat and not my head."

With another laugh and the swinging of his arm once again over the young man's shoulder they entered the cottage.

Peeking from the edge of the window was Michael Nagle now stooping down, then kneeling, then placing his elbows on the window sill and holding his head in his hands and wistfully thinking of how lovely Meghan appeared even in her nightgown. Then turning his head, he blew out the candle and just watched the stars over the O'Grady cottage and the glow of candle light from its window until he slid onto the floor in slumber. His own nightshirt had pulled up to reveal that he slept with no undergarments so as to allow his manhood, as his father called his testicles and penis when they just a few days ago had that talk about becoming a man, to breathe and grow. But that night it wasn't his manhood of which he dreamed but that of a young lass entering womanhood and if she would ever cast an eye his way.

The cottage was virtually ablaze with light and the hum of activity as Colleen had placed a cloth covering on the table and set two candles at its center. The kettle was already brewing the last of the tea until Sean received the stipend for the building of the stone wall around the pastures and overseeing the caring for the crops for the Nagle family who now lived in his family's castle. There would be, however, no biscuits to accompany the tea as Colin and Maggie had grown accustomed to in Dublin.

None of this mattered to Maggie even though her glance about the cottage and her memories of their father's cottage in Enniskillen and even her own simple apartment in Dublin had far better accoutrements than what she saw about her.

"So tell me everything," Colleen began. "How did you meet Colin; was it love at first sight?"

Colin began to blush which made him ever the more attractive to Maggie, Colleen and Meghan too. His fair skin turned bright pink next to his bushy black hair and now twinkling blue eyes which he attempted to shield so as not to allow the blushing to be too noticeable, simply made him all the more adorable to the women and comical to Sean.

Now with his eyes cast down as such and Maggie going on and on about how she was just a weaver in the McBirney factory when Colin came along as an inspector of the newly made fabric meant for exporting, he took note of the fine china of the tea cups and saucers being used.

"Well it was almost noon time when Colin came right up to me and asked to see my handiwork. He looked at each detail, all the while casting an eye over the cloth and into my eyes. I became uncomfortable that a gentleman should look at me in such a manner and well he knew it. Didn't you dear?"

"Oh yes I was quite taken to be sure." And then Colin went back to studying the china.
"Now at that moment of the exchange of glances the noon lunch bell rang and all the weavers ceased their work and went about going to the refectory for the meal of soup and even bread."

"Oh my Auntie, you must be rich to have both soup and bread just for lunch."

"I only wish that were true Meghan. The truth be known, the meal was considered part of our pay. Keep the workers fed so that they can work better is more to the reason for it."

"I see. I'm sorry."

"Not at all lovely one, for if I were not in that factory I would not have met your soon to be Uncle. And for that, I am most grateful."

Now even Sean wanted to hear what transpired in that factory meeting and asked that Maggie go on with her story. Despite the late hour, she did so.

"Now we were alone in the factory, just Colin and me. He began to speak of the fine cloth that I weaved. Then wouldn't you know he just tossed it down and asked me to have the noon meal with him."

"Maggie, you didn't…"

"But I did Colleen."

A hush now fell over those gathered at the table though for Colin it was the china that held his interest.

"Oh stop it. I know what you're thinking all right. And it's true. I was a brazen lass to accept such an invitation. In truth I did think he to be quite handsome but I was also hungry and when he offered the meal to be taken at the Brazenhead Inn right near Dublin Castle how could I say no. Well I said 'yes' and that's when everything began to change in my life."

Maggie flipped her long ringlets of auburn hair and removed her bonnet dramatically as if performing a role on the stage.

"Now look at the man. Those crystal blue eyes, that hair, those long legs holding up that frame of a god from Olympus itself."

Sean and the women looked toward Colin still busily studying the details of the china tea set. Sean shrugged thinking his build not to be far different from his own before the "great hunger" days. Now with his rock building work and lack of substantial food let alone more than a meal and morsel snack in a given day much of that appearance was being lost. Colleen and Meghan saw quite another vision

150

inspired by the story of the meeting and his graciousness outside. They agreed with Maggie's description. And in the candlelight about to flicker off as the last of the wax burned Colin appeared in a romantic light one would read about in the Shakespearean story of Romeo and Juliet. They had no choice but to agree with Maggie's point of view.

In any case they were soon affirming that espoused view, even Sean had to agree that he was a fine gentleman in appearance.

"Tell me Colleen," Colin had spoken but not in reference to any of the story being told. "How did you come to have this china?"

"Maggie, haven't you told Colin about father's side business?"

"I certainly did Colleen. Love, don't you remember?"

"I'm a bit confused. You spoke of a Pottery Shop in the north to help supplement his fishing efforts. This isn't what I would describe as the type of Irish Pottery found in villages."

"But it is indeed," affirmed Colleen. "Da has been carrying the type of pottery business of which you speak for the village for years. This is not his ordinary work as it requires what he calls resources of clay, and chemicals not available readily."

Then she went on to explain that the fine china was created on occasion for landed gentry who had the means to get the supplies he needed. In fact those supplies came from Beleek

151

at the north end of Lough Erne where they first were stranded as children at Caldwell Castle lands in a storm.

"And it's that same Caldwell Castle which now belongs to my boss's friend John Caldwell Bloomfield. Just a few months ago Bloomfield inherited the castle and he told Mr. McBirney about meeting a father and his two daughters as a lad and he mentioned the fine china they brought for their picnic lunch. Throughout those years together at Trinity College he could never let go of that story or the thought of those dishes."

Both Colleen and Maggie responded in unison. "That's us, Colin."

"So it would seem," he replied with a grin. "And at this moment John is arranging a meeting with your father?"

Colleen, Sean and Meghan sat in amazement as Colin went on to explain that he was going to America to introduce to merchants there the prospect of importing a new line of china from the business that John Caldwell Bloomfield, Robert Armstrong and his superior, David McBirney were joining forces to create near the village of Beleek. In fact the building of the pottery factory was already under way they were told.

"And that, my dear sister and brother-in-law, is why our marriage had to be hurried and also why we've come this night to present to you a proposal which may affect Meghan's future." Maggie rose and made her way to Meghan so that she might place a kiss upon her forehead.

As for the young lass, she was in a total state of confusion as were her parents. And still she began to fidget with anxiety despite not having a clue as to what her aunt meant by their visit and her future.

Seeing the rising mix of confusion and anxiety Colin tried to explain.

"Maggie's right. We've come with a proposal which we hope that you will consider."

Before he could go on, Colleen interrupted.

"Maggie again, since when do you let anyone call you Maggie... openly that is?"

Margaret would always use her given name and only Sean dared to call her Maggie openly and that's because she was in Dublin and they were in Doolin across the country from each other.

Now the sisters just looked into each other's eyes. Soon those eyes twinkled. Colleen could see why the change was allowed. It had become an endearing term. Margaret now enjoyed the abbreviated name given to her, this time by the one she loved even more than the properness of society. Maggie smiled at her sister and then at Colin.

"It's rather endearing, the name that is, isn't it?"

Sean just choked and wondered if she had realized that it was how he referred to her, if she would be as enamored with it. None of that mattered anymore however, so he brought the conversation back to the "proposal" which had been alluded to.

"Now that's a pretty name to be sure, but exactly what is this 'proposal' of which you speak?"

Maggie pulled a chair and placed it between Meghan and Colleen. She took hold of the hand of each and nodded to Colin to go on just as the clock on the shelf with the other pieces made by Colleen and Maggie's father struck the midnight hour. Colin took the distraction to breathe deeply and then began.

"First let me state that Maggie and I know how difficult life has become for your family. Evidence of the effects of this blight could be seen as we crossed Ireland from Dublin. But here in County Clare 'tis a great horror that we beheld as we passed those stone walls which the others in the carriage called 'famine walls' built by those who had no work, no way to earn a livelihood."

Sean shifted with uneasiness knowing that he was one of those who contributed to the walls being built just to earn a piece of bread and some soup. This did not go unnoticed by Colin, as he continued with quietness in his speech as if not wanting to call too much attention to the plight of the O'Grady family.

"Now my lovely Maggie told me as the cart passed the castle tower across the pasture from your cottage that it had once been part of the O'Grady family lands. She went on to say that one day you, Sean, hope to gain it back."

"Aye, that's true enough," replied Sean.

"Well I think Mr. McBirney, Mr. Armstrong and Mr. Bloomfield might just have a plan to make that a possibility."

To say that joy pervaded the cottage in an instant, as looks of hope crossed Sean's face for the first time in many months, would be an understatement of magnanimous proportions. And yet, not a word was spoken. Only Sean's shifting to the edge of his chair would indicate a growing interest in this "proposal" as yet to be explained. With a nod to Sean, Colin went on with the grand "proposal."

"Mr. McBirney and the others are seeking men to help establish the factory near Beleek in the north of Ireland. Mr. Armstrong believes that this blight is getting worse and though at first centered in Counties Mayo and Clare, it now affects all of Ireland in some way. His plan will bring Ireland a new economic opportunity in the building of a ceramics factory. Already, Mr. McBirney is on his way to Enniskillen to speak with Colleen and Maggie's father, Mr. McMahon."

Colin picked up the ceramic cup which held his tea. He turned it and lifted it as if it were a chalice for all to see. The candlelight flickered off its highly polished finish.

"Maggie, is this true? What has Da to do with all of this?"

The excitement within Maggie could not be held any longer as she blurted out how the three men desired to hire their father to help supervise the creation of a ceramics line to be exported world-wide.

"And that's why Colin is going to America even before the train tracks are laid down and the factory is up and running. He'll be seeking investors for the project and merchants' orders for the product once it's up and running."

Hugging her sister, Colleen was jubilant.

"Margaret…I mean Maggie, this is just too grand. Da won't have to go out on that boat alone anymore and fish. He can do what he's loved to do all these years. Mom will be thrilled, I'm sure of it."

Colin had to enter this exchange of delight and just as he was about to do so, Sean asked a question which brought everyone back to the initial reason for the late visit, the grand "proposal."

"And that brings me to the proposition. Your parents are aging and have been alone since Maggie left for Dublin and you for Doolin. We believe they would have many years ahead of them should they have family about them. Mr. McBirney agrees and is offering Sean a job in the building of the factory and set up of your father's ceramic facility."

While there was a sudden burst of a smile upon Colleen's face, it soon was gone as quickly as the last flicker of one of the candles as it burned itself out. She had seen a gloom descend over Sean as he rose and walked to the window, saying nothing, just looking at the Doonagore Castle tower up on the hill.

As the sisters held onto each other, Colin joined Sean at the window. At first he said nothing. He looked at the castle tower as Sean did. In silence they saw a light in the tower window go out and the moonlight wrapping itself around its smooth gray stonework. Sensing what such a move would mean to Sean, Colin spoke. But he did so quietly and personally just to him.

"So then that is the castle of the O'Grady family, I'm told by Maggie."

"Aye, it was. But we still own it and one day…" Sean stopped and turned to Colin taking him by the shoulders. "And that one day may come a bit faster now Mr. Logan…Colin mi man, won't it?"

Colin could hardly breathe now as Sean hugged him with the might of a wall builder. He had thought that he'd have to convince Sean as to the job's merits but it seemed that Sean was indeed open to the proposal. At last Sean let go, Colin bent over to catch a breath as Sean rushed to Colleen and Meghan and knelt before them.

"'Tis a new beginning we shall be making my loves. Are you for it?"

The smiles on their faces said it all.

Maggie rose to let them have some alone time and joined Colin at the window.

"Colin, love, what about the other part of the proposal?" she asked softly.

"Not now, love, let them have a moment. What comes next won't be easy for them or Meghan."

And so they stood at that window and wondered if Doonagore Castle would ever see the O'Grady family's return.

The clock on the china shelf was now striking 1 a.m. Colleen went to the cupboard where it sat and opened a drawer beneath the clock shelf. She took out a candle, but not just an ordinary one. It had decorations molded on it. They were of a cross and chalice with a host over it. It was Meghan's First Communion candle.

"This night is a grand one indeed. We shall have more light."

And with that she lighted the special candle and placed it into the holder which held the extinguished one.

"Now then, isn't that just fine? We have much to do. When does all this take place?"

With a firm focus on the practical aspects of moving back to the Enniskillen area, Colleen, ever the practical one, began to state a list of what needed to be done so that they may make the move. The list contained the packing of their things, the arranging of transport for them to Enniskillen, the saying of good-byes to their friends in Doolin and so forth. Finally, the question of funding this move had to be addressed.

It was the part referring to Enniskillen which allowed Colin to rejoin the group and speak of the other part of the "proposal" of which Maggie referred. He began first with addressing the financing of the move question. It was his hope that it would help him ease into the more difficult aspect of the "proposal."

"Now then as for the expenses involved in such a move... Mr. McBirney, from his own pocket has given me a stipend to finance your move. However that will not be to Enniskillen. It's to the village of Beleek that you shall be headed and on your way you shall be able to visit Colleen's parents and prepare them for their move to the village as well. Would that meet your approval?"

It wouldn't be truthful to say that Colleen wasn't a bit disappointed in not being able to live in her town, but then again she would have her parents with them.

"Well then Meghan mi love, you shall see Enniskillen at last even if it's for a wee bit of time."

Meghan expressed happiness in the seeing of the town on Lough Erne and of the adventure to the new village as well. It was in that exchange of what their future in a new town would bring that Colin turned to Maggie and asked her to present the last part of the "proposal."

It was not to be an easy task to perform.

"Now Meghan dear, don't you worry about Enniskillen. It's but a wee town not unlike Doolin, I'm told; though I wasn't able to see much in the darkness as we arrived so late."

"Oh Auntie, anything would be better than here. Da works so hard and every day we have to look at that castle." She jutted out a finger toward the window and shook it at the image of the castle tower just visible through it.

"Oh my dear, I had no idea," a now weeping Maggie said.

Colleen and Sean knew that their daughter would sit upon the ridge overlooking the ocean beyond Doolin and dream her dreams of going off on adventures. Occasionally Michael Nagle would come upon her, "by accident" he would say, but it was well planned out to be sure. Michael would tell her of his plans to cross that ocean and go to the big cities of America. "Maybe even New York," he once told her. And she would say that perhaps their paths would cross for one day she too would seek a new life in a free land. This of course thrilled the lad, for he had, since reaching his year of budding manhood, cast his eyes upon her with the fond wish that she would one day cast back a glance at him; though so far that had not come to pass.

The difference in their dreaming was that Michael's family controlled the lands around Doolin and now lived in the Castle. He had the money to make that dream a reality. Meghan on the other hand, since their days of eviction from the castle had no chance of raising the money needed until Aunt Maggie and her Colin came that night to offer her father a job near the Caldwell Castle lands, the stories of which she had heard since she was a little girl.

Now there was hope that one day, she might be able to seek a new life in a new land of opportunity, America.

"Now don't fret my lovely girl." Colleen stroked her daughter's hair. "Ye shall have a grand time when we move on."

Meghan cuddled into her mother as Maggie continued to weep for now came the unavoidable part.

"Meghan, my lovely one, your mother is right. You shall have wondrous adventures ahead of you." Maggie turned to Sean and Colleen. "Now then, what about the girl's education?"

Colin gulped hard. Sean answered.

"She's a lass who's very smart, says her teacher. She can read and write. One day she hopes to write the history of our castle."

"And that does not surprise me Sean, for she is also a McMahon on her mother's side."

Sean shrugged and offered no counter statement. "Of course."

"Good, then you value her continuing education, I presume." "Well of course, Maggie. Meghan will go on to school in Beleek," added Colleen.

"That's my point. There is no school in the village. The nearest one would be in Ballyshannon and that's quite a distance away. Anyway it's a pitiful excuse for a school."

Meghan, whose only escape from their life of deprivation was her books and classmates, few that they were, shuddered with disbelief. Her dreams seemed to be shattering about her.

"Now wouldn't it be grand should she be able to attend a fine school and learn more than reading and writing?"

"Of course, Maggie," Colleen responded. "But we couldn't afford to send her to one right now. And in any case you said there were no schools as yet near Beleek."

"But I've found one which may be just the right one for Meghan. Only it's quite a distance…"

Before Maggie could finish, Meghan was begging to learn more of such a school where girls could go. It was a struggle for Maggie to get out the words of the school's location. She spoke of its fine curriculum, which Sean and Colleen didn't quite understand anyway. She spoke of it being rooted in the Catholic faith, which did impress Meghan and her parents. Finally, she named it.

"St. Patrick School is a fine one. The best of society send their children there. And it's Catholic. Colleen it's Catholic. Meghan may worship without fear."

"Where in all of Ireland is there such a place?"

"Well now that's the point of it all. It's not in Ireland."

"My daughter shall not go to school in England and that's final," Sean yelled out firmly.

Colin and Maggie cast a nervous glance at each other.

"In that case you should calm down Sean. The school is not in England."

"Well then, that's all well and good. But as mi wife has already said, we can't afford a fancy one even if one existed for a Catholic girl."

"Well now Sean, my love, let's have Maggie finish," offered Colleen rather calmly given the tenseness that had arisen.

"'Tis fine, 'tis fine, where is this grand St. Patrick School and how much does it cost?" asked Sean.

"Well now it's quite a distance to be sure."

"We gathered that fact Maggie. How far is it anyway?"

Maggie was unable to avoid the giving of the answer any longer. Her chest heaved with a deep breath as she then spoke words which would cut into Sean and Colleen's heart just as the sword pierced that of Christ himself on the Cross.

"It's in New York City in America."

There, it was said and out for all to hear. As expected the parents slumped in their chairs hardly able to comprehend the words. Meghan on the other hand jumped into her aunt's lap and shouted for joy.

"America, Momai, Da, 'tis to America they want me to go to school."

Her parents looked upon their daughter with glistening eyes welling up with tears. The lass' dream could be coming true but for them what they heard was the beginning of a nightmare for them. At the same time they did not want to prevent their daughter from seeking such an opportunity when the future in Ireland was filled with hunger and disease.

Sean wanted to lash out at Colin and Maggie with something about bribing them with a job while stealing away their daughter. Colleen virtually read his mind and tugged on his arm for him to be seated next to her.

"Well then 'tis America you're talking about. That's really far away," Colleen stated.

"And what would such a trip and schooling cost?" added Sean.

Colleen held onto Meghan continuing to stroke her ringlets of crimson hair, then fixing the collar on her nightgown, then fussing over how its length lay as she sat upon her knee.

Colin answered. "There would be no cost to you, as you would be setting up the new ceramics factory for us with your father-in-law."

"Oh," Sean sadly replied. "You've thought of everything then."

Maggie went to her sister and niece and knelt before them as if she were in Church.

"As God is my witness, we saw no other way to save Meghan from this place. They talk of religious freedom and equal opportunity for education but you know as well as me that it doesn't exist in Ireland."

Then Maggie tried another approach.

"Think of it this way. Once the factory is successful, you'll be able to come to America too. Won't that be grand?"

"And I'll come home to visit when school is over," added a still excited but also torn Meghan as the thought of leaving for such a long time began to sink in.

Colleen lifted Meghan so as to stand and walk to the hearth. On the mantle the picture of the Blessed Mother, Mary rested against the stones. She took it into her hands and held it to her breast.

"There once was another mother who had to see her child go off from her. What He did in that time was to bring the word of God to all He met and would listen. What He did was spread love and hope. How can I keep mi lovely girl from sharing the love in her heart and the hope in her eyes from those in America, where I'm told there is such a need. But mind you, Meghan O'Grady 'tis mi wrath you'll feel should ye stray from our Catholic ways and 'tis mi love you'll feel whenever you bring that love and hope within you to the people of this place called New York City."

Colin felt a bit uneasy about the Catholic Ways statement as he was indeed a renegade Catholic having been brought up in the Anglican Church in order to receive a better education and business opportunity.

Colleen kissed the picture and placed it on the mantle. Her back was toward the others as she prayed a hasty Hail Mary and crossed herself.

Sean went to her at the mantle and placed his arms around her. They turned to see their Meghan snuggling into their embrace.

"So then it's been decided," began Sean. "And when is all of this set to take place?"

It was up to Colin to set out the time table which was to be right after their marriage in Galway. They would then make their way to the harbor area and then to the ships.

"We'll of course send you a post when we arrive in New York," concluded Colin.

"And I'll write you every day," added Meghan.

"'Tis a grand promise that you'd be making but impractical mi lovely girl," began Colleen. "Ye will need to study and become a grand lady of America. Once a week will do just as fine…in any case if their post is like ours then it won't be the receiving of it in a timely manner."

The flame on the First Communion candle fluttered as a stiff breeze wisped through the cottage. Sean took note of it and placed another peat brick on the fire.

"One more thing before we retire this night," Sean thoughtfully said as he jabbed the peat into the flames with an iron rod. "'Tis a promise you'd have to make us this night Colin and you too Maggie."

The clock was now striking 2:00 a.m.

"Anything Sean, what is it?" asked Colin.

166

Sean opened the cupboard doors of the china hutch and took out a leather pouch. Asking everyone to go to the table, he then joined them to open the pouch.

"Now except for mi wife and me, no one has ever seen this. But this night ye shall promise to preserve it for Meghan so that one day she may return to Ireland and reclaim her inheritance as a great lady of America."

He took out a large folded parchment, unfolded it and spread it out on the table. It was the title and deed to Doonagore Castle which proved that ownership was of that of the O'Grady clan. His own name having been affixed on it when he came of age, Sean now added Meghan's name under his name and had Colin and Maggie witness it.

"There now, it might be the Nagle family living in the Castle but it's us who own it and never forget that mi lovely daughter. Come back to it one day and claim what is rightfully yours."

"Yes Da that I will surely do…one day."

With that Meghan was sent to the loft for the night while Colin and Sean were to share Meghan's bed and Colleen and Maggie would share the marriage bed.

It was with a bit of embarrassment that Sean dropped his pants so as to let his nightshirt full to his knees. He, never having a brother, had no experience in being in a room with another male. To cover his discomfort he tried to carry on a conversation about mundane things with Maggie's beau. Colin was removing his own white cotton nightshirt from

167

one of the leather luggage pieces, the other two having been placed in the other bedroom.

"I hope the bed will be comfortable for ye, Colin."

Removing his coat, as Sean spoke, Colin proceeded to fold it carefully and place it over the top of a chair. He responded as he unbuttoned his shirt and baring a chest with but a tuft of hair at its center.

I'm sure that it will serve its purpose well, given that cart ride from Doolin."

Slipping the nightshirt over his head, he then loosened his belt and lowered his trousers. Folding them neatly, they too were placed on the chair. He had chosen to leave his socks on after removing his shoes. Standing at the foot of the bed he didn't know quite what to do next save to watch Sean who had been watching him undress with some curiosity.

"So do ye need to relieve yourself Colin?" asked Sean. "There's a place outside the cottage and a pot under the bed."

Colin looked out the window, then down at his sock covered feet and chose the pot. Sean placed it in a corner of the room next to a wardrobe closet made of heavy planked wood. This, he thought, would give the young man some privacy.

The tea having made its way through his body now sought to escape. The sound of the steady stream hitting the metal pot ended quickly. With a jerk of his "member" Colin asked if he should dispose of the pot's contents. Sean suggested that he place the lid on it and wait until morning as going outside in the damp air may induce yet another need to go.

"Oh, then to bed it is," an uneasy Colin noted.

"Right, it's quite late," an equally disquieted Sean replied.

The two men now stood at the foot of the bed neither knowing what to do next. Finally, Sean asked what side of the bed Colin preferred.

"I never thought of that as I don't have a brother and…well I didn't have to share a bed at home or at Trinity College as the rooms had multiple beds in them."

"That's nice for you. I didn't go to a formal school." Sean stopped, again not wanting to bring up that Catholics didn't have a school to further their education beyond the elementary years.

"I see."

Sean wanted to change the subject but in doing so ended up in a dialogue which created even more discomfort.

"But once you're married, you'll have to choose a side so that you're comfortable with each other….if you understand my meaning."

A blushing Colin indicated that he thought the meaning was quite clear.

"So then, I guess I'll take the right side since you don't have a preference and it's been my side these years of being with Colleen."

"Brilliant, then I'll go to the left side."

Now it was Sean who began to feel the pulsating rush of blood into his cheeks as he realized that in lifting his legs up onto the bed that there would be nakedness under the nightshirt. He seeing that Colin hadn't removed any undergarments presumed he to be covered in the event that the nightshirt might ride up during the night.

Almost in unison the two men pulled up the cover and slid into bed. Each pulled up the blanket up to their necks as they both stared up toward the ceiling.

"It's been quite an eventful night, God give ye rest Colin."

"And to you as well Sean."

Silence ensued as the two grasped the top of the blanket to make sure that nothing but their head showed above it. Sean broke that silence.

"So do you have a father?"

"Yes, he's in Dublin with my mother. They are quite distraught that I wouldn't let them come to Galway."

Sean chose to ignore Colin's comment about his parents not coming to the wedding.

"Oh good, then you've had the talk."

"I don't understand."

"My meaning is that you and your Da have discussed the differences of ladies to men."

"Well of course, I studied Science at Trinity College."

"Don't be offended sir, I'm not trying to pry into your personal affairs but that's not what I mean." Sean clarified.

"I see, I think. You're wondering if I will be able to perform my marital duties, is that it?"

"In part, yes, but also in the handling of women with tenderness and so forth."

There was no response coming forth. Sean turned to face Colin as both had continued to stare up at the ceiling.

"Well?"

Colin spoke but with eyes toward the ceiling.

"Can you keep a secret?"

Sean told him that he certainly could and had done so on many an occasion as if he were a priest in the confessional. The latter part he wished he hadn't mentioned as it was a Catholic practice. Despite the Catholic reference which in fact hadn't in the least impacted Colin's trust in Sean, the young man confided that he had never been with a woman.

"Good heavens man, that's not what I meant. If you're in good working order, you'll come to know where to place your "member" and all the rest will come naturally."

Colin turned to face Sean.

"But I'm nervous about not being able to….well give my love physically."

They were now face to face in the narrow bed. The fear in Colin's eyes was quite evident.

"You look like a fit young man," Sean said trying to encourage his soon to be brother-in-law. "I never having a brother either had no one to talk to about such things as my father passed away in my youth."

"I can relate, only mine chose not to do so. I'm sure he felt that gentlemen simply didn't discuss such things especially with their children."

"But you went to Trinity College. Did ye not speak of women and men being together?"

"Oh that sort of thing was more like boasting of things we dreamed but never did."

Sean controlled a giggle of sorts but tried desperately not to show amusement as Colin was being quite serious in his concern about performing as a man should in his opinion and living in Victorian society. Then to give the young man a sense of confidence he sat up not caring if his nightshirt was revealed and shared a story. It was one which he never told to a living soul. It was of his marriage night with

Colleen. He spoke of his breaking out in a sweat which made him seek a wash basin so as not to let Colleen know of his nervousness. He told of his first touching of a woman, which as it happened, like Colin, was his first time in doing so. He told of that first marriage bed kiss and how it caused within him a stir never experienced before. He never talked of Colleen by name as that would be un-gentleman-like to speak of one's wife in such a manner. But he did mention how kind she was as he tried to insert his rigid "member" inside her several times before success was achieved. By the end of the story Colin was beginning to understand that his wife to be would understand as she probably also was experiencing that same type of fright to be a good wife as he was at being a good husband in bed. But in the end their love would grow as they came to know one another over time and in each encounter there would be a sense of ease and a fervor that was difficult to put into words other than their love enabled them to accept each other as they were, inexperienced and naïve perhaps but full of love and concern for one another.

"Then Maggie won't be expecting me to know everything about a woman on our marriage night?"

"You come off to be a man full of accomplishment in business and finance but that doesn't mean that Maggie will expect that in your performance nor you should expect that from her. Love has to grow over time."

"Thanks Sean, I feel much better about Galway now. I was dreading that night."

The married man smiled at the younger single man.

"Well then, I'm glad I was of help to ye. So then will you answer a question for me and not be offended?"

"In the Anglican Church were you taught to sleep covered or uncovered?"

The resulting blank stare caused Sean to reframe his question.

"I mean, do you wear undergarments even to bed?"

Colin laughed. "They never addressed that issue in College or Church services. But there's no rule and I go bare underneath but not tonight because I was embarrassed that you might see me."

Sean laughed as well. "Well let's not get into how rigid we get okay?"

"Very all right with me. The guys at school did enough of that and none of it was probably true anyway."

And so the two men rolled to their side butt facing butt and let slumber take them.

All the while this man talk took place the ladies were also in a fervent discussion as to what would take place on the wedding night. The difference is that their mother had actually discussed with them as girls as to what would be happening to them when womanhood came upon them. That of course was quite unusual for Victorian society but then they were really not a part of that strata of class distinction. But as for the wedding night, no one was there to advise Colleen as Maggie was younger and their mother would never address such an issue. Thus the elder sister tried to answer those same types of questions regarding anxiousness over being a good wife in bed and in the home.

"Maggie, men are different from us…"

"That I know Colleen, but what about their parts. How should they be treated?"

"How would you like to be treated in bed?"

"I hope with tenderness and understanding."

"And that my dear is the secret men don't want you to know. That's what they want too. If their "member" doesn't grow as they would like ignore it and perhaps fondle it so that their nervousness may come to an end. You see men want you to think they know all about love making. They've been told that is what is expected. Just let them think so and help them be real men."

They giggled over the fondling of the "member" and so forth. But Maggie was quite receptive of the information about helping her man be a man even though she too was just as inexperienced.

Then having resolved the issues of man and woman together their talk focused on the upcoming trip to America after the wedding in Galway. It would be a trip in which Meghan would be brought to America so that she might have the opportunity to survive and grow in faith and knowledge. But it would also split a family.

It would be this opportunity and family break-up which would soon bring together the lass from Doolin, a lad from Inishbofin and a young fisherman from the Aran Islands.

A Friend for Father O'Malley

Chapter Seven: Farewell Inishbofin

The sea rocked the O'Flaherty boat softly as the sun began to break the black of night. The Captain rolled out of his hammock-like bed to rouse his sons. He was excited to see the lad and the villagers once again, perhaps for the last time. The low tide was setting in. Bishop's rock was almost entirely visible as Father O'Malley stretched out to meet a new yet still ebony day with only the slightest hint of red at the eastern horizon. He rubbed his eyes and tried to find his two new friends. It appeared they had departed for greener pastures or so he thought. He rolled his blanket and replaced it into his traveling sack. Just outside the cavern entrance a rapid stream of water splashed down the limestone wall behind the ridge path. It was the same waterfall under which young James had taken his shower just before meeting the priest for his lesson several months prior to what was promising to be a gloriously bright day by any Irish standard. Looking about to insure no one was about the priest removed his clothes including his undergarments and peeked out of the crevice which formed the entrance to the cavern. Dawn was now making its spectacular entrance with gold, red and orange colored streaks of light. The island was still asleep. All was still; so he made a dash for the waterfall and began to wash himself in that cascading water.

He lifted his face upwards and let the clear water splash across and stream down his broad chest trickling down his legs. Thinking all the while how the day would be the beginning of a new life for his student and candidate for the Order of St. Augustine; yet at the same time it would be a time of farewell. It was that latter part of what the day would become which froze him in the cold waters. He just peered out over the harbor wondering how he could best help young James' parents, indeed as Kiernan had said all the village say good-bye.

As he pondered in this state of undress in which only his God would be privy to a voice suddenly penetrated the sound of the rushing water. It was a voice quite familiar to him.

"Father O'Malley, are you about?"

The priest didn't quite know what to do. He as he was on his day of birth and his clothing hanging on the rocks just in the crevice entrance created a panic within him. *"I should have brought the blanket,"* he now thought.
"The lad couldn't be allowed to see his priest in such a state."

He turned to face the rock wall behind him and virtually became another layer of rock as he pressed himself into the formation. A moment later the lad came to the cavern entrance peeked in and saw nothing except the priest's sack and some clothes hanging on a rock. Proceeding on the boy stumbled over two sheep which had been following him, though he didn't realize that he had company. They were now approaching the priest acting as rock in the waterfall. He stooped down to pet them, realizing that they must belong to Mr. O'Connor as his plot of pasture was closest to the ridge path. They were quite receptive to his attention. While playfully rubbing their necks he looked up and saw the figure of a man in the plunging water. His back had streaks of red which were scars formed after being lashed

179

when imprisoned some twenty years ago. Having never seen a grown man, even his father, in such a state, he froze not knowing what to do or what to say. In a flash of an astounded second the lad knew that the man must be Father O'Malley, for he had heard the story of his being in prison. He stared at the scars and wondered if he could be as brave as the early Christians and now Father O'Malley.

"Could I stand before others and profess my faith even in the face of aggression or worse?"

The man made no attempt to identify himself. The lad being quite astute began to understand that the priest could not present himself in such a state, It would not be proper. So he returned to the cave's entrance, took down the clothes from the rock and walking backwards placed them just outside the flow of water within the man's reach.

Waiting in the cave young James called out to the priest, who had watched the lad walk backwards, so as not to see his nakedness, and then place his clothes on the rocks near him.

"Father O'Malley, I'm here in a cave. If you're around I'll wait for you."

The priest quickly dried himself with his shirt and pulled on his pants all the while thinking what the hermits of St. Augustine did to be clean and modest at the same time. Having restored that modesty he called back to the lad.

"James, is that you? I'll be right there."

The sun had risen to a level as to make the harbor waters sparkle as the priest entered the cave not alone but followed by his sheep friends from the night before. He found the lad sitting next to his traveling sack.

"My, you are prompt James. I was just preparing for the day, a special day for you I might add."

The lad smiled, his cheeks a bright pink as the priest put on his jacket over his damp shirt and began to fasten the collar while the sheep pressed against his legs as if to attract his attention. The clothes he wore would give no hint that he was a priest. Orders had been given to any priest ministering in Ireland that they should not attract attention to themselves, thus they wore not the Augustinian Habit nor cassock or collar. Rather they wore the typical wool suit of a gentleman with vest, shirt and cravat.

He bent down to give them a rub. "These are my new friends James. They were my guests last night," he began, trying to ease the awkward moment. "How are your parents?"

"I've just met them Father. In fact they led me to you."

James suddenly realized that he drew attention to what he saw and immediately stated that his parents were well and looked forward to the Mass and his Frist Communion.

The priest on his part chose to make no mention of his shower but rather focused on the celebration which would be taking place. And yet he wanted to lighten the situation so he spoke of the sheep and how they symbolized Jesus as the Good Shepherd so perhaps it would be fitting to bring them to the celebration. James thought the suggestion to be quite appropriate. So did apparently, the sheep, as they bleated acceptance to the invitation.

The heavens seemed to agree as well as a stream of the sunlight filled the cavern. James interpreted the sunshine in a cave as a sign of blessing. Father O'Malley could hardly dampen such enthusiasm.

"So it would seem lad, but shouldn't we get on our way to the fortress? The Captain should be ready to enter the harbor any time now."

James bubbled over with excitement as he ran to the sheep, which he startled, but who chose to receive his attention. He knelt before them and looked directly into their eyes and gave them instructions as to what must be done.

"We're off to guide the Captain and his crew into Inishbofin Harbor. Now you stay on the path and make sure all goes well. We'll come back for you."

The sheep gave the impression of understanding the direction, bleated, jumped on James and turned to exit the cave. Priest and boy followed. The humans made their way along the path, passing the waterfall with no mention of how it was used and jumped onto Bishop's rock and then onto the ridge which gave them entrance into the ruins. Following them were the sheep. But they didn't make the leap onto Bishop's Rock. Rather they stood stoically watching their new friends disappear behind the walls of the ruins.

James having gotten a boost stood atop the exterior wall which faced the open sea. The sea was calm and the skies clear. The tranquility of the scene conflicted with the turmoil of emotions which were about to surface as the day progressed. But for the lad, the only thought at the moment was that of guiding Captain O'Flaherty into the harbor and to the dock. And so he removed his ragged shirt and began to wave it wildly.

Some hundred yards away, the youngest O'Flaherty son, Aengus, was acting as the spotter for the ship. The make shift flag on the skinny arm of the lad easily caught his attention. The faded blue rag like flag barely contrasted with the bright blue sky behind the lad. His pale skin and skeletal appearance however could not be hidden despite his energetic waving and jumping, which was interspersed with the tightening of the rope holding up his pants, on the narrow wall's decaying stonework.

"Da, there's the lad high on the wall at the tip of the point."

"Aye, so he is. 'Tis a slight lad that he is mi boy. America will fatten him up a bit."

The Captain called out to Aedan and Adam to raise the sail to half-mast. Taking hold of the tiller he turned the ship toward the point. The lad seeing the movement yelled down to Father O'Malley, who could never stay atop the wall like the lad was able to do. What he did do was climb over the fallen section of another wall facing the rocky point and shouted to the ship as it approached.

"'Tis a grand sight you are Captain!" he called out. "God has guided ye here."

Aengus called back. "And glad we are about it."

"The whole island awaits you," the priest yelled out.

"So it would seem," came the reply.

The priest turned to face the dock area and beheld a grand sight, for indeed the entire village seemed to have turned out on this breaking of day arrival of the O'Flaherty ship named "Eoghanacht." Each of them seemed to have a say as to what water path the ship should take but Captain O'Flaherty tugged on his graying beard and looked for the lad, whom he trusted completely to do the job.

He didn't have to wait long, for young James climbed down to the priest at the point and then made his way toward the harbor side where a now more visible mast of the sunken pirate ship could be seen. Then he jumped onto Bishop's Rock so that he'd be in a better position to notice the rocks just under the water level.

Standing at the edge of the dock were Kathleen and James Shields. The lad's father had his arm around his wife, who tightly grasped a white piece of cloth it would seem, but in fact it was a shirt for her son. Staying up most of the night to insure her task of changing part of her wedding dress into a shirt of white for the lad who was to receive his First Holy Communion that morning and then be off to a land that most at the harbor's edge had only heard about from an occasional story brought to them by a visiting ship picking up the sheep's wool.

As the "Eoghanacht" glided toward Bishop's Rock, Aengus jumped out of the boat onto a smaller rock just above the water line. His task was to take the boy, whom he now regarded as a friend, and prepare him for his special day.

The others would be joining him soon enough. It would be a Prince that they would be fussing over that day.

The lad jumped into the strong arms of the young fisherman, who except for his wind reddened face was as pale as the lad.

"You made it, you made it." The lad wrapped his arms around the teen fisherman's neck as if he were greeting a long lost brother.

He was no longer the ten-year-old who first met them. And yet, though a bit taller his weight didn't cause Aengus to lose his footing. In fact he climbed up onto Bishop's Rock with the lad in his arms so that all could see that he and the lad were just fine as the boat eased past them making its way to the dock. On the ledge next to where they stood Father O'Malley had arrived, having made his way from the point when the ship safely entered the harbor. Aengus handed the lad to the priest. In truth it was more of a upward thrust so that the priest could get to the lad. He grabbed young James under his arms and swung him above his head and onto the ledge.

A rather loud gasp followed as all on the pier watched the antics of the jump, the hug and the tossing of the lad upwards to the priest. More significantly the shock was that a priest could be so strong and agile to do what he did in swinging James up onto the ledge.

"Glory be, if that's not our son taking delight in being tossed about like a sack of potatoes."

"Aye, isn't it a grand sight my love," responded the elder James. "To see him laugh again could only be bested by a real sack of potatoes being thrown about."

A sudden sadness covered Kathleen's face. She well understood that her analogy hit her husband in the gut as he had not enough salvaged potatoes to fill even a small sack. She hugged him, encouraging him to relish the joy before their eyes.

"Now then husband," she began so as to divert the talk from food or lack of it. "Ye go meet the Captain and his brood with this shirt. I'll take our friends and the other children to make ready for the Mass."

"And be attentive to the task. Make sure our son is proper in his behavior to receive our Lord. I'll have no shenanigans on this day."

"But love, it should be you who should be dressing the boy."

"Our James is not a boy any longer my love despite how he may appear. He is older than our Lord was when he went to the temple and declared his need to do His Father's business."

She paused and thought of what would happen later that day and became gloomy, then just as quickly perked up and added. "'Tis indeed better to have his Da there with his Uncles of sorts."

Now such a term was not to be given lightly. Kathleen had just bestowed upon the O'Flaherty clan the ranking of family member and that was indeed worthy of note. Well did the elder James realize what she had done. He smiled, turned toward the ship and tucked the shirt carefully under his arm. Then turning back, gave her a hug before all the villagers, who made note of it with a cheer.

Playfully giving him a slight shove, and off he stumbled in dramatic fashion toward the ship, as she made her way to Kiernan O'More, the Overseer. Giving him instructions as to call upon some men to help unload the ship and bring whatever supplies they may have to the St. Colman ruins, she then called to the women and children to follow her. To Mr. O'Connor who stood with donkey and cart at the end of the pier she gave instructions as to how the supplies should be loaded so as to make most of the capacity of the cart. He dutifully made note of it and waited as the others followed the woman in the plaid shawl up the village road, her hair blazing as the sun itself. None had seen Kathleen Shields walk with such determination and joy in her step for the several months since the Captain's last visit.

James Shields was greeting the Captain and his sons as they put down a plank from the boat onto the pier.

"Welcome Captain… lads, to Inishbofin once again."

"Peace be unto you and all of this village," responded the Captain. He was of course offering the greeting to Mr. O'More and some men standing behind Mr. Shields.

"Your wife told me to help if we could," Kiernan told the elder James.

Welcoming greetings having been exchanged, the Captain informed the lad's father and the others of the supplies he

187

brought. These were donated from those received in the first of relief supplies to Fr. O'Malley's Church.

"The people of his parish, deprived as they are, wanted to help ye with your celebration."

"And grateful we are for their generosity," James responded. "May God bless them for it."

"Amen," was offered by all on the pier.

In short order the Captain ordered the sacks and goods to be handed off the ship by Aedan and Adam. Aengus, still being with the lad and the priest at the ruins, watched the goings on and explained to them what Father's parish had done for the people of Inishbofin.

Tears welled up in the priest's eyes as he turned away so as to give thanks to the Lord, he had said.

Across the harbor, the men of the village led by Kiernan were placing the supplies into Mr. O'Connor's cart. He of course, explained the wishes of Mrs. Shields as to their placement into it. Aedan and Adam, having secured the ship to the dock joined their father and the lad's father. In their arms one held a package wrapped in brown paper and tied with string. Over Adam's arm hung a white cotton cloth which he called a towel and in his hand laid a cake of soap, the latter not seen in recent memory. Such a luxury could not be afforded by most anyone in western Ireland let alone on the remote islands off its coast. It was a used bar of soap of be sure but there was enough left for its purpose and then some.

Under the arm of the Captain was yet another smaller package. He tapped it as he began to explain what their task was to be as the sun now brightened the entire island with unusually warm rays even for the July day.

"'Tis the orders of mi wife that I must explain to ye Mr. Shields and it is her hope that ye shall see their value for the lad."

He looked about the harbor. He then called out to Aengus to bring the lad and Father O'Malley to them at the waterfall. It being at the cliff's edge was located about mid-way between those at Bishop's Rock and themselves at the dock.

With eyes on the wrapped packages, the elder James presumed that gifts were to be given to the lad. And in this presumption he was partially correct. But as it turned out there would be more to the orders then the presentation of gifts.

Approaching the cascading water, its coldness could be felt as it splashed onto the pathway and over into the harbor. Aengus noted that the falls would make an ideal place for their task. The lad looked stunned. Looking up at the priest, he could only see in his mind the good Father in the falls in his nakedness with those scars of red across his back. Father O'Malley himself seemed rather apprehensive as he saw in the boy's eyes that which he was thinking but had never mentioned.

The other men approached and stood to one side of the falls opposite to Aengus, Father O'Malley and the lad. The water of the falls splattered over the rocks with a steady stream but not violently as in springtime nor with such force as to wash one under it over the Cliffside. The Captain then began to explain why they were meeting at such a place.

"Now then lad, Mr. Shields, mi wife being the good woman that she is…"

His sons and son-in-law interrupted with comments as to how true a statement their father spoke. The Captain smiled and continued.

"Now we have a bit of a problem. "Tis your wife that should be here to do this not us, but seeing that she is not, it falls upon us men to do the task and do it well to be sure to meet her and mi wife's standards."

Now as panic began to fill the lad, for he had no idea what could be the reason for this meeting at the falls; other than for the washing away of blood after a Circumcision being performed. Such a thought had come to him from his hearing of the Scripture story of the ceremony having been done to the Lord. He having then asked his grandfather what that meant when but a younger lad had him horrified at the thought of it ever since. He discreetly stepped behind the priest getting ready to run off.

The Captain looking about and not seeing the lad called for him. The lad peeked out from behind the priest, who in turn eased him to stand in front of him and face the Captain. Young James began to shudder. His father noted his discomfort.

"Son, are ye ill? Is it too cold for you here?"

"No dadai, I'm fine…it's just." He could not go on.

190

The men were now perplexed, having no idea what could be causing such alarm in the lad. Thus the Captain took upon himself to explain the situation so as to make the lad more comfortable. Taking the bar of soap from his son, he stooped down onto one knee to look upon the lad face to face.

"Now James mi boy, do ye know what this which I hold is?"

The Captain handed the soap over to the lad, who examined it, smelled it and identified it as something he thought he read about but had never actually seen.

"I believe this is what people in the big houses use to wash their clothes."

The Captain nodded affirmatively and told the lad's father that he had a bright boy indeed.

"Now then, knowing that, do ye also know what washing yourself all over is? Mi wife calls it bathing."

Relief came to the lad as he laughed and told them that he knows all about washing and that in fact he had done so right in the falls next to which they all stood. The men joined him in his laughter, especially his father.

"So then you know how to do so with soap."

The lad informed them that he hadn't such an experience as his family didn't have soap. He looked up at his dad, who appeared solemn as the lad's deprivation of ordinary things in life, which he could not provide, came to mind. He stooped down next to the Captain and took the soap.

"Now mi boy, this is how you use soap."

Holding the bar under the water he rubbed it in his hands until a goodly bit of lather appeared to the marvel of his son.

"See, it's easy. Now give me your clothes and I shall wash you. There's nothing to fear save perhaps if you swallow the foam and that you might avoid by keeping that gaping mouth of yours closed."

Once again laughter ensued as the boy turned his back to them and began to unloosen the rope around his waist and step out of his pants, throwing them up at Aengus. Next was his shirt, ragged as it was, he slipped it over his head gently so as not to cause another tear in it.

"Aengus, would you mind keeping these dry. I don't think I can wash them and get them dried before Mass."

"Ye needn't worry about that lad, right Da?" Then he became unusually still as his eyes took in the sight of the pale lad with rib cage quite evident and something else not expected.

The Captain nodded and told all that they would take care of the lad's clothing, but not mentioning as to what that meant. During this exchange the lad stepped under the waterfall. He shivered a bit as the cascading water splashed over him as the water was cold. It splattered on the men in the process. Goose bumps began to appear over his back and rear end as he faced the limestone wall behind the waterfall. Then he turned so that his Dad could soap him up. As he did so his father and the Captain gave out a gasp as they were on bended knee and saw what they saw right in their face.

"James! Why didn't ye tell me," exclaimed his father.

"Lad, ye are no longer a boy to be sure," added the Captain.

Suddenly, the lad realized as to what they referred and covered himself with his hands.

"I meant to but with Momai being sick so often and everything it didn't seem important."

James wanted to grab his son and tell him how anything that was about him was very important to him, even his private parts growing and having a tuft of hair appearing over the penis area. What he did manage to get out was that it was a sign of becoming a man and that he would need to have a man to man talk of what that meant.

"But for now, let's just say that you need to wash all over, for men stink if not properly washed, beggin' your pardon Father."

The priest who had turned his back on the scene as had young James done for him to afford him modesty, turned his head slightly to say, "To be clean is to be pure of heart as well, and your son, this day shall receive the Lord with a pure heart."

"Thank you Father."

"Okay then let's get this lad washed or he'll not be receiving anything," Aengus suggested. "He's already turning blue."

And with that the youngest of the O'Flaherty sons took hold of the lad, plunged him under the waters of the fall, took the soap from the Captain's hand and began to scrub him with it. All the while he thought of how not that long ago it was he who was entering manhood. Now at seventeen he thought of himself as a grown man. The Captain would have another opinion if he were asked.

Everyone else had turned their backs to the lad save his father who was tearing up over his son becoming a man. Each told a story of a day when they first understood how those early days of entering manhood astounded them and wondering if girls went through the same feelings. They exempted Father O'Malley from adding a personal reflection on his sexuality.

"I think all the mud is gone, Dadai."

The elder James came to his senses and took hold of his son. He turned him around to make sure the lad had done a good job. Adam gave him the towel and soon the lad was wrapped and dried as if he were indeed a Prince being prepared to be presented at court.

Aedan having looked about found the campfire of the priest from the night before and rekindled it. Young James was brought to the fire swaddled in the towel. He looked around and asked for his clothes.

"James, we have a surprise for you."

With that being said Adam picked up a package which had been set next to the fire. He opened it and pulled out a pair

194

of long johns. The boy looked at them with a questioning glance.

"What's that?" he asked.

The fishermen were amused as was the priest though he held hid his quite well while the others giggled like wee ones who had seen a girls' petticoat. So he answered the lad's question.

"Those are undergarments. One wears them beneath one's clothes to give added warmth and protection."

"Well said Father," a still giggling Adam blurted out as he handed the long underwear to the lad with instruction to go into the cavern behind him and put them on. The lad obediently did as he was told.

Dadai, what's this flap of material in the back for?"

Another round of laughter ensued as the elder James went into the cave to help his son. In short order the lad appeared as Lazurus must have in the Bible story, clothed in white and still wrapped in the towel.

Aengus, held up what most people would consider a pile of rags and announced that they were best suited to be burned in the fire as the lad gasped and screamed to stop.

"No Aengus, please don't."

"It's all right lad, I won't if you don't want me to."

"But we do have clothes for you, if that's your concern," added Aedan.

Adam then took out a suit of clothes from the opened package. He held the pants and jacket up.

Young James' eyes bulged out with admiration. "Those are for me?"

"Aye James, all for you," replied Adam as he gently took the towel from the lad and put the jacket on him." Then handing the pants to the elder James, they soon had dressed him in a wool suit of black tweed which was recently donated to the parish by a merchant from Galway upon hearing the plight of many young people without decent clothing.

The only problem evident to all was that the jacket was placed over the underwear. The lad had no shirt. Adam pulled out the white cotton shirt from the package and was about to offer it to James when the lad's father remembered what his wife had made for their son.

"If you don't mind, Kathleen has made something for the lad's First Communion day." The elder James reentered the cave and brought out the shirt. "Momai would like you to wear this shirt, my boy."

Now all that was taking place filled the lad with emotions which he never knew he had. He laughed at his own appearance, naked before grown men. He marveled at the fine suit which only a Prince would usually wear, in his thinking that is. He shivered in the soap suds until he turned blue but wouldn't disappoint the men who thought to make him clean and pure for his Frist Communion as best they knew how. Now he wept as he removed the suit coat, handed it to Adam and took the shirt as if taking Communion with reverence and piety. He caressed it to feel each woven thread of fiber. He rubbed it against his face.

"Gosh, it's really soft."

Then he held it up to let the sun shine off it and slipped it over his head. Tucking it into his new pants, he smiled. Adam held the coat up as a valet might do so the lad could slip his arms into it, but the Captain stopped him.

"There's just one more item, we wish to share lad."

"Holy Mother of God…oh oh, sorry Father."

"This is a special moment lad, savor it," the priest replied.

The lad could hardly get any more words out. He stammered that never could he have dreamed of such a day as the one he was enjoying. But when the Captain held up a knitted Aran wool sweater such as worn by the fishermen of the islands, his words froze on his quivering lips. Struggling to keep his emotions under control, his glistening eyes brought the men into his very soul which was leaping for joy and filled with gratitude. Soon they were in the same struggle to be the strong men of Olympus which the lad had elevated them to be.

"Oh Captain, it's just like yours." The lad took the sweater and squeezed it next to him. He examined each pattern formation of the natural colored fibers. "I'm going to be a fisher of men you know, so this will always remind me of that call Jesus made to his followers."

The Captain could hardly bear the words and wept openly as he hugged the lad and told him that he would always be one of them no matter where in the world he might go to be that Fisher of Men. He helped the lad pull it over his head as Adam held up the jacket.

"No Adam, but thank you. I want everyone to see that I'm one of you."

"Sure lad, whatever you say." Adam folded the jacket and held it as if he were holding a baby.

"But I'll wear it on my way to America, don't worry about that."

"America, surely that will be grand."

"But first there is the Mass for the First Communicants that we'd be celebrating this day," reminded Father O'Malley.

"And it will be quite the day to be sure," Aedan added as he swooped the lad up and placed him on Adam's shoulders to be carried along the path back to the dock and onto the village road.

By the time the band of fishermen, farmer, priest and youth arrived at the ruins of St. Colman's, Kathleen had organized the entire village to help prepare for the mass. Once again the altar was covered with Mrs. O'Connor's handiwork tablecloth and lined with Shamrocks from candle stick to candle stick, which were brought by Kiernan. Six children, scrubbed and dressed in the best of what their families could provide stood at the entrance to the ruin waiting to be called forth in procession. They waited with excitement pounding in their hearts for their final member, young James. His arrival on the shoulders of Adam brought about a great cheer as his mother turned to see her son in a sweater she recognized at once to be the creation of the O'Flaherty clan and with the shirt she had made peeking out of the collar and sleeves.

She wiped her hands on the white apron hanging from her waist, talking to herself. *" "Tis plenty of time for tears Kathleen Shields, now it's to the mass we must get the lad."*

She placed her hands on her hips and took a dramatic stance to give emphasis to her words.

"Now the entire village has been waiting James Richard Shields for ye to arrive." She turned and spoke with softer tones. "Father, all is ready."

"Yes Mrs. Shields, thank you so much for attending to the preparations."

Adam lowered young James, who immediately ran to his mother to place a kiss and hug of thanks for the shirt. Mass or no mass, Kathleen Shields wept as the pipes and fiddle began the musical prelude to the Eucharistic celebration.

With his mom on one side and his dad on the other, James was escorted into the ruins to take his place with his friends. Each set of parents stood behind their child in front of the altar. Father O'Malley had placed the gray habit of the Order of St. Augustine over his clothes, then a green chasuble and stole. He had asked the O'Flaherty men to serve the mass, thus they escorted him from the ruins entrance to the altar area.

The ancient hymn of St. Thomas Aquinas was intoned and all sang the Latin words:

Godhead here in hiding, whom I do adore
Masked by these bare shadows, shape and nothing more,
See, Lord, at thy service low lies here a heart
Lost, all lost in wonder at the God thou art.

With the hand of the lad's Mom on one of his shoulders and that of his father on the other the emotions of all began to surface. As the hymn resounded throughout the ruins the hands tightened on those shoulders pressing against his boney frame despite the fullness of the woolen sweater acting as padding. He sighed, not in pain, but in remembrance of all that had passed which brought him to this day of celebration but also of farewell. He looked to his left and took in the solemn expression on his Dad's face. Then he did the same to his right, gazing at his Mom. Her eyes for the first time in many weeks seemed to sparkle. Her gaze was returned to him with a smile which hid the feeling of dread which in a short time was sure to follow after the Mass concluded.

As the Alleluia was intoned to announce the Gospel reading, the lad made a concerted effort to pay attention. He listened with every fiber of his being to the story of Jesus on the Mount preaching to a huge crowd of over five thousand people who had to be fed. Then with but two loaves and three fish the Lord fed the multitude. Having fed their bodies, the Lord then gave them spiritual food in the form of the Beatitudes. When Father O'Malley placed the book of

Scriptures down, he looked to the people of Inishbofin slowly casting his gaze across the gathered assembly finally stopping as he reached the face of the lad. Looking upwards to the boy's parents he repeated one of the Beatitudes as he began his sermon on the Sermon on the Mount.

"Blessed are the Pure of Heart, for they shall see God," he proclaimed.

Pausing to give the restatement a dramatic impact, he placed his hands on the Gospel and announced that each of the young people who were about to receive their Frist Communion were a shining example of what Jesus meant by "Pure of Heart." Young James could feel the eyes of the priest searing into his very soul. He took that explanation to mean that he James Richard Shields should always strive to keep his heart pure. He gulped hard and pledged in his heart to do exactly that for his Mom and Dad to be sure but also for Father O'Malley, who risked so much to make his mother's hope for him to be fulfilled.

Shocking those assembled, Father O'Malley left the stack of rocks serving as the Pulpit and walked amongst the people. A murmur arose but soon quieted as he stood first next to Captain O'Flaherty, then at the side of each of his sons, Aedan, Adam and Aengus. This youngest of the O'Flaherty sons had taken the words of Pure of Heart quite personally. He stood with glistening eyes praying that he would be a good example for James. With two of the men on each side of him, he added a twist to 19th Century Theology by pointing out that the people of Inishbofin were on that day like those on the Mount with Jesus. They hungered to be fed on the Word of God but their humanity also needed sustenance.

"On this day as in the past you have gathered to be nourished by the Word of God and the Bread of Life. And once again the Lord has provided the O'Flaherty clan; who have come with their loaves and fish to meet the needs of our humanness."

By the end of the Sermon not a dry eye could be seen within the ruins of St. Colman's. For he had concluded with an analogy of how the multitude must have felt when Jesus left them in order to bring his message to others and also how the Lord, Himself, must have felt as he departed to carry on his ministry.

"So too must a lad, whom you have loved and cherished, take his leave from this land of his birth, to carry that same message to a land across the sea. You know that I speak for young James Richard Shields when I say that you of Inishbofin shall always have a place in our hearts."

The hands once again tightened on the lad's shoulders as the priest returned to the altar and the piper played a solemn anthem which sounded much like "Londonderry Air" which was becoming popular in the northern area of Ireland but new to the western area.

The words of Institution of the Eucharist, which the lad had learned to refer to as the Consecration of the Bread and Wine, began while all in those ruins knelt. Captain O'Flaherty rang the ship's bell as the Host appeared over the priest's head. This time unleavened bread baked by the Irish Sisters of Mercy in Galway was used. The same was done for the elevation of the Chalice, which as in the previous visits was once again a pewter goblet.

All rose as the Lord's Prayer was chanted. The time had finally arrived. In the 19th century Church, a child had to be twelve years old to receive Communion. Given the circumstances, Father O'Malley was allowing any properly trained child who was at least ten to receive. That day there were two girls of age 11 and four boys ranging in age from 12-14 who received their First Holy Communion.

Each set of parents presented their child; that is all but those of Mary Catherine O'Connor. She was presented by her grandfather as her parents had passed away at the beginning of the blight years from a combination of malnutrition and what would today be called pneumonia. They formed an arc in front of the ancient sanctuary. An embroidered pillow had been placed on the ground in front of the stack of stones serving as the altar. The brown corduroy cushion was embroidered with a golden Harp and a green shamrock. Aengus was given the duty to move the cushion after each youth received so that the next one could kneel more comfortably.

James Richard, his Aran knit sweater fresh and bright in the sunlight entering the ruins, folded his hands with fingers pointing upward as his mother had taught him. He was at the end of the line. He watched his friends one after the other reverently kneeling and tilting their heads back so as to have the host placed on the tongue. Father O'Malley looked regal in his bright green chasuble of cotton and silk with the outline of a gold cross on front and back. He moved from child to child holding a ceramic plate which belonged to Mary Catherine O'Connor's family. On it were the consecrated hosts, enough for all who filled the ruin, save that of Kiernan O'More who could not receive as he was no longer Catholic. That however did not stop Father O'Malley from offering a blessing on him as a sign of his gratitude for keeping his mouth shut during the preparation time and for the candlesticks and cushion.

Kevin Sweeney was next to last. Young James would be next. For some reason his palms began to sweat. Beads of perspiration formed on the lad's brow. Aengus was now in front of him placing the pillow on the ground and looking up and giving him a wink. This only made him hesitate more. Why he hesitated his parents were hard pressed to guess. Perhaps the sunlight bouncing off the white host which Father O'Malley now held up in front of him caused a distraction; so thought his father. But the lad knew very well why he stood frozen, his knees unable to bend.

For three years he regularly climbed into the Cromwellian ruins, at first as an ignorant boy with a dream of pirating. Now the very descendent of that Pirate Queen held the Body of Christ before him. He began to wobble a bit as he felt pressure on his right shoulder. It was being applied by his father as a reminder to kneel. His face flushed with embarrassment as he plopped down clumsily thus disgracing his family or so he thought. In point of fact, the kneeling was not done with the gracefulness such as done by Mary Catherine but it wasn't terribly irreverent. A quick glance out of the corner of his eye toward his friends who had done a much better job caused him to think of how this would be the last time he would see them for many years, if at all. The beads had now become sweat dripping into his face despite the day being a cool one even by Irish standards.

His mother, noticing the lad's anxiety, took the corner of her apron and really ignored all ritual by wiping her son's brow simultaneously with her husband pushing him down onto the cushion. Father O'Malley waited patiently for the drama to end.

The lad looked up into the scruffy crimson bearded priest's face. He knew that if anyone understood what his innermost thoughts were at that moment it would be him. After all, wasn't it he who brought him from dark ignorance into the light? Now he could read and write with quite the flair, but also he could do so in Latin as well. True they were simple sentences but they were written in the language of the Church.

"Corpus Christi," Father O'Malley began.

"Amen," young James responded as he remembered to tilt his head back as the others had done.

A tug on his arm reminded him to rise so that his parents might receive the Eucharist next. He offered a weak smile then chided himself for lack of proper piety. So he bowed his head to avoid eye contact and stepped aside. But it was too late, his priest, mentor and teacher had looked into those sparkling eyes. And what he saw were deep blue pools filled with that youthful light of innocence, excitement, and that something else one finds difficult to put into words. Perhaps it could be called "admiration" for that descendant of the Pirate Queen, who had opened the world to him. Perhaps it might be labeled as a "yearning," that is the lad's desire to be a man like the O'Flaherty men, who now flanked Father O'Malley. They too had seen those qualities sparkle in the lad's eyes and moved next to the priest so as to be close to young James on his special day; a day which may never have come to pass were it not for their involvement. Yet another quality, an emotion really, comes to mind as well.

It's that of "love." It's the love he felt he hadn't expressed openly as he should for his Mom and Dad.

"And now it was too late," he thought. *"For in a short time I will be boarding the fishing vessel and leave my island home."*

All of these possible qualities were reflected in those orbs of sea blue. He needn't have tried to hide them from view. None who knew him would ever deny that they were there. Innocence, enthusiasm, admiration, yearning and love were all part of who he was. They filled his heart and soul. And they made him that adventurous youth who mounted the wall of the ruins on that fateful day on which he guided the O'Flaherty ship to safe harbor and met the one person, other than his parents, who would have a pivotal impact on his young life.

As his mind twirled with these thoughts, he hardly realized that he was the last First Communicant to receive. He certainly hadn't noticed that the entire assembly also took Communion. His mind was dancing now, moving from the ruins of St. Colman's to a view of all of Inishbofin and then to his call to serve the People of God. Not until the chanted words of "Ite Missa Est" (the Mass is ended) boomed through the ruins and a thunderous "Deo Gratias" (Thanks be to God) was echoed by the assembly in return was he brought back to the sacred ruins in thought as well as in body.

The pipes began to play once again as Father O'Malley left the altar area but this time there was to be a procession which would take all present on that familiar path leading the lad and his family to their cottage. There he would make his final farewell to his family and home, pick up his meager belongings and be escorted to the dockside harbor basin. It would be at the harbor where the meal would take place so that as high tide came in, the O'Flaherty clan, the priest and young James might board their vessel and set sail.

Upon arrival at the cottage, the procession stopped and with such quietness so as one could hear only the bleats of two distant sheep, the very ones which had befriended both the priest and the lad, was heard as if they were within the cottage itself. Kathleen and James led their son through the roughly hewn wooden door. The lad sensed the heaviness in his parents' heart. His mother began to cough again, a sure sign of not only her weakened condition but her concern and anxiety over what was about to take place.

She poured a bit of hot water from the kettle set over the hearth into a cup and took a sip.

"Now then," she began. "Let's make sure all your things are in the sack."

To the side of the fireplace was a sack, the like of which one would see a sailor carry as he went out to sea. She placed the canvas like sack on the table next to a small shoulder bag made of the same material but empty of contents. Father and son watched her from their place in front of the hearth, knowing full well not to disturb her enterprise as she was on a mission to insure that all was as it should be.

"There, all is well." She then fastened the sack shut and joined her husband and son at the hearth.

All three turned in unison. Their eyes fixed on the Bible and the Crucifix symbols of their faith to be sure but also of their family history. The elder James took the Holy Book off the narrow stone mantle. He opened it and walked the few steps back to the table around which their last meal together, such as it was, took place the day before. He read out the family names written on its inner first page ending with that of young James Richard Shields. Then he closed it and prepared to place it into the empty shoulder bag.

"Wait dadai," the lad shouted. "Where are my clothes?"

"Love, they're in the large sack, here," answered his mother.

"No momai, not those, the ones you took off me dadai when ye dressed me earlier in the waterfall."

"Good Lord mi boy, I do believe that young Aengus O'Flaherty set out to burn the rags."

Now the lad was quite distraught.

"No, no!" He was now virtually in tears. Certainly not over his worn and torn raggedy shirt and pants but over what they meant to him. "I told Aengus not to burn them."

The lad ran to the door, swung it open and called out to Aengus, as the entire village looked upon the scene in confusion.

"Aegnus," he yelled out with tears streaming down his face. "Where are my clothes?"

All eyes turned toward the youngest of the O'Flaherty clan. What they saw was not the controlled young fisherman with the appearance of a Celtic warrior but one beside himself as he had completely forgotten about the saving of the clothing.

"Oh my God, da," he whispered to Eion O'Flaherty, his father. "I thought Aedan had them for the lad."

"But I do," called out Aedan. "Here in mi bag."

The two rifled through the bag of not his personal belongings but those items they brought on shore to help prepare the meal. Adam, Kiernan and Mr. Sweeney had already gone ahead to begin the cooking along with several women of the village. Fortunately, they had not taken Aedan's bag with them.

"Here they are lad." Aedan held up the faded gray rags which served as the lad's every day clothes and his school uniform of sorts during his sessions within the ruins at the harbor entrance.

Aengus feeling guilty that he had not kept better watch on them took them and brought them to the relieved youth. James took them into his hands with such tenderness that Father O'Malley had tears running down his cheeks. Holding his clothes next to his chest, he thanked Aengus with a smile that melted his heart and re-entered the cottage, leaving the door wide open.

"Praise be to God, they did save them for you," called out Kathleen, his mother.

"Yes momai, Aedan and Aengus saved them."

"Good lad," the elder James said. "But why in heaven's name did ye want such pieces of cloth when you have such a fine suit of clothes for your travels?"

The lad was stuffing his old pants into the big sack and looked up at his parents still holding onto the ripped shirt. Each of those rips held special meaning for the lad as each came from an adventure in learning on the ruins.

"I'm ready dadai."

"Then you've figured out my intent, have you?"

With a crooked grin came the reply. "I think so"

"A smart lad we have Kathleen, mi darling wife."

"And haven't I said that long before he became educated and speaking in Latin?"

"Yes dear that you have."

The proud father took the Bible in his hands and held it out to his son.

"My son, one day may you read those stories often told to ye by mi own father, your granddad, to your students."

The elder James paused and with a smirk of sorts across his face continued.

"You do understand that if you do become a priest, then it won't be to your own kin that you'd be doing the reading." He winked at the boy.

The lad shuffled and nodded his understanding as his dad continued with an alternate scenario.

"However, should you find a woman who might take your heart such as your mum has done to mine, then do so with my blessing."

"James Shields, you make me blush in front of the boy."

"He is a boy no longer. You warned me of that and it was only today that I have come to realize it to be true."

With pinkish cheeks the lad took the Bible from his dad and wrapped his old shirt around it before placing it into the empty shoulder bag.

"The Holy Word on these pages will speak of our faith to me. The Holy Book itself will always remind me of my family, you dadai who work so hard to keep us alive; and you momai, who gave me love every day and a dream which now comes to pass. As for this shirt, it shall symbolize my roots; that is where I came from no matter what the future has in store for me."

The weeping mother responded.

"He already speaks like a Bishop."

The three laughed, embraced and then walked to the doorway outside of which stood the villagers awaiting to

211

continue their procession. As soon as they appeared, a rousing cheer erupted. Mr. O'Connor pulled on his donkey to bring the cart to the three Shields standing at the opening in the small stone wall surrounding the cottage. With the Bible bag slung over his shoulder, the lad was lifted onto the wagon by Aegnus and Aedan. Then they helped Mrs. Shields to board. The elder James refused all help and made his way onto the cart by his own power.

"'Tis not an old man that I'd be yet," he had said.

Mr. O'Connor cast him a look with frown lines forming across his forehead.

The sun had reached its zenith and was on the wane when the meal ended and the fiddle playing was in full swing. The fiddling hardly gave note that the celebration was that of a farewell and better that it served to distract family and friends from what was about to take place. It was Captain O'Flaherty who signaled that the time had arrived for their departure. This he was informing Father O'Malley while the lad was above on the Cliffside path with his friends saying his good-byes.

"We cannot afford to wait another hour Father, if we are to catch the tide."

"I understand. We shall make our farewell then. Where's the lad?"

Up on the hillside, Mary Catherine, speaking for all, told young James that he would make a fine priest one day. Claps on the back from the other lads suggested their agreement with her. The six of them ran down the path back

212

to the gathering at the dock just as Father O'Malley was making his farewell to the lad's parents.

"Your son is becoming a fine young man," he began. "Have no fear. I shall watch over him as if you were right there with me."

"'Tis a great comfort that ye will be with him Father."

Kathleen nodded her agreement with her husband.

Captain O'Flaherty gave orders to his sons to make the vessel ready. Aedan holding the ship's bell rang it out as they headed for the boat. The sound attracted the attention of all as well they knew what it meant.

James and Kathleen looked about for their son who having squeezed through the crowd of well-wishers now ran to them. Wrapping her shawl around the boy, Kathleen kissed him. Hidden from sight for that brief moment, he kissed her back and told her that he loved her. Adam then lifted the lad up and onto his father's shoulders and they walked onto the pier. Lowering the lad at the plank leading up onto the boat, father and son embraced.

"I love you dadai."

"And I love you, my son."

With that the lad took Adam's hand and was led aboard. Aedan rang the bell once again as the lad boarded. Father O'Malley called the youth to him on the bow of the ship. He blessed the villagers and called upon them to sing that tune of Daniel O'Connell which he first heard on that visit so long ago.

The O'Flaherty boys raised the ship's sail slightly and the men of the village pushed on the boat so as to let it slip away from the pier. The sail caught a breeze. The Captain took hold of the tiller and worked it to swing the boat around toward the rocky point which opened to the sea beyond. The lad taking the priest by his hand led him to the rear of the ship so that they could continue to see his parents and the villagers at dockside who sang of the great hunger and their hero, Daniel O'Connell. As the boat slipped past Cromwell's Fortress ruins, a shadow crossed the ship and it seemed briefly to be in darkness and yet light was all about them. From that darkness into light the lad peered out and thought he saw his mom collapse into the arms of his dad. He grabbed hold of the bag which held the family Bible and prayed.

14th Century Castle Keep Ruin, County Galway

Chapter Eight: Galway Bound

Still clutching that bag with the family Bible, young James made his way to the bow of the fishing craft. For under its wooden railing there was a crawl area in which rope was stowed most of the time. For the lad, it was just enough room to squeeze in his boney body if he curled up with his head between his legs. This he did rather effortlessly so that his emotions would not be revealed to Father O'Malley or the O'Flaherty clan. After all, they thought he was a brave lad at the threshold of manhood; that they all saw for themselves under the waterfall in the early morning hours of that very day. He couldn't be teary-eyed in front of those he idolized and wished to emulate. So he sought solace and a quiet space in which to dwell on those last images of his Mom and Dad on that pier in Inishbofin Harbor with all the villagers surrounding them. His heart sinking into his stomach with the beat of a somber drum as played at a military funeral would be his alone to feel.

Now that very scene was also seen by Father O'Malley, who having his hand laying upon the lad's shoulder could feel him tensing up as his mother collapsed into the arms of his father as they made that turn around the fortress ruins. When the lad took hold of his Bible and slipped away to the bow, he chose not to follow but to allow him to deal with his sorrow alone so as not to embarrass him.

What neither the priest nor the boy realized was that the eyes of the youngest son of the O'Flaherty clan had also seen what happened on that pier and how James reacted to it. Aengus O'Flaherty, just four years older, tethered the rope to the sail beam and made his way to the bow of the vessel.

Aedan and Adam worked on preparing their nets so that they may attempt to bring a catch home to the Aran Islands and their own families. They waved Aengus on, seeing that he was on a mission.

The "Eoghanacht" steadily made its way along the western coast of Ireland, a route that the Captain had found to be easily followed to and from the Aran Islands. They were headed for Kilronan, the main village of Inishmor, the largest of those islands just beyond Galway Bay. Captain O'Flaherty tightly held onto the tiller ensuring that the vessel took full advantage of calm seas and a fair wind. Gazing up at Father O'Malley, who stood next to him, he pondered as to whether or not he could give up one of his sons, especially at such an innocent age. The lad was just about to turn fourteen and he was indeed pure of heart and without guile.

"Father, where's the lad?"

"Just there at the bow. See Aengus is there as well." The priest became silent, watching Aengus stoop down and then sit on the deck. "I'm afraid our lad is having a bit of difficulty with departing his island home, his family."

"Aye, to be sure; I was just wondering how I would deal with leaving one of my sons, and James is so young to be alone in the world."

"It will be, at first, a sad time but he will not be alone Captain. I will be there for him whenever I can."

"Yes Father, I understand. It's not your role that I question. You are an honorable man who serves our Lord. Yet something is tugging at mi heart."

The priest sat himself on a small water barrel so that he could be head to head with the Captain, who had to steer the boat with the tiller. There was no wheel on such a fishing vessel as his. Those would only be found on the great mast ships which crossed the ocean. It would be one of those on which the priest and the lad would soon travel.

"Mi heart is struggling with how the lad will handle being in a strange land which is even stranger to one such as he who has never left his tiny island home. I hear that America is huge. It takes one many days just to travel from one of their towns to a nearby city."

"My heart is also filled with fear Captain…that is I've heard stories of America, in fact…" The priest became quiet, looking away toward the bow. There he could see Aengus holding James who still clutched that Bible bag.
"I would like to share something with you about that fear, if I may."

"Of course Father, anything."

Father O'Malley pulled out an envelope from the inside pocket of his black wool coat. He gently opened it and unfolded its contents so as not to have it swept away by a gust of wind

"This is a letter from my superiors in Rome."

The Captain's eyes widened with interest and curiosity.

"All the way from our Holy Father in Rome?"

"Well not quite the Pope, but the leader of my Order. But that's not what makes it so important. It gives me the instructions as to where the lad and I will travel in America, of where to catch passage in Cobh near Cork City. But it's this passage which is of concern to me. It says here that there is trouble in America for us."

"'For us'… who's the us?"

'I'm afraid it means those who are Catholic and immigrants like the Irish. I was hoping that you would have heard stories from America. You do get to Galway for supplies and to bring your catch on occasion don't you?"

"Aye, that's true. And there always a tale about things…I mean stories full of the blarney, you know what I mean."

"I do, but I also believe that in those tales are seeds of truth. They may give me some insight into what to expect. Would you share them with me?"

The Captain nodded affirmatively and began to relay a story which was spreading across Galway and all the way to Dublin. With each detail the priest would shudder. Each image imagined caused his face to lose more of what little color it possessed.

Some of what Father O'Malley incredulously heard he was familiar. That is, it was common knowledge that landowners and the government would make it impossible for many tenant farmers to remain on their land. They would offer them passage to North America and a promising future of jobs and money for their families. What he didn't know was that the ships which were made available to them were hardly more than cattle ships. Like a herd of sheep or cattle they were crammed into "holds" most of which had no bunks, no sanitation, and no availability to get on deck for a breath of fresh air. Jammed in such a filthy environment they were given only a pound of food, hardly enough to keep them alive. When they became sick from the 27 day voyage and disease they brought aboard, there were no doctors. They were given watered down rum. This caused many to become violent and outlandish in behavior.

The dream of a bright future for the lad began to darken. *Surely, there was a better way to cross the ocean to America,* thought Father O'Malley.

"Captain, surely the government knows of such conditions and is taking steps to improve such conditions."

"I can only tell you what I've heard Father, as you requested. Our people are being lied to. They are being brought to a city called Montreal in Canada and then made to wait in long lines of ships for permission to leave the ships. Thousands are dying before even a foot had been placed onto the promised land of opportunity. These they dump into the St. Lawrence River without so much as a priest to pray over them."

"Mother of God, can this be the trouble of which my superior spoke?"

"I can't say Father, but if even a bit of this is true ye should not take the lad to Cobh. Can ye find a way to travel to this place you spoke of called Philadelphia in the United States right away and not go through Canada first?"

Once again the priest cast his gaze toward the bow. James and Aengus were now sitting side by side and engaged in a spirited conversation.

"So you see Aengus, in America all things are possible. Father taught me all about the Declaration of Independence. It says that all men are created equal."

"Can this be so? No one is better than another?"

"I think so. I can't say that for sure but if you would read their Declaration, I think you would agree with me. And that's why I must leave our land just like our Lord had to leave his mother and hometown, even though it hurts my heart."

"James, ye are far more brave than me, that's the truth and no blarney."

Aengus took hold of the lad and squeezed him; not too hard for those bones would surely crack under his grasp. The boy laughed out loud and squealed. Hearing the laughter helped Father O'Malley to keep a positive thought on what he must do to insure the happiness of the lad and his dream to serve the Lord. He shifted his position and sat looking directly into the Captain's eyes.

"I think I have an answer to our problem. We have an Augustinian parish in Galway by the name of St. Augustine, have you heard of it?"

"Aye, that I have and I've been to mass there as well."

"Good, then we shall go there upon arriving in Galway. There must be ships which sail to America from Galway and they may be able to help procure our passage on one of them. We shall avoid Cobh all together."

"I think I may be able to help in that regard as well Father for I have a friend whose son serves on a ship named the "Cushla Machree."

A wave of relief crossed Father O'Malley's face as the lines in his brow began to fade away almost instantly. For now he was regaining his conviction that a safe passage was possible. This was reinforced as he noticed the lad and Aengus in serious conversation, one sided though it was with the youngest of the O'Flaherty sons listening intently to every word coming forth from the lad as if it were Gospel.

While the "Eoghanacht" made its way down the western coast of Ireland, the clattering of a coach's wheels made its way past Queens University in Galway City. Inside the coach drawn by two horses were the O'Grady Family (Sean, Colleen and Meghan), Maggie McMahon and Colin Logan. Meghan stuck her head out of the window to see the marvels of the only medieval city in western Ireland to survive into the 19th Century. Coming from a village the size of Doolin in which most people knew each other quite well to a city with the population of five thousand was unbelievable to the excited girl. Her flame hair blew in the breeze and soon tangled as it filled with the dust of the road.

"Meghan, get yourself into this coach," called out her mother.

Meghan hardly heard the command as the clattering of hooves on the cobblestones was so loud despite the slow pace they now traveled upon entering the more populated area of the city.

"Let her be Colleen," Maggie said while interrupting her sister. "She's just excited about being in a big city. Imagine her thrill upon arriving at New York City next month?"

The sudden silence was deafening as Colleen, like a swan folding its head under its wing, did something akin to it as she dug into her husband's shoulder. Sean had to change the subject but feared to even open his mouth so as not to say the wrong words which might ignite yet another bout of tears even though both he and his wife knew that Meghan going to America was for the best. He took solace in his upcoming job with the new pottery enterprise being formed in Beleek by John Caldwell Bloomfield. The business leader being known to Colin, Maggie's fiancé, made him feel at ease with the decision. Already their belongings were on the way to Enniskillen, to the home of Colleen and Maggie's parents. They would leave for her hometown after the wedding and the departure of the ship which would take the newlyweds and their daughter to America.

None of this now mattered to Colleen. She was Meghan's mother and needed to enjoy that role for the limited time left to her. And so she wept snuggled into her husband's shoulder.

It was Colin who then broke the stillness interspersed with intermittent sobs.

"I wonder what Gary has in store for us when we arrive?"

Finally, a question which could be questioned and lead a discussion away from the ship and Meghan's unladylike behavior. Sean took to be the questioner.

"Who's this Gary person?"

"I'm sorry Sean. He's really the Archdeacon Gary Hasting, the Rector of St. Nicholas Church and a friend from my time in Dublin at Trinity College where he also attended."

The snuggled head popped up. Colleen had no intention of wedding talk taking place without her involvement.

"So 'tis he who would perform the ceremony, I take it."

"Yes, and we have to meet with him tomorrow for some kind of paper signing and rehearsal," Colin answered.

Both Maggie and Colleen looked at each other, both thinking the same thing. *"This non-Catholic wedding is really going to happen."*

It was a look of solemnness not joyfulness as one would think when a wedding was being discussed. And both men saw it that way and neither knew how to address the issue behind the expression without causing more grief.

With tears now streaming down her cheeks Colleen looked deeply into her sister's eyes. Maggie returned a gaze of confusion then emotion. She knew that in the 19th Century Catholic Church what she was about to do simply could not be done. She knew that it couldn't be done in the Church of

Ireland of the Anglican Communion either. She knew that the rector who was to meet with them was risking his entire ministry to marry a Catholic to a Protestant. And yet what can be done? That was the question. The answer in her mind was that, her love for Colin was more important than anything in the world. His love for her allowed him to call in favors which not only jeopardized his friend's ministry but also his immortal soul.

Then she recalled a passage from Scripture. *"God is love and love is of God,"* she spoke in her mind. *"If that is true then what they were about to do is a sign of His love, of Him."*

"Colleen, I know how difficult this has been for you. I've seen you pray the beads for my soul. But please believe me. I am at peace with this decision. Love comes from God, so it can't be wrong to marry someone who is not a member of your religion." She reached out her hands to grasp those of Colleen.

The men didn't know where to turn or what to do. They may have thought these very same things but never in their wildest dreams, even as they lay in the same bed in nightclothes confessing of sexual concerns would they ever address the condition of their souls. So they kept their eyes averted and heads turned to the openings in the carriage door.

"I know how you feel Maggie. And my Rosary was not to save your soul but to bless your marriage."

The sisters embraced and cried and then began to giggle, why neither knew. In that last phase of easing of tension and emotions, Colleen decided to share something.

"Oh and by the way…I hope you and Colin don't mind, but I invited Mommy and Dad to come to Galway."

A scream from Maggie could not be ignored. The men turned toward the women and Meghan plopped back onto her seat.

"Aunt Maggie, what's wrong?"

"Nothing child… nothing at all. It's just that your mother has invited your grandparents to meet us here in Galway."

"So then you're just happy, right? I know I am. I don't really know them."

"She's right Maggie. Before she leaves us she should have a memory of her grandparents, shouldn't she?"

Maggie wrapped her arm around her sister and her other arm around her niece.

"Yes my dears, they should indeed. That is if they should come at all."

Meghan didn't understand the meaning of "at all" but she was pleased that her Aunt was happy as well. The men smiled and joined her in that feeling.

"Well then, I guess that we'll soon see how powerful love really is, won't we?" asked Maggie with a smile and a wink to Colin.

He gulped deeply while conjuring up an image of his future father-in-law coming into the Church and shooting him on sight.

The jolt of the coach coming to a stop and Sean grabbing his shoulders and shaking him, then giving him a half hug of encouragement brought Colin back to them.

"Well look at this, it appears that we've arrived at the Inn," said Colin.

After a journey which took them along the sea side which was often muddy, they crossed the stark barren lands of the Burren into the beauty of Kinvarra at the eastern end of Galway Bay. This offered a view of ships going into Galway harbor. Also visible on a clear day were the Aran Islands at its western opening and cliffs which rose at ninety degree angles out of the sea. When they finally arrived, Meghan having never been past Doolin was thrilled. The jostling and bumpy ride may have made the traveling quite uncomfortable for the adults but for her, it was an adventure no matter how sore her butt was from being bounced up and down as each hole in the road seemed to be found by the wheels of the coach.

The coachman was already climbing down and securing the horses to a metal post which had a horse's head as ornamentation at its top. The riders all looked about, expecting some type of canopy or covered portico under which the carriages would drive to disembark their passengers. None of those types of hotel-like features was evident from their view. What they did see was a series of two to three story houses attached one to the other in a row. In point of fact they were "row houses" built in 1641 for the gentry of Galway. Between riots, Cromwell and now the blight much was changing in Galway. The row houses were being transformed in their interior into an inn, affording the great number of people, now coming to Galway to get out of it and all of Ireland by ship, a place to rest before the perilous journey. Those were the people who had some means of payment and livelihood.

Hundreds of others crowded along the harbor hoping to find steerage passage on one of the ships set to cross the Atlantic to North America. These were the evicted tenant farmers and their families, penniless and promised a new life by agents whom they paid twelve dollars, all they had in most cases, for the privilege of being crammed into a dark musty hold of the ship with little ventilation, no decent water and sub-standard food at best. All they had was what was on their backs and in a small sack holding a memento of their life back on their acre of rented land in County Mayo or Clare and perhaps a change of shirt. Many were in rags not even having that much to bring with them. These sickly and half-starved people had sold every personal belonging to get the fare for passage. They hadn't as yet realized that they were really entering their coffin. In fact those ships were called "Coffin Ships" for well over a third of its passengers would never make it to America and were thrown into the sea without so much as a service as there were no priests aboard in most cases.

It was this sight which Meghan first beheld as she was lifted from the carriage doorway in the arms of her father and lowered to the stone pavement. She had walked up to the driver so as to thank him for the splendid journey. The balding gray-haired man blushed with pride at the compliment and thanked her for being so kind. She patted the head of the horses so as to thank them as well, though they were not the same ones with which they left Doolin, having had to change horses at Kinvarra. Nonetheless they had done their duty well and were deserving of her praise as well. Looking up into their eyes with that smile which could melt the hearts of any man or woman for that matter, she caught a glimpse of the squalor of the green park like square across from the Inn.

She gasped and turned sheet white at the sight. Her family busily being greeted by the Innkeeper took no note of her condition being distracted as they were. The Innkeeper was known to Colin. He like Colin worked for the McBirney Company, which in turn had an interest in the restructuring of the row houses into an Inn. Unfortunately, due to one crop failure after another that enterprise would be slow to prove successful.

The driver, Jonathon Finigan by name, seeing the lass so frozen with fright went to her. Taking his cap off thus revealing his graying bald head he gently approached the lass.

"Come young lady. I'll show ye the way."

"Mr. Finigan, what has happened to Ireland? I thought only Doolin had such unfortunate people."

"Now lass, 'tis not just your town suffering. All of Ireland suffers from hunger and now this sickness called cholera."

The girl could not take her eyes off the sight of scores of people lighting fires to keep warm in the open air, stretching blankets and bits of sheet into tent like coverings to protect their children from the elements as best they could.

"And all of this in the middle of Galway City," she murmured.

"Come lass, you shall have a bed this night and from what I hear a happy time at Miss McMahon's wedding to the chap from Dublin."

Somehow, the thought of a joyous wedding was the furthest thought in her mind, not only because of what she had seen and learned about the vast effect of the crop failures and the blight but also because she had indeed heard of the controversy of the interfaith marriage. She didn't quite understand what it all meant. But she did realize that if her grandparents didn't show up for the ceremony, then they were indeed rejecting their daughter, her Aunt Maggie. All of this collided with such a dramatic sight as what she saw on Eyre Square on that bright afternoon, which would soon turn to a stormy night. A line of black clouds had formed beyond the harbor and by the looks of their movement were headed right to center city.

With a final glance toward Eyre Square, she allowed Jonathon to return her to her parents. They, having made the introductions all around, now brought the lass into their small circle of greeting, to present her as well.

Now those billowing coal like clouds had indeed given a good soaking to the Aran Islands and had moved toward the mouth of Galway Bay. The fishermen of the islands having taken the warning of the thunder had heeded the signs of the coming storm and made their way back to Kilronan harbor on Inishmor. All save one vessel. For that was the "Eoghanacht" and it was not fishing that afternoon but carrying a precious cargo of lad and priest headed for the very city to which the storm threatened to soak as well.

Though by Atlantic Ocean storm standards, it was a brief one without much long lasting winds, it was at that moment tossing about the O'Flaherty vessel as a child might do with his wooden sail boat in the bathtub. Aedan and Adam were hastily battening the hatches to the hold where the small catch they had managed to net was stored. The last thing they needed was the sea water of the ten and fifteen foot waves now pouring over the sides of the craft, to spill into the hold and thus sink the boat from the weight of the water. Drenched to the skin, all on board were helping to steady the craft. Young James never having experienced life at sea let alone such a storm took to helping Aengus secure the sail so that it would not be ripped from the mast. Climbing on the broad shoulders of the Celtic-like warrior, the lad was pulling on the rope which was stuck in the pulley. It let go and with a crash the sail fell as did the boy. With the quickness of a parent charging to save his child, Father O'Malley jumped over Aengus' body, he being knocked over by the crashing of the sail canvas, and caught the lad in his arms.

"James, what on earth were you thinking?"

The lad looked up into the priest's face. Water poured over it from thunderous waves exploding over the boat's sides. But it wasn't only sea water which streaked his face.

"You could have been killed. Aengus, have ye no sense whatsoever?"

Now the seventeen-year-old son of the Captain, himself covered in more than just sea water was distraught that he might have caused the lad's demise.

"I'm sorry Father. I didn't mean no harm."

Father O'Malley, feeling the eyes of the Captain behind him, looking at his son with fiery eyes ready to chastise as well, readily understood the error in judgment. Aengus had been setting sails since he was younger than the thirteen-year-old lad was. But James was never at sea, save in his adventures on the walls of the fortress. He took the lad from the priest's arm and embraced him with apology after apology.

"As God is my witness James, I am so sorry. Truly I would rather die than have you harmed. I'm just a dumb cluck I guess. But you, you are smart, you speak Latin and everything."

A ten footer chose that moment to crash over the side. It caused the three to be washed to the other side, holding onto the very rope which the lad had loosened, lest they go overboard. Aengus, still holding onto the very sweater which his mother had knitted the boy, just in case, grabbed the lad into his arms once again. The lad would have none of it and pushed himself away. Speaking as loudly as he could, given the thunder above and crashing of waves at sea level, he told them that it was his idea to climb the mast not Aengus.

"If I am to be the man you say that I am becoming then I must do manly things. I must carry my own weight…"

The lad paused, looked at himself from feet up and shrugged. "Such as it is."

That broke the tense situation and a bit of laughter followed. James joined in and hugged Father O'Malley thanking him for saving him from a bit of a fall and then returned the embrace of Aengus with words which told him that he was to him like the brother he never had. The tender moment did not last long. Another wave came splashing over the sides of the boat.

Aedan and Adam called to them for some help. Soon all was back to battling the effects of the storm. As fast as it came upon them so too did it pass over them. Sailing out of the blackness into the light of bright sunshine they found themselves at the mouth of Galway Bay.

The Captain steered into the Harbor proper. James sat at his side while he pointed out the Aran Islands seen at a distance to the rear of the vessel. Aedan and Adam were raising the sail once again to catch the now softer breezes entering the Bay. Flying from the mast were five Aran knit sweaters, one for each of the O'Flaherty men and that of the lad. Father O'Malley sought out a barrel over which he hung his frock coat. His shirt he never removed. The bare chested sons began to tease each other as to which of them was strongest, when their father asked to be relieved of the tiller duty so that he might "put things in order," his meaning being that the boat was not tidy enough to be seen by strangers clearly seen on the docks of Galway.

The contest ended as Aedan took the tiller and asked James if he would like to have a try. The lad jumped at the chance to steer the craft. However, the Captain had decided the time had arrived for a chat with the lad. He had seen the boy and his youngest son in deep conversation and wondered as to what was so interesting as to captivate his excitable son so as to rivet him in a motionless state with eyes glued to those of the lad.

He began with a story of the prehistoric fortress of Dun Aengus, high above the Kilmurvy village on Inishmor not far from Father O'Malley's parish Church. It was after that ancient clan leader that his youngest son, Aengus, was named he told the lad.

"It was a truly sad day when the parish bade their farewell to the good Father. He will be missed, that's the truth."

"The people of Inishbofin will miss him as well. If it wasn't for him none of my friends would have received Communion, and I would still be climbing the walls of the ruins dreaming of the world but never seeing it.

"Aye, that being the truth as well, lad."

They sat in silence for a bit of time. The Captain was reflecting on that farewell on Inishmor and the lad bolstering up courage to ask about what he saw under the waterfall on that morning of the Inishbofin farewell.

"Captain..."

The aging fisherman adjusted his cap, wiped his eyes with the back of his hand. He may on the exterior exhibit a rough-hewn demeanor but on the inside, ah that was soft and gentle, full of feeling and love.

"Yes lad, what is it?"

"I need to ask you a question. It's kind of personal and you don't have to answer if you don't want to and maybe you don't even know the answer anyway, but…"

"James mi boy, just go for it and ask away."

The lad fidgeted, looked about for the priest so as to make sure he wasn't able to hear what he was about to say. Noticing that he was seated at the bow of the boat and engaged in what would be a similar serious conversation with Aengus, he felt confident in his asking of the question. The Captain scratched his head while watching the lad and thinking to himself as to what could be so important as to make him anxious as he was. Finally with a deep breath, James asked his question.
"I…I saw something yesterday morning not far different than what you and mi dadai saw of me in the waterfall."

Now it was the Captain who became anxious and embarrassed.

"Now lad don't you fret over that. We had no idea that ye are on the threshold of manhood or we would have turned our backs and given ye more privacy."

The Captain squirmed and his face became flushed, not having such a talk since his lads were boys ready to take their first voyage as fishermen. In fact in the case of Aengus, no such talk had he made as his brother and brother-in-law took it upon themselves to teach the lad the ways of being a man or so they thought. The Captain had stuck to the teaching of the use of nets and line for the catching of fish.

James with bowed head so that his flushed cheeks might not be too noticeable tried to assure the Captain of his trust in him.

"It's all right Captain, I'm good with it now. After all you have sons and must have helped them understand what was happening to them at my age."

"Thank you lad… 'tis gracious and mature that you are. So it's the talk of men and women together that ye are seeking."

"Oh no Captain O'Flaherty, not at all…I'm going to be a priest and such matters will not be for me, if you get my meaning."

The Captain cleared his throat so as to conceal his laugh.

"So at thirteen ye thinks that women will not have a place in your life, is that what this is about?"

"I'll be fourteen sir, in a few days. But that's not it at all. It's just that I saw someone in that waterfall washing himself and in a manner just as mi dadai wanted me to do."

"I think I understand lad. Ye have never seen a full frown man in his all together as it were."

"That is the truth, not even mi dadai. But that's not it either. You see…it was Father O'Malley in that waterfall."

The "Eoghanacht" was now making its way past several merchant ships and sea faring ships in the Galway Harbor as the Captain thought about what to say. After all, the looking upon a priest in such a way was sinful in his mind. At the same time he didn't want to scare the lad with talk of hell and such. He made the sign of the cross over himself and approached the subject.

"Now James mi boy," the Captain paused to build up courage for that which was to follow. "'Tis a natural thing to want to know how ye might look when you become a full grown man. But I must ask this. You weren't spying on the good Father were you?"

The shocked look of innocence upon the lad's face gave great relief to the Captain.

"Oh no, it was not like that at all."

James explained how he came upon the priest by chance as he was to meet him at the ruins to signal the Captain to come into the harbor at dawn. He told him of how he even walked backwards with a set of clothes for the Father so as not to see him. But see him he did and what stuck with him was streaks of red across the priest's back. In the Scripture story of Jesus being scourged at the pillar, such an image came to his mind.

"They weren't scratches like I have gotten when climbing on the rocks of the ruins."

"Well then, you acted like a gentleman. I wouldn't let the encounter worry you. Now as for those red marks on Father

O'Malley's back. He never shared his story with you, I take it."

With a nod of left to right the boy indicated "no." Knowing that the lad's time with the priest would be for many months if not longer, the Captain felt that he should understand the fiber of the man, what made him so respected and praiseworthy. He began to tell the story of Father O'Malley having just been ordained and sent from Rome back to Ireland in secret as priests were still under persecution and orders existed for their deportation to places like Australia, Bermuda and so forth.

"Now these were the days before the Act of Emancipation which helped us practice our faith in the open. The 'penal laws' as we call them wouldn't let Catholics own land or even live within five miles of a town. All we believed was done under the cloak of darkness and secrecy."

The lad learned of how Father O'Malley would travel on a donkey from place to place along the western coast of Ireland in County Clare, Galway and Mayo. In village after village in hiding he would celebrate the Mass and teach the Word of God.

"Then on that fateful day he had come to Galway City itself, a courageous thing to do. He, like others in his Order of St. Augustine, no longer had a Church. It had been destroyed centuries before by the likes of Oliver Cromwell, cursed be his name. 'Tis to that very Church, now rebuilt that we shall be taking you lad."

It was on the edge of his seat that the lad sat amazed that his priest had used such strong language, but he thought it to be justified. He was mesmerized by the tale of the brave priest who was his teacher and mentor. With open mouth and wide eyes he listened to the tale of how the young priest had taken an interest in the oldest Church not only in Galway but most of Ireland, even though it had long since become part of the Church of Ireland and in such places a priest was not welcomed under the law.

"I know of it Captain. It's called St. Nicholas Church and the Italian explorer Christopher Columbus prayed there in 1477 just before seeking funds to find a route to the east side of the world by going west."

"Indeed, Columbus you say…not an Irishman to be sure but a good Catholic I'm told. Ye have learned your lessons well mi boy, and that too is a credit to the good Father."

"I try not to disappoint him, that's for sure. So then what happened?"

"Well on a day not unlike this very one after a good rain and sunshine following, the good father had a notion to visit this St. Nicholas Church and see for himself the place where the man who would change the world's notion from being flat to that of being round first sought the guidance of God. In any case at the time it was raining and getting inside seemed to be a prudent thing to do."

"Well he always tells me to have the good sense to come in out of the rain."

"Well said. In any case he tied up George just outside the cemetery."

The boy looked at the Captain with questioning eyes.

"Who's George?"

"The donkey of course… Now I've since told him not to be so familiar with such beasts of burden. But he was young and loved to walk in the pastures with the sheep with George following him. He told me that such times offered him a quiet time for prayer, though I'd say that beast was a noisy one; and a stubborn one at best."

"I only know Mr. O'Connor's donkey. He's a pretty good listener but sometimes I can hear Mr. O'Conner losing his temper with him."

"My point exactly, lad…now as I was saying the beast was tied to the post and Father O'Malley entered the great Church standing there for centuries of time. Oh and what he saw, lad, was grand indeed. We have no such place to worship that's for sure. Great gray stones with huge windows to let in the sunlight and a tower soaring to the sky greeted our good Father. He told me later that it was built in the year of our Lord 1320."

"That's pretty old, Captain, over 500 hundred years."

"Aye that's true and back then it was a Catholic Church. It wasn't until Henry VIII had his dispute with the Holy Father in Rome over a certain wife of his that things changed and that is when the Irish got caught in the mess. You see, we didn't want to give up the faith for his new religion."

"Oh I know all about the lust of King Henry VIII, Captain…"

"What? I think your education is going too far lad."

A silence fell over James while the Captain blustered about his youth and innocence being threatened by such knowledge. It wasn't until the lad had a chance to clarify that he meant only the sin of lust that was in the King's heart which was known to him. The relieved elder stopped twisting his cap in his hands and placed it back on his head with a snort.

"Well then, that's better. In any case if you are to become a priest, you needn't know of such things."

"You mean stay pure of heart right? I don't even know how babies are made."

"Is that so? Well we'll save that talk for another day if that's all right with you?"

The youth was intrigued by this idea of men and women together and the making of babies but right now his thoughts were focused on the tale being shared of Father O'Malley. It was to that tale that he directed the Captain.

"Yes of course, if you think I should know. Now you were saying that Father had entered the Church?"

The storyteller fisherman continued his tale. In his mind's eye James was envisioning the scene as the priest entered with caution onto holy ground. He could hear each echoing step on the stone floor and see the amazed awe on his face as he looked about the great Cathedral-like Church of arches and pillars. The darkness of the clouds made the feel of the

Church despite its large windows to appear as it must have in the Middle Ages, dark and mysterious. Thinking he was alone, not a soul could be seen as he looked about, he walked first to the Baptismal Font made of stone and marble, he dipped his hand into the Holy Water and blessed himself knowing full well that such an act in a place that was not of his faith could be questionable to his superiors and to the Church of Ireland. One striking aspect of his visit to St. Nicholas was in the studying of the sculptures and stone reliefs found within the walls. He couldn't help but to see that some heathen had damaged the statues and stonework and in a place holy to all believers.

"You see the statues were headless and the hands of the saints were cut off. And that's when he realized that he wasn't alone," the Captain added.

"Who would do such a thing?" a shocked James asked.

"And that's what Father O'Malley asked aloud as well."

It turned out that a young gentleman was praying off to the side. It was in the Lynch family aisle that he stood. It was they and the French family which were great powers in 16th Century Galway. Each had added a side aisle which expanded the Church to its present state. The priest's question had stirred him to realize that he wasn't alone either. He walked to the center aisle, where Father O'Malley stood and told him that the blasphemy was done by the troops of Oliver Cromwell when they used the Church as a stable during the rebellion which brought down King Charles I and made Cromwell Lord Protector.

"It was he," the priest was told, *"who brought the final destruction of many of the holy places of Ireland."*

"And it was this young gentleman who brought Father O'Malley to a reckoning with the authorities over twenty years ago."

"But why? What had he done? Did this man betray him?" asked the astounded James.

The Captain told the lad that all his questions would be answered. He went on with the story; first by identifying the man as being around the priest's age. "He was a descendant of the very family who built the side aisle in which he prayed. His name is Patrick Lynch. His family once lived in the Lynch Castle, the very one which was serving as a prison back then.

"So it was this stranger who betrayed Father?"

"Not at all lad, he was only there to pray where his family once worshiped and could no longer. That castle was lost to them centuries ago when Cromwell took control of Galway. He befriended Father O'Malley. Why else would he tell him about Cromwell's destruction of the art in the church? Sadly though, because of that connection, the good Father, was indeed, found out."

What the youth learned was that the Lynch family was under a watchful eye of the authorities. They constantly feared that they might try to rise up again and flex their muscles to incite rebellion. Their reputation was still that powerful in Galway. When Patrick Lynch walked the priest out of the Church, those very spies set to watch Patrick followed

Father O'Malley. They were led down Lombard Street and then to the Forthill Cemetery. It was there that the priest knew he would be able to seek out fellow Augustinians for fellowship. It was in that cemetery that guards appeared and he was arrested as attempting to incite rebellion with a known member of the Lynch family. It was later that they also found out that he was also a priest. That alone would allow him to be imprisoned and deported.

"And that's how our good Father was thrown into prison without so much as a trial. Those lash marks which you saw lad, were given to him as they tried to get information from him. He would give only his name. But when they heard O'Malley fear rose up among his captors, for all had heard the stories of Gracie O'Malley, the Pirate Queen. They became harsher in their treatment of him. That's when he betrayed himself as he called out in Latin a prayer to our Blessed Mother, Mary, for her intercession."

The lad on the verge of tears crossed himself and looked over toward Father O'Malley who was still in a deep conversation with Aengus. The Captain watched not only with emotion but also with the thought that this lad had a heart full of love. He was destined to make a difference, and perhaps even so young, he would serve the Church.

"Aye lad, he is a good man as you can see plainly and a brave one too."

James stood with the conviction of a soldier ready to face anything. For him that anything was to actually tell Father O'Malley how he felt. To share his feelings was not easy for him. He held all things in his heart and tried to control his emotions. That's why he hid himself from view after losing sight of Inishbofin. But all that was changing as he saw his teacher, his priest in a new light.

"Captain, he's a hero really and should be proud and not hide his courage."

"Aye, perhaps…but that's just it; the good Father is also a humble man, not one to boast. Drawing attention to those scars when others all about him suffered in silence is not for him."

The lad began to understand those jokes about his own mother's battle with humility. Of course were it not for her forcefulness, he also realized that the adventure he embarked upon would not have come to pass and he would not be sailing into Galway harbor to board a ship for America.

"Thank ye Captain, excuse me please."

Walking toward the bow of the ship, which was not a distance by any stretch of the imagination he soon heard Aengus' excited voice. How his father and brothers didn't hear also he attributed to their concentration on running the boat between those great ships about them. What he heard would come to impact his own journey.

"James tells me that in America all people are equal, not like here in Ireland."

"The lad speaks the truth," responded Father O'Malley.

Aengus' voice did get softer but James still could catch the words.

"Then Father, I want to go to America. Will you take me?"

The priest didn't know how to respond. Such short notice would make booking a passage difficult at best. Then there was his family who depended on him for their fishing business and caring for their sheep. Yet, how could he say "no?" Aengus saw that look of strife within himself across the priest's face.

"I can pay my own way once these fish are sold, Father."

"That's not what worries me son. What about your family? You would be leaving without even a farewell to your mother."

"Aye, that troubles me. But one day I shall bring them to America. That is once I make mi fortune."

James stood rigid as stone. Once again he was privy to something which was not meant for him to know. He held onto the "boom" to steady himself and turned to make a hasty retreat back. A shift in the wind caused the "boom' to move causing him to stumble forward.

"There you are James," said the priest in greeting. "Is all well with you? You'll have to get used to the rocking of a boat lad, if we're to cross the ocean on one of those ships."

He pointed to a rather good sized ship with three masts alongside of which the "Eoghanacht" was passing. A little too close observed Aengus; for they could read the name of the vessel clearly on its bow. It read "Cushla Machree."

James offered a crooked grin as if feigning seasickness in the harbor while when in the storm he took the rough sea as well as any sailor. And well did the priest realize what was going on; so the lad built up his courage to say what was in his heart.

"Ah…yes Father, I know and really I can do it. It's just that I had something to say and I don't know quite how to put it."

"It's always best to say what's in one's heart, lad."

That heart stuff again was causing this lad who had faced hunger and concern for a sickly mother, ignorance and restricted faith expression to have to put it all out there for all to see and in this case to hear. He placed his two feet firmly on the deck allowing his body to move with the gentle rocking of the boat to avoid another mishap.

"It's just this. Captain O'Flaherty was telling me a story back there at the tiller."

"Lad, it appears that it was some tale that it has caught your tongue. Would you not agree Aengus?"

"Aye Father…come on James mi boy, spit it out now."

In an instant it all came out short and succinct but hitting the priest in his very own heart.

"All right then…all I can say is that Father O'Malley is far braver than his ancestor, The Pirate Queen."

The priest looked aghast and yet also confused. He had no clue as to why this was said and even more so what provoked the compliment. He slapped Aengus on the back and laughed.

"It seems Aengus, that our lad here has something in common with my ancestor. That is the using of the gift of blarney."

As the two enjoyed the diversion from the true meaning behind the compliment, James too began to laugh so as not to embarrass the priest. Actually, James was rather relieved that they chose to make light of his comment as if coming from an admirer or hero worshiper. He didn't have to explain the source of this admiration. He didn't have to talk about the scars which could have only been seen when he saw much more under that waterfall.

"Come on James sit here." Aengus patted the deck beside him. "I'd like to tell ye about the plans for mi future."

Relieved that what he overheard would be made known to him he parked himself between the fisherman and the priest. He listened intently to Aengus' telling of this new dream of going to America, the land of equality, opportunity and freedom.

The Spanish Arch next to the ruins of the medieval stone wall which once surrounded Galway loomed before them as they were now near the docking area for fishing boats. The great merchant ships and vessels which would take the hordes of people now swarming the docks across the Atlantic Ocean barely rocked at anchor in the harbor. No horror story as had been retold by the Captain would deter

Aengus nor the priest from their resolve to sail across the sea. As for the lad, he could only think of Christopher Columbus, whom he now admired as well since his learning that he had come to Galway before his journey of discovery of a new world when he sought a western trade route to the East Indes. Now he would soon be like the great explorer, he thought while once again looking at the "Cushla Machree," which would be his "Santa Maria."

Aedan and Adam masterfully guided the "Eoghanacht" alongside the dock. The Captain called to a couple of seamen at water's edge to catch the rope for tying the vessel to the dock. He jumped onto the pier and checked the lines much to the chagrin of the seamen. The Captain announced that he would be taking Aeadan with him for the selling of the fish in the hold. Aengus and Adam were to watch the boat and its cargo of fish. Eying the people milling about the docks, it was clear that some were in desperation for any kind of food, even raw fish.

All were seeking to leave Ireland. Some were dressed in proper traveling clothes and had with them leather pieces of luggage and small trunks. Most, however, carried canvas sacks or small cloth sacks over their shoulders and were barely clothed at all. These were the ones who stood in long lines to speak with agents who were selling passage with a promise of a job in North America when they arrived. The fee of six British pounds ($12.00) was all most of these men had to their name. Whether any of these hopeful people heard of the stories which the Captain had shared was unknown. It was doubtful that even such stories of bodies floating down the St. Lawrence River near Montreal would deter them either. In any case the ship most would board was sailing to New York City in the United States and that made them even more hopeful.

As for Father O'Malley and James, they would be headed for St. Augustine Church near the Forthill Cemetery where the priest had been arrested some twenty years prior. This time a Church had been actually built and Augustinian Friars served the people of Galway. Once the catch was sold, then the O'Flaherty men would join them there. They would have to walk as carriages would be expensive and at the harbor unlikely to be found. And so the priest and lad made their way, sacks slung over their shoulders to the City Center.

Up Queen Street, which ran alongside of the dock area they strode. Never had James thought that such a city existed let alone that he'd be walking along its streets paved with stones and lined with shops, row houses and two story manor houses surrounded by whitewashed smooth stone walls with white painted iron gates leading to their entrance. For the lad, Galway was a grand city. For any other 19th Century traveler it would be a modest sized town in the stage of decay and neglect due to the impact of the blight, a decreasing population and poor economic conditions in no large part as a result of a failing fishing industry. The latter was said to be caused by the lack of government support and investments for the fishing business.

None of this mattered to James, not that he wasn't noticing the throngs of people obviously in distress nutritionally and for simple comforts of proper clothing and housing. Yet in comparison to Inishbofin, it was a hub of lively activity and seemed to be thriving.

While this walk took place, at Eyre Square the O'Grady family, Aunt Maggie and Colin Logan still stood in front of the hotel. The passengers were weary given the rough mud filled Cliffside road on which the coach had to travel. All around Galway Bay from Doolin through the Burren to Kinvarra and finally to Galway City they had traveled. The five had watched the coach fade away on the other side of the square. It was for them the severing of the final attachment to their home in Doolin.

With heavy hearts they had watched the coach depart. The sight of the square filled with people living under deplorable conditions, created an all too real image of Ireland's suffering. It reminded Sean and Colleen as to why they were allowing Meghan to go with Maggie and Colin to America. The sight had impacted Meghan particularly hard.

Present Day Eyre Square, Galway, Ireland

Chapter Nine: A Chance Meeting

The dark clouds were approaching the harbor area creating a line of black against a vividly bright afternoon sky over land areas.

"Don't you think we should get inside?" asked Colin.

"What? Oh…of course Colin," answered Sean.

"Maggie are you ready? We should go in."

"Yes love, I'll be right there. You and Sean go ahead."

The men walked up the few steps and waited as Maggie went to Colleen and Meghan who stood at curb side just watching the people in the square milling about and talking with one another. Squeezing between them, she grabbed their arms. The younger sister instinctively felt their emotional state.

"Come dears, we need to get inside. Rain is almost upon us."

With that they joined the men on the stairs and entered through the red painted door into what was the reception area of the Skeffington Inn. By Victorian standards it was quite plain and simple. The registration counter was made of flat oak panels with no designs. The back wall, save for its trim, was also made of oak panels. A cubicle of the same wood held keys and mail for guests behind the counter. The reconstruction of the row houses was still in progress on either side of the central building. That center building was of smooth white washed stone while the flanking buildings were constructed of red brick.

Behind that austere counter stood a tall young man with dark hair brushed back off his smooth shaven face, which was unusual for the Victorian man. He was dressed in a black suit of wool with a white shirt and black cravat and smiled broadly as he welcomed them and assigned their rooms.

Off to the side was a lounge area in which two plush sofas faced each other and were arranged perpendicular to the hearth. A table with a flower arrangement on it stood between them. On one of the sofas sat an older man dressed in non-Victorian style, in fact not in a frock coat at all. Rather he wore a jacket as one might see on a traveler hiking on a trail, brown wool pants and a flannel shirt with no tie. The woman was also around 60 and had no headgear covering her gray streaked auburn hair pulled back in a bun. Her style of dress was more formal compared to the man, who was obviously her husband. The floor length full skirted dress with lace over the bodice was more Irish style than Victorian. She had a knitted shawl of dark green about her shoulders. They were talking of the difficulty of their trip to Galway from Northern Ireland, when the sounds of the commotion in the reception area filled their ears with a voice readily recognized.

The woman squealed with delight and ran toward the archway leading into the other room. Her husband followed and stood next to her under the arch. Both watched waiting for the right moment to make their presence noticed. The woman was tugging on his arm urging him to say something.

Dennis McMahon did as his wife asked. "Could these lovely lasses be our daughters Catherine?"

Maggie and Colleen turned in an instant having recognized that husky voice despite so long a time being away from their parents.

"Da, Momai," screamed Maggie.

She and her sister ran to their open arms. Maggie entered into the embrace of her father and Colleen into the arms of her mother.

"You came Da, you came. I just learned that you had been invited," exclaimed a weeping Maggie.

"Oh Momai, you and Da have made Margaret so happy," Colleen whispered into her mother's ear.

They being of the same height, about 5'2" and slender figured with ample bosoms made them at first glance to appear as sisters were it not for Catherine's graying hair pulled back in a bun.

The men stood with Meghan in-between, several feet from them so as to afford them the opportunity to reunite. Sean was anxious to reintroduce his daughter to her grandparents whom she had not seen since she was eight years old.

"And why such a shock look on your face daughter? Should not your mother and father at least meet this man who would make you his wife and then take you off to America?"

"Well it's just that…" Maggie began but couldn't finish her thought. Rather she went to Colin and pulled him to her father.

"I am honored to meet you Mr. McMahon. 'Tis a great business enterprise in which you have agreed to participate with Sean."

Now Dennis McMahon was not a tall man. He barely stood two inches above his wife. But his presence was very dominating in the gathering of family though both Sean and Colin were at least six inches taller than he. As such he looked at the young man, who proposed this involvement in a ceramics business, up and down as if approving his appearance as a gentleman. Of course Colin was, if anything, a prime example of a Victorian gentleman. He nodded his approval, smiled graciously and nudged Maggie to her mother while pausing to give Colleen a hug before extending his hand to shake that of Colin. They shook hands heartily. He went on to do the same to Sean ending with a hug. In that embrace he took notice of his granddaughter standing behind her father.

"Can this be little Meghan?" asked Dennis.

The women gathered about them with Catherine Mary taking the lass into her arms before she had a chance to finish her curtsy.

"Mi lovely girl you are radiant like the rising sun," Catherine exclaimed. "Now then, you must tell your granddad and me all about Doolin and this grand adventure upon which you are to go."

"Good idea Catherine, how about some tea. They must have some kind of service in this place."

"Dennis, let Sean go ask. You'll scare the poor boy behind the counter again."
"I'd rather chat with Meghan anyway," Dennis replied as he and Catherine escorted Meghan to the sofas.

His daughters followed with Colin in tow. The grandmother nuzzled Meghan between she and Dennis on one sofa while the others sat opposite of them. Sean was entering with the desk clerk and a female server who was pushing a tea cart. The clerk welcomed them to the hotel on behalf of Mr. McBirney of Dublin.

"We at the Skeffington are most pleased to offer you this refreshment after your long journey to us." He then nodded to the server who began to pour the tea into china tea cups.

What Meghan was most caught up in was the bread rolls and cookies on a three tier tray. Never in her life had such elegance ever been experienced. But it wasn't the prettiness of the china set or the treats which impressed her. Rather, she thought of how many mouths in Doolin could be fed by just this one tea serving. Then her thoughts went to those people right outside in the square. Many of them were obviously in need of decent food, really any kind of food just to survive another day.

When the server reached her and inquired as to what she would like with her tea, milk or lemon, she was hard pressed to imagine such a choice as such choices simply weren't ever available in Doolin. When she was handed a small white china plate trimmed in blue on which a roll and cookie

257

was placed she could hardly contain herself. As for the server, she apologized for   being able to offer butter and jam as the only condiments. Meghan smiled and told her that the oatmeal cookies and rolls looked scrumptious.

Everyone having been served the cart was placed behind the sofa on which Meghan sat. The clerk and server left without further words having been told by Catherine that she would take care of refilling the tea cups as needed.

Once they had left the retelling of that now familiar story of Dennis and the girls first meeting John Caldwell Bloomfield as a lad began. As the tale was drawing to a dramatic conclusion ending with that very boy becoming the man, who with Colin's boss was about to begin a new ceramics company in response to the declining conditions of the Irish people due to the blight, Dennis observed how such a business would eventually be of great value.

"But," he added. "That will take time and I suppose that's why you have to go to America."

Catherine was not pleased that he brought up the journey to America. She knew how difficult it was for her to lose her daughters for long periods of time right in Ireland but Colleen was facing the loss of her daughter to a land of which they knew very little and as she had put it, *"Only God knows how long it would take Colin to get business leaders in America interested in the Irish enterprise."*

What came next however would really cause her to become upset.

"Now then, we've had a bit of tea and have gotten to know each other a bit better eh Colin?"

Colin smiled politely but couldn't help feel that more was to follow. And he was quite correct.

"Good lad, so then perhaps you and Maggie might enlighten me as to why this marriage is to take place in such a fashion."

Gasps were followed by silence. Catherine gave Dennis the look of disgust, rose and took Meghan by the arm, suggesting that perhaps a breath of fresh air might be needed. Meghan followed her grandmother pausing at the tea cart and loading the remaining rolls and cookies into linen napkins to be taken with her outside.

They were at the hotel door when Colin finally broke the silence and began to address the issue of a marriage between a Catholic and Anglican. Catherine hustled her outside.

The lass and Catherine stood on the steps overlooking Eyre Square with its temporary residents of those seeking passage to North America from Galway as the possibility of going to Cork City or Cobn seaport was out of reach for them even though they had far more ships sailing from their ports to Canada and the United States.

"Thank you Granny for taking me outside."

"Not at all child… my you must be starving by the looks of your bundles."

"Oh these aren't for me. I thought that some of the children in the square might be hungry. Would you mind if I went into the square?"

Now while this discussion was taking place, coming up to Forster Street were Father O'Malley and James. Another sight of people in distress and in want met their eyes as they rounded a corner which bordered Eyre Square.

"Father, look at all those people. Is all of Ireland desiring to leave?"

"We are in trying times. There is no doubt about that. Soon we will be very close to them on our ship. Perhaps in the sharing of our stories we might bring a bit of Erin with us."

James had stopped and was rifling through his sack. He pulled out what appeared to be a book. It wasn't however a novel but a journal made up of blank pages. Father O'Malley had stopped at a bookshop along Queen Street for the purpose of finding a book on America from which both he and the lad might learn more about the United States. The search was fruitless. But he did find the journal which James now held. He thought the writing down of the experiences they had already shared and were about to as well would not only provide James with practice in writing but also in the creation of story-telling. For the gift of telling a good tale even those filled with blarney was indeed something which would bring a bit of Ireland with them.

"Lad, why do you need the journal now?" asked the priest.

"Would you mind terribly if I went into that park and talked with some of the people. Maybe they don't have a journal or even paper or pen to write with. I could take notes of their tales."

Father O'Malley just looked at the lad and questioned how such a youth could have such insight into the souls of others as to feel the need to preserve their stories. At the same time he had to be realistic. Often the stress of their plight caused short tempers and a vision of others who might have a bit more than them as being superior snobs. He cautioned the lad but allowed him to enter the park. He soon found himself not having a care for his safety for they were welcomed warmly. In fact once they had learned that he was a priest, an improvised prayer service was arranged at which he prayed for a safe journey for all in the square and on the dock. As the final blessing was given, James took note of a young girl around his age handing out something to young children at the edges of the square. Like him, she had someone looking after her. Slipping through the crowd who gathered around Father O'Malley, the lad made his way to the girl.

"She has a tale to tell," he thought as she handed out what he could clearly see was some kind of bread and something else which he couldn't identify. He was within arms-length of her as she forced that unknown food into his hand which he held outstretched to touch her to gain her attention so that he might speak with her.

"Ah…thank you," the lad began. "But I don't need whatever this is."

"It's called a cookie. Surely you know what a cookie is?" asked Meghan.

"Actually, I never heard of such a term. It's a food of some type, isn't that so?"

Meghan's face turned sheet white. She had insulted the boy, she thought. He standing there in that Aran knit sweater which she had seen on many a fisherman coming to Doolin looked uncomfortable in his own skin as he lifted up the cookie to examine it.

"It's made from oats and a bit of sugar."

"Oh, well on Inishbofin we don't have oats."

"I've studied the geography of Ireland so I know of the island but not what's grown there."

Just as James was about to tell her about his island home, her grandmother came between them. "Meghan, I think we had better return to the hotel as the skies are getting quite dark with storm clouds.

"Yes, granny…oh young man, do take a bite of the cookie. I think you'll like it."

James was now tongue tied but managed to smile as Catherine with her arm around Meghan led her off across the street toward the hotel. The lad watched with cookie in hand at a vision of a girl. There was nothing like what he watched on Inishbofin. Meghan's skirt swished as she trotted across the cobblestones, and her flaming hair around her shoulders swayed from side to side. Just as he bit into the cookie, she stopped on the stairs turned her head, spotted him biting the cookie, smiled, then disappeared into the hotel.

"Wow, this is tasty!"

A hand on his shoulder startled him.

"Father O'Malley! I was just eating this…it's called a cookie."

"Indeed, thank you. In Italy, I found those to be most tasteful and have missed them since my return."

"You mean they have oats in Italy too?"

"And wheat and corn as well, but I'll save that lesson for another day. It's time to move on to St. Augustine Church or we shall be wetter than we were from those waves splashing upon us at sea."

The lad broke the remainder of the cookie in half and handed a piece to the priest.

"James, I didn't mean…"

"I know Father. But I want to share my good fortune with you."

Once again the priest felt that purity of heart; that humanness sparked by the Divine from the lad of Inishbofin. He could only accept the cookie piece and say "God Bless You."

The two walked along the fringe of Eyre Square receiving greetings from its residents as they made their way. They had many blocks to walk before they would reach their destination. Each of them presented a new insight into urban life for James and a glimpse of what was to come in America, where the cities were larger, more complex and populations much greater. Though they were unaware at the time, one of those streets would bring back the memory of that fateful day when Father O'Malley was arrested.

Back in the hotel the voices from the lounge area filtered into the reception area, not so much due to anyone shouting as to the number of people speaking at the same time. Catherine hastily explained to her granddaughter that a discussion was under way regarding her Aunt Maggie's marriage.

"Now child, 'tis been quite a long time since you have seen your grandfather. What you need to understand is that tradition and faith are very important to him."

"I think I understand granny. It's like what we do at Christmas or Easter time."

"Yes, love but even more so, for he sees all life as run by traditions even to the way a line is baited or the price for his fish is…shall we say discussed at market."

The girl nodded not entirely knowing what she meant. As for those voices the lass was only half listening anyway as her thoughts were still on that lad in the square who looked like a young fisherman, for in Doolin such sights were plentiful. Somehow he didn't act like one despite the Aran knit sweater many of which she had seen when going to town, more frequently done before the bad times. She was envisioning his bushy black hair and those sea blue eyes just as he bit the cookie. That image caused her to smile and that's when Catherine realized that her mind was miles away from that hotel lobby. She took the hand of the lass and they entered the lion's den.

"Well now, there's my sweet granddaughter. Granny has kept you away from us too long. Come sit by me and tell me about this journey to America."

Both the lass and the grandmother stood for a moment saying nothing. It became quite clear that the discussion had been about America and each was sharing a story they heard about that country across the ocean. Some were fantastical ones, not unlike their Celtic legends, such as the streets being paved with gold. Others were of commerce and industry and how their buildings were each several stories high and attached one after another for many blocks. And then they shared horror stories of people who actually owned other people. They were relieved when Colin had told the others that slavery was not allowed in the north where New York City was located.

As for the marriage issue, they came to learn that it was dealt with quite satisfactorily when Dennis McMahon placed his stamp of approval on the union with the hope that in America, where all people are equal, "at least in the north" he said in amending his position upon hearing that slavery existed. "And they are free to worship as they see fit. In such a country, your marriage would not be looked upon as sinful."

Meghan now bookended between her grandparents listened intently as Colin had to inform them that the basics of the ceremony itself would need to be addressed and that would be with the Rev. Gary Hasting, Rector of St. Nicholas Church. It was he who had been the soon-to-be bridegroom's classmate at Trinity College. It was he who had published the bans, which announced the coming nuptials. They were to meet with him that very afternoon to go over the wedding service since their departure would take place soon afterwards. The "Cushla Machree" would wait for no one when it was time to set sail for America.

Since Colleen was to serve as Matron of Honor and Sean as Colin's Best Man, it was decided that the entire family should go with them to the Rectory.

"Gary may want us to get familiar with the church environment," Colin had concluded.

The desk clerk entered as the proposal was offered.

"Sir, the carriage has arrived."

"Thank you, we'll be out presently," responded Colin.

Droplets of rain pitter pattered across the stone walkway and streamed down the tent like structures in Eyre Square across from them. They boarded the carriage giving thanks that it had a canopy over it. However, it had no side panels.

Raindrops had spread across the city and some of them hit James on the head just as they were passing a large limestone church surrounded by a short wall of field stone. Across the road a series of decaying buildings were being demolished. James took an interest in how the buildings were being dismantled when he noticed the plaque on the church's outer wall next to the doors. It read St. Nicholas Church and listed service days and times. Wiping water droplets which now plunked down onto his face from the mop of wild hair, the lad finished reading the sign's message. His conversation with Captain O'Flaherty came to mind and he hesitated to bring attention to the church. And yet he supposed that his priest would have been aware of where they stood, so he spoke matter-of-factly.

"Father, this is St. Nicholas Church. Isn't this where Columbus prayed?"

Father O'Malley nodded affirmatively. His reluctance to pause was not to quell James' enthusiasm; nor was it because of it not being part of the Catholic Church. Rather, it was his need not to relive that fateful day when shortly after leaving the church with Patrick Lynch, he was arrested. Though that was twenty years ago, the event was seared into his memory and scarred across his back as if it had been yesterday.

"May I go in and see where Columbus prayed?"

Thomas O'Malley OSA had no desire to enter St. Nicholas and be further reminded of that horrific day in his young life as being newly ordained. At the same time the lad was so excited about paying a visit that he was hard pressed to say no. So he took a deep breath, looked at the beaming boy with rain drops running down his face and forced a smile. He would sacrifice his discomfort to bring joy to the lad who would serve the Lord.

"Of course James, in any case it may save us from being rained upon."

Through the huge oak doors still bearing the marks of swords and vandalism of Oliver Cromwell's troops when they used the church as a stable, they walked into an environment created in the 14th Century. To their left was a marble and stone Baptismal Font. In front of them at the end of the main aisle was the sanctuary. Huge stone pillars held up arches which drew the eye along the nave toward the sanctuary, which they noticed had a group of people engaged in conversation in front of the peaked window being transformed into stained glass from clear glass. Their steps echoed as they moved forward toward the marble pulpit which from their view stood to the left and elevated so that the preacher may have a view of all the assembly. Visible too were the results of Cromwell's vandalism as the depictions of the saints had no heads or hands.

Halting about mid-aisle down the nave, Father O'Malley paused to conduct a short lesson for James. He was explaining that the Church was named in honor of St. Nicholas of Myra.

"He is the patron saint of children. However he is also the patron of Mariners. Since we have become mariners of sorts, it might be worthwhile to offer a prayer for his intercession on our behalf as we begin our voyage."

James was wide-eyed at the thought of the voyage now having conjured up a rather adventurous and almost romantic notion of what that journey would be like with St. Nicholas at the wheel guiding them to America.

"I can't wait until we sail Father. It will be a grand adventure."

Father O'Malley being privy to those stories from Captain O'Flaherty cautiously replied that sailing can be dangerous as well. Then once again noticing a clergyman giving instruction in the sanctuary, he suggested that they move off to the side aisle. At the front of that aisle was another huge peaked window. This one was almost complete in its stained glass rendition of Jesus with his apostles as he Ascended into heaven. Never had the lad seen such beauty in expressions of the faith. He stood in awe with open mouth and crossed himself.

That gesture not being commonly used by Protestants was noticed by a lone figure standing in the shadow of one of the pillars. He too was admiring the window. The tall man with broad shoulders and light hair sported a full beard trimmed close to his face. His hazel eyes looked at the boy as he made the sign of the cross sizing him up and then was doing the same to the man with him. It was in the studying of the man's face that he gasped so loudly that the people in the sanctuary looked over toward the area where the sound emanated.

The dark clouds now covering Galway City obliterated most of the direct sunlight of late afternoon so much so that the glorious stained glass window was not filtering sunrays to create that solemn light so expected from such windows in most Medieval Churches before the Renaissance Era introduced wider and brighter worship spaces as evidenced in St. Peter's in Rome. Nevertheless a lone direct ray of sunlight managed to escape the cloud cover and make its way through the window and came to shine on James' sweater.

Another gasp was emitted, but this time it came from Meghan, who with her family was being instructed on the various aspects of the wedding service.

"Oh dear…excuse me, I just saw something."

"Ah, the Lynch window no doubt, it is beautiful isn't it and it's not quite finished as yet," the Reverend Hasting observed. "Why don't you go and take a closer look at it. We're almost finished here."

With a proper curtsy, Meghan moved slowly toward what is called the Lynch aisle as that family created the extension to the Church. They were also the family which was donating the window restoration. She approached the aisle slowly seeing a lad and two men in excited but quiet conversation.

"It is you," began Patrick Lynch as he stepped from the shadows. "I thought I'd never see you again."

Patrick embraced the stand-offish priest, who stood stunned at first, took a deep look into those hazel eyes and recognized the exuberant Patrick. He could hardly speak and his emotions were mixed with those of shock and resentment in that it was because of Patrick that he was arrested or so he thought all these years.

"It is you, Thomas O'Malley, is it not?"

"Yes, I'm he. Further words failed the priest.

James stood to their side not knowing what to do. It was clear to him that his friend, teacher and priest was experiencing a high degree of discomfort. In the end he thought it best to let the scene play itself out.

Patrick, around three years the senior of Father O'Malley held onto the priest's shoulders at arms-length.

"You look well Thomas or should I be calling you Father?"

"Then you knew that I was a priest," a now smoldering Thomas O'Malley OSA replied coldly.

"Aye, I do know," Patrick replied, feeling the tension rising. "But not when we met here some twenty years ago. Every day for those many years I have come here to pray that one day you would return and we would meet."

"Then you didn't...I mean you were unaware of my status when we first met?"

"That's very true, lost friend, hopefully now found. It wasn't until your arrest that I learned of your true identity. I tried to see you when the news came to my attention. I should have known that a priest being in the company of a Lynch gave authorities the jitters."

Patrick informed him that though he wasn't allowed to see the priest, his family still held some clout. When the Act of Emancipation was promulgated, the family used that influence to secure O'Malley's release from prison. However there was a catch; the Lynch family wasn't allowed to seek him out.

"And so I come here daily to pray for you. Even this grand window which my family is donating has not dispelled the government's fear of our influence. But they couldn't fault us or you, I thought, should we happen to come upon each other in a Holy place."

Now it was Father O'Malley, tears streaming into his beard, that took hold of Patrick in a sustained embrace.

"I'm so sorry Patrick. All these years I've harbored a harsh attitude. Yet it's because of you that I was freed and am able to walk these streets all these years later. Forgive me."

"There's nothing to forgive, Father."

The two walked arm in arm off to the side, Father O'Malley telling James that he needed to have a private chat with his friend long lost to him. As they walked toward a pillar behind which they would be out of sight by those in the sanctuary, Meghan arrived. James was studying the detail of the Lynch window.

"So it is you."

James twisted around so quickly that he stumbled forward toward her.

"Huh…oh my God, it's you!"

"Hush, you blaspheme in God's house."

James crossed himself and asked God's forgiveness.

"How, why and what brings you here?"

"My Aunt will be married here tomorrow. What about you, boy fisherman who isn't a fisherman at all?"

"Oh, well that's nice for her…huh, how do you know I'm not a fisherman. I have you know that this is an Aran sweater of the O'Flaherty clan."

"Well boy, you may be wearing an O'Flaherty clan sweater but that look of yours, such paleness with no ruddy cheeks from being at sea says otherwise."

James grabbed his now reddening cheeks. "Oh it's that obvious then?"

"Quite so boy," she responded with a manner not quite haughty, but close enough.

"Stop calling me 'boy,' my name is James Richard Shields."

"Well James Richard Shields, my name is Meghan Catherine O'Grady. I'm pleased to meet you."

She curtsied politely as he bowed. Then both laughed.

"There we're all properly introduced. Now then, did you enjoy the cookie?"

"Indeed I did Miss…I mean Meghan. I have never tasted anything like it."

"Then I am pleased that I took them from the hotel and shared it with you."

A short silence followed as James processed her sin of stealing from the hotel. Both looked about for adult eyes which might be watching. The adults were otherwise occupied.

"Really, I didn't steal the cookies. They were left over from our tea at the hotel." She could sense the lad's relief. "Now tell me James, what brings you to St. Nicholas Church?"

The lad was all too pleased to share his knowledge of the Church's history and its special guest, Christopher Columbus.

"So I just couldn't wait to visit and walk in the great explorer's footsteps for I shall be one soon myself."

"Really! Then you intend to be a sailor then?"

"Not at all, I'm going to be a priest."

The glow on Meghan's face faded instantly and she became bleached white.

"Oh, I see. Then I shouldn't be talking to you at all. You're much too holy."

Her words had become cold with disappointment.

"I don't get you. My teacher, Father O'Malley over there, says that our ministry is for all people, even girls like you."

"So you think I'm a sinner. How dare you."

Now he'd done it. He insulted her first by implying that she was a thief and now that she needed salvation because of the type of girl she was. How to regain his footing became the challenge for the lad of Inishbofin who never talked to a girl his age.

"I'm so sorry Meghan, what I meant is that we are all imperfect because of Original Sin."

The glow came back to her cheeks.

"My, but you are really quite a learned one. I'm sorry for treating you…" she couldn't go on.

His cheeks glowed as brightly as hers.

"I like talking with you. When I get to America to continue my studies maybe you might consider writing to me."

"You are rather forward for a person who is to become a priest."

"Am I? I don't get your meaning but will you write?"

Her broad smile answered his question. She tugged on the scarf covering her head nervously.

"Perhaps if I knew where you plan to be in America then I would consider it."

Just as James was about to talk about Philadelphia, Father O'Malley and Patrick came out of the shadows and seeing James with the lass called to him. At the same time Sean had come to seek out his daughter. After a brief introduction and an explanation that they were discussing the merits of the window, Sean led Meghan away. The lad and two men stood below the Lynch window, its colorful glow bathing them in holy light. But James wasn't feeling holy; rather he felt a weight on his heart that he had never experienced before. He wouldn't and couldn't move. He watched Meghan being escorted out of the sanctuary with her family.

He couldn't have heard the specifics of their conversation when she returned but he presumed that it was about him. It wasn't at all. The Rev. Gary Hasting had invited them to dine with him. Colin was hesitant, at first wondering if Dennis would refuse because of the minister's religious affiliation. However, Maggie's father was most gracious in his acceptance of the invitation. Not a word was spoken about the lad under the window with Meghan and she was glad of it.

A tug on his arm brought his eyes back in focus on Father O'Malley and Patrick Lynch.

"It sounds as if the rain has passed. Perhaps we should get on our way," Father O'Malley suggested.

After a brief glance back to the last spot where he had seen the lass, James exited after the men. They made their way on Taylor's Hill toward St. Augustine Church. Patrick had asked if he might accompany them as far as their Church. He would not have presumed to intrude on their meeting with the O'Flaherty clan who was to meet them there. The talk was of America and the journey aboard a ship which was to take a month before arrival at New York City.

The conversation had brought a sullen look across Patrick's face. So evident was it that James couldn't help but ask if he didn't like America.

"Heavens no lad; it's just that Thomas and…I mean Father Thomas and I have been renewing a friendship which now appears not to be possible."

"Patrick, we'll write. One day, when James here is ordained we may be back." Father O'Malley had deliberately made it known for James sake that he would be with him until he fulfilled his vocation.

Patrick brightened. "'Tis a way off to be sure, but then it's been twenty years since our last effort, so what's a few more years, eh lad."

Patrick brushed his hand across James' bushy hair.

"The girls will be sighing when this lad gets ordained, that's for sure."

James blushed and the men laughed as they continued on their way to meet the O'Flaherty clan at the Galway Augustinian Friar's house of St. Augustine Church.

St. Nicholas Collegiate Church, Galway

Chapter Ten: Friars and Riots

Father O'Malley and Patrick continued their conversation about James' future and the likelihood of his ordination which would be years away. Their pace was so quick that the lad was hard pressed to keep up. Suddenly, the men came to an abrupt stop. James crashed into them but didn't move them. They were too consumed with the building in front of which they stood. For it was Lynch Castle, once the home of Patrick's family in past centuries. It was then turned into a temporary prison, the very one in which the priest had been placed upon his capture for a brief time. As for Patrick's family, they no longer were part of its history even though their Coat of Arms was clearly visible on its exterior wall. Built in the 15th Century, though called a castle, it was more like a Castle Keep Town Home for use when in the city.

"God help us, if I didn't forget that we would pass this place. Thomas, please forgive me."

The priest stood stoically just looking at the edifice. James saw him reach his hand towards his back but said nothing. Rather he moved in so that he was actually touching him so closely was the lad to him. The affectionate move did not go unnoticed. He placed his hand on the lad's head patting it.

"There's nothing to forgive Patrick. It stands here idle. Maybe one day it will be used for the betterment of the people of Galway. I think it's best to move onward, we have several more blocks to go."

It was growing darker as they reached St. Augustine Church; not because of rain clouds but due to the lateness of the afternoon hour. The sugar from the cookie began to wear off and James, who had rarely had more than one meal of sorts on a given day, now experienced a craving. He said nothing as that was not in his nature. The men however noticed that he was getting lethargic.

"The lad looks a bit worn out and he toting along that sack around his neck and another over his shoulder. When was the last time he's eaten?"

"Patrick, I think he needs nourishment. The Friars should be able to scrap up something for the lad."

Since the Act of Emancipation, being a practicing Catholic was tolerated. At the same time it was not wise to flaunt allegiance to the Pope. Thus the Friary was quite plain and unobtrusive in appearance. It appeared not unlike any other of the two story stone buildings around Galway. The Church itself was located on Middle Street and not attached to the priests' house. A short trim elderly Friar answered the bell which Father O'Malley rang by pulling a chain which penetrated the wall to the interior and was attached to a small bell.

"I have never met you Father Thomas, but your reputation is the talk of the House in Rome. Welcome to you and your companions."

"Thank you Father…"

"My name is Francis Fitzgerald. Do enter and meet the other brother priests."

The threesome followed the older man into a sitting room which was dominated by a stone fireplace around which several sofas were arranged in a semi-circle facing it. Unusual for Ireland, all the Friars were wearing the gray habit of St. Augustine. It consisted of a floor length robe with a short cowl with hood commonly worn in Italy and around Europe but not in Ireland so as not to draw attention to them being Catholic. James was quite impressed by their appearance though quite shy during Father Francis' introductions. Seated on one of the sofas was a woman in her mid-fifties and dressed in a long green skirt of wool with a white cotton bodice. She held a knitted shawl around her shoulders, having lowered the shawl thus revealing her dark hair with gray streaks. The man next to her was perhaps a year or two older than she. He was tall, lean and obviously a fisherman, given his Aran Knit sweater which even James recognized as having the O'Flaherty pattern.

"Father Thomas O'Malley, Mr. Patrick Lynch and Master James Shields may I introduce Father Anthony Biscotti and Father Henry Mooney."

The lad took the hand of each priest with a loose grip but a fervent shaking of the hand followed.

Father Anthony was newly arrived from Italy, where the Italian cooks were creating sauces made from tomatoes grown from plants originally imported from America. These sauces were combined with the pastas they created from wheat not potatoes, though the latter had been used to make Italian dumplings before the blight hindered European crops as well. After a quick look at the lad, followed by that handshake, Father Anthony immediately excused himself. So moved was he by the pale appearance and sunken features of the lad, who had actually been eating something more regularly in the last few days than in the three years of his first meeting Father O'Malley, that he had to remove himself to the kitchen to find something for the lad. The parish was quite poor especially during the recent years of the blight. The Friars did have a garden and a few chickens but otherwise depended on the generosity of their human flock for their source of food.

Poor James felt that he had insulted Father Anthony because he had made a remark to Patrick that he was a foreigner for his Italian accent was quite thick, though he spoke English fairly well.

Father Francis then came to the woman and man, both stood as he approached.

"And may I present, Mrs. Nancy O'Flaherty the wife of someone you know quite well I am told as she is a member of your parish as is Mr. Liam O'Flaherty."

"Indeed I do, Father Francis. James, this is the Captain's wife and his brother from the Aran Islands."

Nancy took hold of the lad and squeezed him though tenderly.

"So this is the lad who my husband calls the Hero of Inishbofin. I thank thee for saving mi husband and sons."

James could hardly move in her grasp. Her face was so close to his that she could kiss him easily which she then did several times. Only the snickering of the men moved her to release the blushing dumb struck lad from her hold.

While his head was still reeling from the spectacle, Liam O'Flaherty came and grabbed the lad's hand hanging limply at his side. The jolt of the energetic greeting at first stunned the youth and yet it was welcomed after the kissing episode. In any case the Captain's brother looked so much like his older brother that it was uncanny. It was on those features of scruffy beard and long auburn hair that the lad dwelled. It made him feel more comfortable given the fuss made over him.

"Well lad, you need a bit fattening up but otherwise you have a strong hand shake to be sure."

"Thank you sir, I am pleased to meet you and Mrs. O'Flaherty as well."

The lad turned his head and smiled at the Captain's wife, who then took it as a cue to embrace him again. The re-entrance of Father Anthony with a tea cart mercifully stopped her in her tracks.

"Well then, it's been quite the day for you lad and all here. You must be hungry after being at sea, then walking here. It's not much but hopefully it will help fatten you up, as Mr. O'Flaherty said."

With that the other Friars helped him to serve tea to all while he focused on cutting the brown bread and offering it with jam to James. It was another new experience, for he had never seen jam made from fruit on Inishbofin. In that regard he was most correct for it was Father Anthony who brought the grape jam with him from Italy.

"James, the Friars of Rome hope that you enjoy this special jam made from grapes which didn't make it to the winery."

James was already licking his lips, having consumed the bread and jam while the Friar was giving his explanation. He grinned at Father Anthony with embarrassment, but accepted another piece of bread and jam readily.

"It appears that the lad did need some nourishment," Patrick observed just as the bell on the door sounded.

Father Henry excused himself to answer the sound of the tinkling bell.

"'Tis a quiet one he is," mentioned Patrick.

Father Francis, once Henry had left the room, then addressed Patrick's comment. "He is indeed and with good reason, I think. That young Friar newly ordained accompanied Father Anthony here. He is to be your replacement Father Thomas."

"He is a bit shy to stand before you, one who saved the people of Inishbofin and this lad while also reestablishing a Church on the Aran Islands," added
Father Anthony.

"And don't forget that Father O'Malley is a descendant of the Pirate Queen herself," James added between bites of the bread.

"Indeed lad, and who is this Pirate Queen?" Father Anthony asked while looking at Father Thomas with a warm smile. For he already knew the tale as Father O'Malley had been

284

quite thorough in his letters to Rome about the lad and his stories of Gracie O'Malley.

James' eyes lit up like the oil lamps on the tables set at each end of the sofas. "Well she was the terror of the seas here in western Ireland and to Queen Elizabeth I she was taken and stood up to her for all the people of Ireland, that's the truth...."

The boisterous voices entering could not be ignored by James or the others for that matter. The lad jumped up and ran to the entrance hall to greet the Captain and his sons. Right behind him were Nancy O'Flaherty and Liam. The Captain raised his arms in greeting then resting them on the shoulders of his wife whom he then embraced. Adam looked about for his own wife but was to find out that she being with child could not cross over to Galway. Aedan and Aengus tossed James playfully between them as if they had not seen him in many months.

"Woman, what are you doing here in Galway?" the Captain then gave her a peck on the cheek. His sons howled.

"Captain O'Flaherty, and in the house of the Friars....control yourself," Nancy said as she pushed him aside to greet her sons and son-in-law.

The quiet Friar then spoke. "I think it would be more comfortable in the sitting room. Please follow me."

The troup of fishermen immediately quieted themselves, the Captain setting the example by taking his wife's arm and escorting her into the parlor. Aedan and Aengus did the same to James, but his feet didn't touch the ground as he was lifted and carried forth. Adam walked with folded hands next to Father Henry through the archway to meet the other Friars.

The young fishermen's eyes went directly to the tea cart. As introductions were made, Father Anthony brought them a cup of tea with bread and jam, a delectable taste for them as well. It was Father O'Malley who asked if all went well with the sale of the fish as they were rather late in arriving.

"We are lucky to be here at all," quipped Aengus, as he held his hand up to his eye.

Nancy O'Flaherty became distraught seeing that it was bruised. "What have those beasts at the port done to ye?"

"Oh Ma, it wasn't the guards exactly," answered Aedan.

"And who would treat ye in such a fashion then?"

Adam then explained that as sacks were being loaded onto one of the merchant ships, one of them fell from the pallet which was being hoisted up onto the boat. It bounced onto the dock were a number of people had gathered to seek passage on the ship bound for England. They had hoped to get a job such as what they were seeing, as dockmen.

"Well that sack split open and what do you think was inside?" Adam didn't wait for an answer. "It was full of grain, corn or wheat I think."

To say that the people became outraged at the sight of a food substance being shipped out of Ireland while the people were starving would have been an understatement to be sure.

For in that parlor shock and disbelief pervaded as the tale went on.

"The men went wild grabbing handfuls of the grain and shoving it into their pockets. The dock-men ran onto the ship for fear of their lives while the guards came forth to calm the crowd. It was to no avail as the men now shouted for justice and food for their families and jumped aboard the ship throwing other sacks onto the dock which also split open."

"Lord in Heaven!" screamed Nancy. "Beggin' your pardon good Fathers."

"A brawl broke out and what a sight it was." Aedan now took over the story telling. "Fists flew to and fro…and one of them hit poor Aengus here right in the face. We who just came upon the scene having sold our catch of fish had not seen what caused the fight at first that is."

"I'm truly sorry Momai but I couldn't just let them do that to me…so I swung back not caring if it were an Irishman or a guard."

"Well it turned out to be a guard and soon we were considered part of the problem when we were not at all," continued Aengus while his mother was dabbing a napkin into water and applying it to his eye. "Owe, Mom, take it easy."

"And you should be offering your pain up to the Lord, for having been so involved in such goings on."

James now inserted himself between Aengus and his Mom. "So did ye get him good Aengus?"

"That I did lad, right back in his face and a tumbling he went, but then it got really bad." Aengus looked about at the horror on the faces of the Friars and the glee on the face of James. "And let me tell ye that no one this day was in the right."

Father O'Malley smiled. It was one of those, *"that's right Aengus, that's the right thing to say to this impressionable lad who would glorify fighting and rioting."* At the same time there was indeed an issue of justice which caused the riot in the first place. And this he addressed as well.

"Now fighting aside, for one should always try to find a peaceful solution first, we must find out more about this shipment of food out of Ireland when the people are in great need."

Patrick Lynch looked about the room and then settled his eyes on those of Father O'Malley.

"Thomas, our family doesn't have the influence it once did, but I shall insist that what it does have should be used to investigate as you suggested."

"That's a great commitment, sir. What a shame that the people or those guards hadn't heard what I had when arriving at Cork City on my journey from Rome," Father Anthony shared.

James was disappointed that the story telling of the fight came to an end as the Friar from Italy told them that he had been in Cobn, "now called Queenstown in honor of Queen Victoria's visit," he added.

"So the Queen has come to Ireland. Now she'll see what's really happening here," a pleased Nancy O'Flaherty said.

"Hopefully, though in Cork so festooned with banners and flags and such, she might have thought that all was well, when in fact many of the hundreds who waited to cheer her on were about to leave the country."

In any case, it was felt by most seated around the parlor that Her Majesty's visit was a good omen that the plight in Ireland would be addressed. They were soon to learn that relief efforts were already being started and that the "use of land" laws were being re-evaluated so that changes could be made. None of these would soon impact the people in County Clare, Galway and Mayo.

"But it is best that you have decided to leave for America from Galway, Father O'Malley. For the tales I heard in Queenstown of those ships taking the unfortunates to North America were quite chilling. And yet the people flock to board those ships to seek a better life." Father Anthony added no more graphic details as James sat at his side taking in every word into his heart.

For Father O'Malley, the Friar had just confirmed the tales which the Captain had shared with him. He too was pleased that they would be departing the next day on the "Cushla Machree" which sat in anchor in full view of those on the docks who were engaged in the fight over food. It was with relief that the O'Flaherty clan had escaped the scene before more damage was caused to them or worse their capture for inciting a riot, which they had not.

The talk moved from that of the rioting and the royal visit to that of the journey to America. The time had come to speak of the details for Father O'Malley and James' departure. It would be during that discussion that the conversation which Aengus had with Father O'Malley just before docking in Galway would come to light. However there was to a bit of other news which Father Anthony had traveled all the way from Italy to be shared first. Part of that was that Father Henry Mooney OSA was to replace Father Thomas O'Malley OSA.

Father Anthony patted the lad on his head and rose to whisper something into Father O'Malley's ear. Whatever that message was, it brought a bleached white color to his face. But first, James would have to leave so as not to upset him just before the trip overseas.

"Father Henry," O'Malley began. "Perhaps James would like to see the Church. He's never seen a Catholic Church."

"James would you like to help me set up for Vespers?" asked Father Henry.

The lad was only too delighted to do so. He explained quite emphatically in the process that since he was to be a priest like Father O'Malley, thus like the Friars he should learn about such things. The two left with James asking questions about the term "Vespers." He would be given a quick lesson on the "Divine Office" or the "Liturgy of the Hours" which the Friars would pray during the course of a given day. Later James would add this lesson to his journal along with the passage of departing Inishbofin and the storm at sea and not yet written but soon to be, the meeting of the girl who gave him a cookie.

He learned that these prayers (Matins) were to be said by all ordained and by those in Religious orders and the people in general as able.

These began with "Lauds" in the morning, "Terce" at mid-morning, "Sext" at midday and "Non" in the mid-afternoon. "Vespers" was prayed in the evening and was followed by "Compline" the night prayer. It was evening prayer which they would prepare to pray when the others joined them in the Church. The two left by the back door of the Friary and cut through the garden upsetting the chickens in the process as James couldn't resist trying to catch one of them. He failed save for a few feathers stuck to his jacket.

Back in the parlor, Father Anthony had begun to share the news he brought from Rome. The Prior had received a message from Father Ashe OSA of St. Augustine Church in Philadelphia. There was trouble brewing in America against the new immigrants and Catholics in general. A political nativist group locally called the "Know-Nothings" was inciting protests and even riots for several years against the newcomers and their Catholic religion. It seemed that they feared the Pope was seeking to run the United States. These anti-Papists were native born Americans set on preventing the spread of Catholicism and further immigration to the country. They saw such immigration as a threat to their jobs and the faith which came with them as a blasphemy. Not since Oliver Cromwell had such horrific language and actual attacks on Catholics been so wildly received as necessary to cleanse the Church of Romanism and a nation of those who followed such beliefs.

Horror filled the parlor as this tale of prejudice and mayhem of the past few years in America had finally come to the attention of the Prior in Rome. The Prior was of the belief that Father O'Malley should be aware of the tense conditions existing in the United States so that the lad might be protected from possible harm. Since the riots seemed to have calmed down, if not the political talk, the Prior felt that their plan to educate James at St. Augustine could continue as proposed.

"However, Father Thomas, our Prior cautions you not to dally in New York for too long a period. And be cautious when traveling to Philadelphia to not appear as a Catholic Priest. Nor should the lad speak of being a candidate for the Priesthood." Father Anthony finished with an apology for bringing such disheartening news just before what was to be a voyage of hope.

"Not at all, Father Anthony," responded Father O'Malley. "All will be well. I shall watch over the lad, as if his parents were beside me. Now perhaps we should go and pray for what appears to be a much needed safe voyage and journey to Philadelphia."

"Aye, that sounds like a good plan to me," added the Captain.

"And not to worry about protection Father, I shall be there to help out as I did this very day on the docks."

All eyes turned to Aengus O'Flaherty. Nancy demanded to know what he meant by such talk of protection and being with the good Father. Amidst tears and protest from his Dad and brothers, did Aengus relate that he wished to go to

America to make his fortune and send for his family. Nothing his father said regarding the fishing business or the family's sadness as evidenced by his mother's tears could sway him from his mind set.

"Da, don't you see," he countered. "The fishing business is going down as is all of Ireland. They're sending food out of the country when we need it right here. I'll be able to send you money to help out."

"Oh mi precious babe," a tearful Nancy began to say. "'Tis so fortunate that I brought ye this bag with your things, for you shall need them for such a journey, that's the Lord's truth." She again begged the Friar's forgiveness.

"Oh Momai, you're wonderful. How did ye know?"

"'Tis a deaf ear I appeared to give whenever you brought home stories of the lad and his vision of being free in America to be a priest or whatever he wished to be. I saw those green eyes of yours glowing with wonder and excitement that such a future could be yours."

"Love you said nothing to me, why?"

"Mi darling husband, how could I when you depended so heavily on the lads for the fishing. I held hope that you would be able to convince him to stay with us. But that is not to be and we must accept that he is a man now and must seek his future."

"Well if ye must go, then be sure to watch over James, like he was your little brother or I'll hear of it."

"Da, thanks." Aengus hugged his father and then his mother and brothers. "Let's go pray as the good Father suggested. 'Tis the 'Cushla Machree,' which will be greeting us on the morrow."

"Amen," said all the Friars as they led the way to the back door and into the garden.

Lynch Castle, Galway

Chapter Eleven: O, God, We Praise You.

The *Te Deum*, a hymn of praise to God, was still ringing in the lad's ears as he entered his assigned room for the night. Not only was it his first time in a Catholic Church, but it also culminated his lesson on the praying of the Divine Liturgy. He mulled in his mind how the Saints Ambrose and Augustine must have felt as they composed the verses which would become this most sacred hymn of praise. Great composers such as Mozart, Verdi and Haydn set its words to music. The Friars, because it was a special occasion, chose to sing the Mozart version of the hymn. The lad was hard pressed to understand every Latin word, but his training proved to be successful as part way through the hymn, he joined the Friars in their song. He couldn't fully understand why this hymn of all those that he learned over the three years of studying with Father O'Malley, struck him with an arrow of devotion and exaltation. In fact, he couldn't describe his feelings at all as the Vespers ended with a blessing from Father Anthony in the name of the Prior General of the Order of St. Augustine for a successful voyage.

He just stood in his "cell" as the Friar's rooms were called and looked about its austere and simple environment consisting of a bed, bureau on which was a wash basin and pitcher of water, and a small desk with a wooden chair with a straw woven seat and back. The chamber pot was hidden under the bed. On the wall over the bed was a Crucifix and over the door was an image of the Blessed Virgin Mary holding the infant Jesus. Never in all his life had the lad slept in such a room in such a house, which even when compared to the Overseer, Kiernan O'More's house, overshadowed it. To him it was like a palace though quite small and simple. The best part was that he didn't have to share it with anyone.

James removed his sweater and folded it tenderly, making sure each fold was laying just as he wanted it to be. Then he placed it into the top drawer of the bureau. It wasn't as if he had to do so. After all, he would be wearing it the very next day. But this is what he wanted to do with all of his clothes just because he wanted to do so. Standing in nothing but his Long Johns as the Captain called the long underwear in the American language fashion of speech, he reached for the sack holding his Journal. Removing it after patting the Family Bible, he placed the journal on the desk on which was an ink well and a petal tipped pen next to it. Just as he sat to put his thoughts of the girl with the cookie onto a page of the journal, a strange sensation rose in his groin area. His male member for no reason grew and became rigid. The lad thought that he had sinned because of how he wanted to describe the girl with the cookie in his journal. He began to pull at himself hoping that it would make it go away. The action only made it more swollen. Next he tried pacing around the room while thinking of the ship which would take him across the ocean and not on his condition. His thoughts were jarred when a knock on the door startled him.

"Yes…" he hoarsely responded in a whispered tone.

"James, are you decent?"

"Ah…I don't know."

"What does that mean? What's the matter lad? Are you ill?"

"Not exactly…I mean I really don't know."

297

With that Aengus flung open the door fearing that the lad was in some kind of distress. He entered as James grabbed the desk chair and placed it in front of him. Luckily the knock on the door did the trick. His rigidness began to soften, but not before Aengus got a glimpse of the lad's situation. He controlled his laughter.

"Mi mother needs your long johns. She insists on washing our undergarments as she calls them so that we don't stink."

"Huh…I can't… I mean right now."

"James, I can wait 'til you're decent."

Aengus turned his back to the lad and made for the bureau and began to search its drawers coming upon the sweater which his mother knitted for the lad.

"So you'll be wearing the sweater mi Mom made for you, is that your plan?"

"Ah, yes, it's a wonderful gift. It will help me to always remember Ireland as we sail."

So the lad had revealed his heart to a guy not that many years older than he and Aengus realized what had just happened. James was already getting homesick.

"I see. Well look what I've found, a nightshirt. This is what the swells wear when sleeping."

Aengus pulled out the nightshirt with a flair, swinging it around so quickly that his own nightshirt flipped side to side as he called attention to how he looked in one.

"See, I'm wearing one just like this too. We'll just have to be a couple of swells this night only. On the ship I wouldn't be caught dead in one."

Having said that, he pulled up his nightshirt to his thighs and laughed.

"Too drafty, eh lad?"

James let out a laugh, finally relaxing.

"Now that's much better. So are you ready to change into this?"

The lad stepped out from behind the chair, looked down and announced that he was.

Good…here…I'll wait outside. Call me when you're ready."

"It's okay Aengus, I'll make do. And thanks for not poking fun at me."

"Huh…why would I do that?"

"Well first there was the discovery under the waterfall and now this…this growing."

"James… 'tis not a sin to grow. It's just what happens to us…ask Father O'Malley if you don't believe me."

"You mean this happens to you too?"

James had pulled down the top part of the long johns to his waist, took the nightshirt from a now embarrassed Aengus and pulled it over his head. Then he sat on the chair and pulled off the long underwear. The older teen now sat on the edge of the bed stifling a laugh at himself for being so red cheeked.

"You should have seen how mi big brother made fun of me when I first entered manhood."

"Aedan! He seems…well so nice."

"And that's the truth James. He is, but he's also mi big brother and well he's a man and likes to make that well known."

James didn't get it but accepted the explanation at face value.

"Now then, mi mom is waiting for our undergarments, smelly as they may be."

"I think mine are all right, in that regard."

"Aye so they are, then again you've only worn them for two days."

Aengus rolled the long johns into a ball, rose and made for the door.

"So if ye have any more questions regarding our condition, you know the growing thing, just ask me. I'm not afraid to tell ye about becoming a man. God grant ye a good rest James."

"Thank you Aengus. God bless you for your kindness."

Aengus closed the door behind him while asking himself if he was being a good big brother to the lad as his mother asked of him.

James stood for a moment looking at the door and thinking, *"So this is what it's like to have an older brother."*

Then he pulled the chair to the desk, pulled up the nightshirt to his knees, moved the candle on the desk closer to the journal, took the pen, dipped it into the ink well and began to put his thoughts of the day which held so much revelation of life, suffering, praying and family ties.

At the top of the page he wrote:

July 28, 1849

Then he began to write his heart out.

Never had I seen such a sea, even from the fortress ruins. The waves came upon us like a great waterfall cascading down the slope on Inishbofin. But I didn't have time to think of my Da's discovery in those waters. I was fearing that before I did became a man I, along with Father O'Malley, Captain O'Flaherty and his sons, would be drowned. Then the good Lord caused the storm to cross over us as quickly as it came upon us. Into Galway Harbor we sailed with a hold half full of fish for selling. The youngest son of the Captain, Aengus, told Father O'Malley and then me of his desire to come to America with us. It will be a good thing, I think, to have someone who has become like a brother to me. No…even more than that. He is a friend too, someone I can talk to about manly things. Some of those things the good Father is too holy to hear about.

We got off the "EOGHANACHT." Father O'Malley and I began walking to St. Augustine Church where we were to meet others of his order and the Captain and his sons. On the way I met this girl, a pretty one she is with long fire red hair and bright green eyes so as to pierce your heart. I didn't know her name, we weren't properly introduced but she took pity on me. To the poor wretches in the park, she was handing out morsels of food. She called them "cookies." Our hands touched when she offered one to me. I didn't have a chance to thank her when Father came to me and a woman came for her. But she looked at me from the Hotel steps. I froze, not knowing what to do. So I bit the cookie and she smiled and then was gone. The cookie was sweet and I enjoyed the taste. Later at St. Nicholas Church, I met her by chance as I visited where Columbus had prayed. Finally, I know her name. It's Meghan. A lovely name to be sure.

Tonight, I had another taste never before having encountered. It's called jam. The Friar from Rome, Father Anthony, brought it from Italy. I think one day I'd like to visit this place which has such wondrous foods like jam, pasta and fruits of all kinds. Also this night I met the Captain's wife and brother. She kissed me like my mother did when I left Inishbofin. I almost cried but held it in as she reminded me of my Mom. But she was a stranger and I think I didn't welcome it as she would have appreciated. I'll do better tomorrow and thank her for her kindness just as I did to Aengus this night. He helped me to understand what this growing of manly parts was all about.

I think I'll like being a priest. The Friars seem so kind and holy and when they sang the hymn called "Te Deum" all present thought we were at the gates of heaven. Father Francis let me take the book he called the Divine Office back to my room. It's so I can pray "Compline," the night prayer. I'm writing down the Te Deum prayer so I won't forget to pray it when we sail tomorrow.

May our Lord be with us on our journey to America, where I can tell everyone that I'm going to become a priest without fear.

James breathed over the writing as there was no blotter on the desk. He reread his words and then closed the Journal as if it was a holy book. Taking the Divine Office, he got into a bed which not only had a mattress but also a feather pillow. He began to pray the opening psalm prayer…

"God come to my assistance,
Lord make haste to help me."

He drifted off to sleep after a day of being tossed about at sea, exposed to the ravages of the blight and discovering girls and his developing manhood. The candle served witness to his slumber until it too was exhausted having given light to his words and night prayer.

While silence fell across the Friary, across Galway City in the Skeffington Hotel another family was settling in for the night. For the O'Grady family, Dennis and Catherine McMahon and Colin Logan it had been quite the day

303

culminating with something which no one save Colin and recently Maggie had ever experienced, that was a dinner prepared for them at the Medieval King's Head Inn. It was a simple fare of mutton stew and brown bread but it seemed like a feast to the O'Grady's who were driven to live in hardship as the land laws and tax laws became too difficult to follow. This inn called "King's Head" was in reference to King Charles I who was beheaded when Oliver Cromwell overthrew him in a bloody rebellion called the English Revolution. That event was to have a devastating effect on the Irish Catholic population as the destruction of all things Catholic, even ancient monastic sites such as Clonmacnoise near Galway, were destroyed. It was an attempt to destroy the faith and culture of Ireland. Despite laws prohibiting Catholics from living within five miles of a town, ownership of land, imprisonment of their priests and utter obliteration of their places of worship, Cromwell failed. The faith and culture of the Irish persevered to the present day in which the Queen of England, Victoria, was then in Ireland to see for herself what the people were enduring. Unfortunately, she was brought to places of natural beauty such as the Ring of Kerry and to homes like Muckross House which most viewed as a small palace near Killarney.

Despite this restricting of what the Queen saw in regards to the devastation of the blight, she was receiving commissions who presented her with ideas for Parliament to change the land laws, expand the Act of Emancipation and create relief efforts for the suffering people of Ireland. Among these delegates was Daniel O'Connell of whom the Irish people sang.

For Meghan O'Grady however, all the talk of the Royal visit was of little interest. She was dreaming of a wretched lad with big blue eyes and wildly thick black hair who bit a cookie for her. She sat before a mirror on a dressing table brushing her flaming hair as instructed by her mother even in the hard times. She admired her new nightgown of pink cotton trimmed with lace at the collar, sleeves and hem. It was a gift from her Aunt Maggie, who actually made it when a worker at the McBirney Mill in Dublin. Not since she was a toddler had she been given such a fine gift. The brushing being concluded she blew out the candle reflecting its light in the mirror, prayed an "Ave" (Hail Mary) and slid into bed.

The moonlight filtered through the window and visions of her Aunt's wedding formed before her. Then a hand reached out to touch hers in that dream. It was that wretched boy who spoke to her in a manner which her would-be friend Michael Nagle would not dare to do; but alas, this James would be a priest and lost to her forever.

The Friars including Father O'Malley made their way across the garden path to the Church for the praying of "Lauds" the early morning Liturgy of the Hours. The clouds of the day before had been swept away and the rising sun was promising a bright day for the departure of the ship. Only Mrs. O'Flaherty was up and about, having insisted that she would collect the eggs for the Friars and prepare breakfast for all as a thank you for their hospitality. The O'Flaherty clan would also be leaving, only they would be returning to the Aran Islands and bring with them the quiet Friar, Father Henry. She was humming the tune of the "Te Deum" sung at the previous night's "vespers" service while finding the eggs. On a line stretched across the far end of the garden near the Privy were nine pairs of long johns and shirts. Four of those belonged to the Friars. She had been quite busy when all others retired doing the washing and hanging of the wet clothes knowing full well that through an Irish night little drying would be done. She however wanted the full morning sun to have its time with the undergarments to insure that they would be ready to be worn when they departed for the docks. It was her opinion that the freshness of the day was better for them than the warmth coming from a fire in the hearth.

As for the O'Flaherty men and James, she left them to their dreams, not wanting to be disturbed. This day would be a holiday of sorts for them as all save the lad would have been up and at their boats readying it for a day of fishing. This was her quiet time as she busily went about the testing of the condition of the undergarments and approving their state, gathering the eggs in a basket and going off to the kitchen to clean several fish kept from the sale for the Friars. She had planned a substantial breakfast for she knew not when they would eat again or if the "Cushla Machree" provided any type of decent food for the month long voyage.

The Friars gave her a silent wave as she scurried about the garden.

Upstairs, a thin ray of sunlight peeked through a slit in the heavy drapes covering the window in the lad's room. It struck him directly on his face. He turned and squished his face into the pillow, but light had done its duty, that is to bring a greeting of a new day to those who still slumbered on such a fine day. Pulling down his nightshirt which had crept up to his chest during the night, he was about to throw off the blanket when he noticed the Divine Office book at his side. A glance at the candle burned down to exhaustion gave him notice of what had happened to his attempt at praying "Compline."

He decided to do better with early morning "Lauds" and looked for the proper reading. His bladder, however, gave him notice that relieving himself should take priority. He jumped from the bed and searched out the chamber pot. Looking about, he pulled up the nightshirt decided to kneel to make sure that his aim would enter center pot and did what nature intended at break of day. A quick shake and the pulling down of the night shirt completed nature's call. He covered the pot quite proud of himself that his first time using a chamber pot was successful. On Inishbofin it was no problem to step out the back and water the flowers so to speak. Now it came to him that its contents had to be dealt with.

The "Divine Office" book lay in the ray of sunlight still upon the bed. He glanced at it and said aloud that he'd be praying soon. First he had to take a peek into the garden from his window which overlooked it. The scene was quiet, no one was about. The long johns were flapping in the breeze like sails on the "Eoghanacht." A wooden walkway stretched from the back door past the Privy to a rear garden gate. Beyond that was the road and across it the Church.

"It shouldn't take me but a minute to run this out, dump it into the Privy and get back before anyone is about," he planned.

Holding the ceramic pot carefully in two hands he crept to the door and stopped. *"Not too brilliant an idea to open a door while holding a chamber pot,"* he mused. Placing the pot on the bureau he ever so gently opened the bedroom door. Again with pot in his two hands he stepped into the hallway and to the stairs but a few steps further. Each creak in the step caused him alarm. He feared to disturb those who still slept. Fourteen stairs later he was at ground level, turned right and entered the kitchen preparation area off which was the back door. Once again he placed the pot down, this time on a counter on which was a basin with a pump to bring water directly into the house. He marveled at the sight for a moment and then began his trek to the Privy. No sooner had he reached the wooden walkway than out from behind the long johns stepped out Nancy O'Flaherty.

"Oh my, James, you gave me such a fright."

The lad couldn't speak. A fright indeed, he was shocked into frozenness and not knowing what to do, caught as he was indecent in a nightshirt now flipping up in the breeze revealing his backside which he quickly turned toward the Privy. Finally the human spoke, though not like his usual eloquent self.

"I...I was just..."

"Yes indeed, I can see that. Well go about your business. I have a meal to prepare. The undergarments are not as yet dry, but they should be by the time ye must be leaving." She became quite still when those last words poured forth from her lips.

James saw her jovial expression vanish in an instant.

"Yes...I mean I will...you know just going to do my business as you say."

The woman said nothing further but forced a smile and left with eggs in hand for the back door. Soon enough a song of praise the "Te Deum" was issuing again as her sweet voice carried through the house. For now it was time that the others were stirred to greet the new day.

James listened, thought of his own "Lauds" which should be prayed and quickly dumped the contents of the pot into the Privy and ran to the outside pump to wash it out. Turning to re-enter the Friary, who should appear at the back door but all of the O'Flaherty men, each in a night shirt and each holding a chamber pot ready for disposal.

"Good Morning lad," they offered in unison.

"'Tis to be a grand day to be sure," added the Captain with his brother, Liam, agreeing.

"Da, look there." Aedan called his father's attention to the fluttering long johns.

"Mom did get them washed," Aengus added but then looked at the lad in his nightshirt and to himself in his. "What are we to wear until they dry. We can't have breakfast with the Friars like this."

The entire clan walked to the lad and stood staring at the line of long johns.

"Well now, did ye not bring the other undergarment worn a hot day?" asked the Captain.

There was a stuttering of words from the three sons which indicated that they hadn't thought of such clothing as they hadn't expected to be out of their undergarments until back home.

"Then mi nephews, it would appear that you will be indecent beneath your outer clothes."

The Captain agreed and added. "It may cause a bit of discomfort but it will only be for a short time. So James, what about you? How did ye sleep in this fine house?"

"Ah…just fine sir, I was just out here to…"

"Yes lad, we can see that. We are all here for the same purpose so that the good Friars will not have to take care of our business. Now get back into the house before ye catch a chill and mi Missus gives me what for about not caring for you properly."

"Aye Captain, see you at breakfast." And off James ran toward the back door his bare arse briefly exposed as a stiff breeze caught the hem of the nightshirt and wildly lifted it as the lad scampered off.

This time James took the parlor route back to the staircase to avoid the kitchen and Mrs. O'Flaherty. At the stairs Aengus caught up with him, having been the first to dump and then wash out his pot.

"So how are you feeling about today?" he asked sincerely. His manner wasn't its usual self-confident self in the questioning. It was as if he just wanted to talk. Man though he thought of himself, his seventeen years often said otherwise.

James having been focused on the praying of "Lauds" hadn't given the day much thought at all. The question brought the ship and his boarding to mind. He too became uneasy and the climbing up stairs in nightshirts had nothing to do with his feelings. So he avoided the question entirely.

"I was just going to pray "Lauds," would you like to pray with me?"

Aengus looked at the lad quizzically but soon realized that the lad didn't want to address the rest of the day.

"Yeah, I think I do. Last night's prayer was grand wasn't it?"

"Oh wasn't it! I liked the "Te Duem" the best of all, what about you?"

And so speaking of prayers and hymns they entered James' room, put their pots on the floor, pulled back the drapes to give them light, opened the window to let the warming morning air filter in and shared the Divine Office book to pray "Lauds." In the distance the voices of the Friars could be heard coming from the Church and doing the very same thing in Gregorian chant.

That same morning air fluttered the lace curtains of Meghan's hotel room and the sunlight made her stir with a stretch to greet a rather special day. Rubbing her eyes, she then lifted the covers off her and replaced them neatly as she rose from the bed. *"Never in all my days, had I slept in such a bed,"* she thought as she knelt at the bedside to offer a morning "Ave" and "Pater Noster" (Lord's Prayer) for the blessing of her aunt's marriage to Colin. A matching robe to her pink nightgown hung over the chair at the dressing table. Wrapping it about her as if a Princess preparing to be presented at court, for never could she remember such softness and elegance in anything she ever wore, she peeked out the door, looking up and down the hallway.

The Skeffington Hotel had installed, before the full brunt of the hard times fell upon Galway, an indoor Privy (toilet) and a bathing room as well. They were at the end of the hall on each of the three floors. A sign hung on their doors. When a person was using it, it would be turned to read "occupied" and when the person left it, the sign would be turned to read "vacant."

Her room's location, being near the end of the hallway, made those signs easily read as she peeked out.

Grabbing a towel, she ran to the Privy first. There she took delight to pull a chain hanging above the wooden toilet seat and watch the water flush away the waste. Tying the pink silk ribbon about her waist once again to hold close the robe, she next went to the bathing room. Back in their Doolin cottage bathing was done from a wash basin filled with water from an outside pump. The pump was a luxury for many cottages got their water from nearby streams and such. A stove in the bathing room held kettles of water being warmed on it. The occupant would pour its contents into the metal bathtub which would first be filled with water from the pump. She worked that pump rigorously until the water flowed out into the buckets provided. A lone window provided light for the activity, though indirect as the glass in it was colored yellow to provide privacy to the bather and yet give light.

With great care she removed her robe and nightgown and slid into the tub. A bar of white soap lay on a tray next to the tub. Her towel she had placed on a hook on the wall next to it. She sighed with delight thinking that this would be how she would live in America every day. She felt like a true lady and even had the developing features of a woman to prove her maturity. Quite proud was she of her burgeoning breasts. *"A true sign of womanhood,"* she sighed. Suddenly she covered them with her arms, as the image of the lad with her cookie flashed in her mind.

"Good grief Meghan O'Grady," she said aloud. "Have the decency to keep that wretched boy out of the bath."

A knock on the bath door ended such thoughts quickly.

"Meghan, I heard a loud voice. Are you all right?"

"Yes, Momai, I'm fine, just a bit too cold in the water," she lied, then asking for God's mercy.

The wedding was to be held in late morning. It was to be a private ceremony given the circumstances of keeping the mixed marriage from the eyes of both Catholics and Protestants alike. Despite this effort, Colin wanted to make Maggie and his wedding day as memorable as was possible given the situation. Thus he, Sean and Dennis wore attire befitting such an occasion along with silk top hats and matching capes which Colin had procured from the McBirney Merchandising department. They waited patiently in the lounge sipping on ale. It seemed ludicrous to Sean in particular as he could never have afforded such an expense. And on a moral level for him, he did not want to be on display in silk hat and frock coat with cape while the people

313

gathering in the park and his own daughter were about to leave Ireland just for a chance to survive. Grateful he was to be sure, that John Caldwell Bloomfield was doing his part to improve the economic conditions in Ireland with the ceramic enterprise in Beleek and the building of a railroad line from Dublin to the site of the factory which was yet to be built. At the same time all that was years away, the reality in the present was that his neighbors and friends were suffering and he felt that he shouldn't be adding to that pain by a display of wealth no matter how good the intention for doing so was. In the end, he swallowed his convictions for the sake of Colleen's family and his daughter.

Upstairs Catherine was fussing over her daughter, Maggie. The dress brought from Dublin was created by McBirney and Co. employees most of whom Maggie was well acquainted. It was a simple gown of Irish white lace overlaying satin. The neckline was just that, at the neck. The long sleeves were just of lace. From a tight fitting top the skirt flared out in the typical 19th Century fashion with many petticoats underneath to keep it symmetrical and extended in fullness. Maggie had decided not to wear a veil in the traditional sense. Rather a friend of Colin, who ran a millenary shop, had designed a bonnet trimmed in flowers and white lace resembling a short veil as it flowed off the back of the hat. Maggie was well aware that soon after the ceremony she would change into her traveling clothes and board the ship. The time frame for that to happen was well planned out by Colin.

David McBirney and John Bloomfield were taking a big risk in sending Colin to America to stir up interest in a product not yet designed for a business not yet built. At the same time it would take a considerable amount of time to lay the

314

ground work for the importation of the Beleek line which Dennis McMahon and Sean O'Grady would now have a hand in creating. The new Mr. and Mrs. Logan may not have been leaving Ireland as those devastated by the blight but the taking of Meghan with them was most definitely an effort to save her from a most difficult future.

Meghan returned to her room to find her mother busily laying out the dress she would wear for the ceremony. It was pale green but with only one petticoat under the floor length skirt. Only the bodice was of Irish lace. Maggie had purchased it in Dublin with the thought that one day her niece would be able to wear it in America as she was presented to society. Meghan's eyes were drawn to the dress's starched broad brim hat trimmed with an emerald colored ribbon which matched the broad ribbon at the waist of the gown. She lifted the hat with a gentle twirl as the towel under her robe was slipping a bit.

"Momai, it's gorgeous. Aunt Maggie should never have been so free with her money, not in these times."

Meghan reflected her father's moral position that all of Ireland should stand in solidarity with those who suffered and that meant to share in their want and not make a display of their good fortune when so many were deprived of even the most basic needs. Colleen was well aware of her husband and daughter's opinion on such displays in desperate times. She however, knew that in America this would hardly be considered a display of good fortune but rather routine and ordinary. For she had heard those legends of streets paved with gold and money so plentiful that hunger and want was unknown throughout the land. She saw for her only child an opportunity to rub elbows with the gentry in such a country. This dress would certainly draw their attention to the lass' serene beauty and charm. In any case she was only thirteen and had the right to enjoy life if she could.

"It is lovely isn't it? Your Aunt wanted you to have a fond memory before..." Colleen couldn't go on.

Meahan placed the hat back on the dressing table and went to her mother, who sat on the edge of the bed holding the dress gently adjusting the flow of the ribbon. She sniffled back her emotions.

"Don't cry Momai, I'll be fine in America. I'll be going to school and make you and da proud."

"My darling girl, 'tis not a doubt in my mind nor that of your father's that you shall make us proud. Tears are wonderful things really. They show sadness and joy as well. My heart is broken that I shall not be with you as you become the lady I know you will be and that same thought brings me joy too."

The two took advantage of this brief quiet time to share memories of family times in Doolin as well as imagining that which would lie ahead in America. All those latter ideas came from stories heard at Church or at the market for they knew no one personally who was an eye witness of life in the United States. Their conversation inevitably had to touch on the voyage. Colleen was advising Meghan as to how to behave on the ship and what to expect. The news of the food riots right on the docks where they would board already spread across Galway City.

316

"People are desperate dear. All they want is an opportunity to better themselves and feed their children. Some however seek to take advantage of those who are so in need. Beware of the sweet talkers. They are up to no good."

"And that's the truth."

Mother and daughter looked toward the doorway from which came the voice. There stood Sean ready to affirm what he had just heard.

"Sean! You could have knocked, the lass is still in her robe."

He immediately turned his back to them.

"Oh, I hadn't realized. I'm sorry but everyone is getting impatient to get this done. I was sent to fetch you."

The embarrassed father closed the door behind him as his wife informed him that they would be down shortly. His wife's voice filtered out into the hallway as he approached the staircase.

"And thanks love for the reminder."

Sean turned his head toward the hotel room door and mumbled, "You would have thought it was the wedding of the lass what with all the fuss."

Then he virtually skipped down the stairs with a broad smile thinking: *"And why shouldn't there be a fuss for mi very own Princess?"* Then he became quite somber as he reached that last step. *"And I only wish that I could have done this for her."*

He walked into the lounge filled with the anxious family smiling again and with a prayer of thanksgiving in his heart for Mr. David McBirney for making the day for Maggie and for his own daughter possible.

Such mixed emotions of joy and sadness were now filling the very soul of young James. He sat in the Friary cell with pen in hand and was rereading the letter he had written to his parents. Father Francis had assured him that he would see that it got posted quickly and sent off to Inishbofin.

July 29, 1849

Dear Momai and Dadai:

Pax Vobiscum. That means Peace be with you. I guess it sounds like I'm showing off. But I thought it would be good practice as now I must learn how to pray what is called the Divine Office. It's really a beautiful singing of psalms and prayers. I like the "Te Deum" best of all. In fact just a while ago I had to pray "Lauds," that's Morning Prayer. I can go on and on but I am happy, I think.

I already miss you. I wish I could be with you today. Turning 14 is not quite what I expected. One day we shall be together again and then I will have my first Birthday cake with you, even if it's not my real birthday.

I met this girl in the park and again in St. Nicholas Church in Galway. She has pretty long red hair and flashing green eyes. Aengus makes fun of me becoming a man but he doesn't mean it. It's all in good fun. Anyway he tells me that priests are not allowed to get married and that I shouldn't be eyeballing...that's what he called mi telling him what she looked like. Well I told him what I told her, that I will be a priest for all the people even girls like her. She didn't like that I said it but I explained it was meant in a nice way.

The ink well is almost dry. Father O'Malley bought me a Journal in which I could write my thoughts as we begin this journey to America. I wrote a copy of this letter in it so that I remember what I say to you. I hope that they have ink on the ship. We will sail on the Cushla Machree this day so I must go now.

Say hello to Mr. O'More and Mr. and Mrs. O'Connor for me.

Your loving son:

The lad signed his full name, *James Richard Shields, just to practice* he thought in case he had to sign anything before boarding the ship.

His room door swung open just as he was blowing on the letter.

"So James are ye ready for the grand adventure?"

The lad turned and saw that it was Aengus. He folded the letter carefully and was about to place it into an envelope which was already addressed.

"I am now, just writing to mi momai and dadai."

"Oh..." the now tongue tied Aengus replied. Then he came to the lad and playfully jabbed him lightly in the stomach.

James doubled over in great dramatic fashion and then pounced on Aengus with a leap of a gazelle. They both landed on the floor with a loud thud which brought Father O'Malley running up the stairs.

"Good God James, for a scrawny lad you certainly know how to take down a big bloke like me."

They laughed and were rolling across the floor as Father O'Malley stood in the doorway.

"Good heavens lads, we don't have time for such shenanigans? The Friars are ready to say their farewell to us, as are the O'Flaherty's I might add."

The lads jumped to their feet in an instant, brushed each other off and apologized for disturbing the house with the dour look of a puppy caught in a wrongful act of emitting waste in the house. The priest placing his hands on his hips let out a great howl of a laugh. The lads looked at each other with a confused expression.

"I'd say that puppy dog look was all the penance needed for such goings on. But now we really must leave. James are you ready?"

A meek smile crossed the lad's face. "Yes Father. I just finished this letter to my family." He held up the letter which Aengus snatched.

"Here James let me take care of this for ye. Get your Journal into the bag."

Aengus glanced at the letter as he slipped it into the envelope. His eyes began to water for he realized he had written no such message for his folks to remember him by and that the lad had done so on his birthday without so much of a mention of it. This didn't go unnoticed by Father O'Malley when Aengus handed the letter to him.

The priest quietly asked if he was all right.

Aengus looked over to the lad, who was slipping his Aran knit sweater over his head. "It's the lad's birthday Father and we didn't even know."

The priest leaned into Aengus and whispered that he should keep the lad busy for a moment longer before coming to the parlor area. "I'll take care of the letter." He then left without a further word.

"So… Father is taking the letter for you. Are you sure that you have everything?"

"Ah…I think so."

"Well here, let me check the bureau and the bags to make sure. There's no running back if something is forgotten now is there?"

Not waiting for a response he began to check the drawers in the small bureau. All of his searching was just to delay the lad but in doing so he found nothing except for one item.

"James, look here," he held up the nightshirt which had begun the entire talk of becoming a man. "Did you forget to pack it?"

The lad hadn't forgotten at all. He was afraid, after hearing Aengus say that he wouldn't be caught dead in one on the ship, that someone might think he was a swell or worse. So he had decided to leave it. After all it wasn't his in the first place. It belonged to the Friars.

Aengus had decided that he had indeed found a delaying tactic and so he played it up.

"You aren't going to sleep bare-assed in America are you?"

Now the lad was really red cheeked. He nodded "no" as he responded.

"Of course not…but you said…"

Aengus halted him in mid-sentence.

"Oh that…that was just idle talk to look tough. You'll need this in America in order to be a proper gentleman."

The young fisherman waved the nightshirt about imitating a sail in the wind or so he intended.

"Anyway, ye might want to use it as a sail if we sink and have to finish the voyage in a life boat."

That did it. Never had it dawned on James that sailing across the Atlantic not only took a month's worth of days but also could be quite dangerous. He plopped down on the bed while uttering a heavy sigh.

"Holy Mother of God, do you really think that our ship might sink?"

The seventeen-year-old stood rather stoically as he now realized that his "little brother," as his mother referred to James, was now a nervous wreck thanks to his nonsense. He had to do something to recover the joy in the upcoming adventure. And it was back to the playful jabbing and the tossing of the lad like a rag doll onto the bed. He followed suit and jumped onto the bed as well landing in a straddling position over the lad.

"'Tis only fun James. I'd hear tell that the Cushla Machree is most seaworthy indeed."

Rolling over onto his back Aengus was now side to side with the lad, their feet were overhanging off the side of the bed and their heads almost rubbing against the wall on the other side. Lying flat they both looked up to the plastered white ceiling which had no ornamentation whatsoever to cause a distracting conversation. Well did Aengus in his efforts to delay going downstairs realize that fact. So the young fisherman had to improvise. He did so by calling attention to manly things as done previously.

"So about that girl you met in the park, have ye written to her as well?"

James bolted upright and playfully punched Aengus a bit too low at the waist. A quiet scream of fake pain resulted so as not to bring back Father O'Malley to chastise them again.

"Holy Mother of God, I don't even know where she lives!"

Aengus rolled over and grabbed James by his shoulders and brought him back down flat on the bed.

"I don't think the Blessed Mother would appreciate you calling out to her twice and it being over that girl in the park."

James rolled over and looked into the face of his would-be brother which featured a wide grin. The lad however was quite serious.

"Aengus, you're right, I have sinned not only in calling the holy mother's name but in even thinking about this girl…me who is to become a priest, me who should be praying the Divine Office, me who lays here joking about bare asses and indecent thoughts. Tell me truthfully, how might I remain Pure of Heart if I do such things?"

The befuddled Aengus was experiencing discomfort as he found himself being the Father Confessor to the lad.

"Now it seems to me James, and I'm no priest or philosopher type, that ye are just learning about life and the world. And I'm learning too. But think of this. How could you really know if your call to be a priest is true if ye never have a chance to see other things in life…like girls for instance?"

The sea blue eyes lit up with understanding like a sun filled sky. He jumped off the bed only to turn and leap upon the prostrated Aengus just as had been done to him. Now the seventeen-year-old had a good four inches in height on the lad and a physique like a Celtic Warrior to the lad's emaciated frame, which in truth had begun to fill out now that a positive food change had come into his life. Nevertheless the impact of the pounce on his middle section was minimal and no pain accompanied it though a bit of his breath was knocked out of him.

"Glad to be of help," Aengus gasped out, again in a dramatic fashion.

"I haven't said anything."

"You didn't have to. Your eyes spoke for ye."

"Oh…I'm that…what's the word called…ah…transparent. You can see right into my very soul, is that it?"

The older lad grabbed the younger and rolled him off, then sat up. With all sincerity he told him that what he thought was as true as the Gospel.

"One good look into those glowing eyes of yours and people will know your true feelings."

"I'm doomed then."

"I don't get your meaning," responded Aengus.

"That girl in the park, by the way her name is Meghan, she probably knows how I feel about her."

"Saints preserve us…I mean, James how do you feel?"

"That's what I'm trying to say. I'm confused. I liked talking with her. I like the way she looks and how she tosses that fire red hair over her shoulders. But I want to be a priest Aengus so aren't I committing a sin?"

"Whoa James, this is way over my head. I never met anyone on Inishmor or the other islands who made me feel the way you do about this lass. But in any case, all I can say is that 'tis grand that you are coming to know how men feel for you will be counseling us when you are ordained."

"Maybe…I guess you're right."

"I am indeed, so how about packing this nightshirt?" Aengus went to the sacks on the floor by the door. He opened one and crammed in the nightshirt as James shuddered as he made no attempt to fold it properly. In doing so he came across what he thought was a rag of some kind and pulled it out.

"Why on earth are ye bringing this thing?"

"It's not what you think. It's my shirt worn most of mi life on Inishbofin and also when I first met you and your family and Father O'Malley. I'm bringing it with me as a reminder of where I came from no matter how grand a man that I may become in America."

"Oh, that's a good man, and by the way, now that's a priestly thing to say."

The lad smiled while Aengus neatly folded the raggedy shirt and returned it to the sack.

"I think we're done here. How about going down to say our farewells?"

James placed the small sack with the family Bible and the journal over his shoulder. Aengus took the larger one, opened the door and gave a sweep of the hand with a bow as if the lad were a grand gentleman passing. No sooner had the lad reached the bottom step than a rousing rendition of "For he's a jolly good fellow" rang out in honor of the birthday boy.

While the O'Flaherty clan and Friars serenaded James, the organist in St. Nicholas Church pumped out a rousing rendition of Mendelsohn's OP. 61. It would become a standard for over a century as The Wedding March. Maggie was escorted down the medieval church's aisle by her father and up into the sanctuary. The Archdeacon Gary Hasting, robed in alb with a gold embroidered stole and matching white and gold cloak stood waiting. To his side was Colin and to his side was Sean. Colleen preceded her sister as did Meghan in the procession. The only person in Church besides them was Catherine McMahon. Colin stood as in a trance as Maggie made her way down the aisle. Dennis took the groom's hand hanging limply at his side and placed it in his daughter's hand. Then with a kiss for Maggie he joined his wife.

Twenty minutes later the final blessing was given and the service ended with the family gathering about the bride and groom.

"Gary, what you've done for us today cannot be repaid. I don't know how to thank you."

"What are friends for Colin. Jesus said that there is no greater gift than for a person to give one's life for a friend.

327

But I would still prefer that the axe doesn't come down on either of us. So let's get you on your way."

"Yes, of course, may we change somewhere around here?"

"Certainly," said Archdeacon Hasting. "Come to the Rectory with me."

It was walking out the rear of the ancient church that Meghan observed that the reading about the Marriage Feast at Cana in which Mary the mother of Jesus pointed out that the bride and groom had run out of wine, was the same one she had heard in Holy Rosary Church in Doolin.

The Archdeacon overheard her comment to her grandfather and stopped the bridal party in their tracks.

"My dear girl…Meghan isn't it?"

"Yes, sir…I mean Father…er I mean Archdeacon."

A gentle smile dispelled her pain of having put her foot into her mouth.

"A day will come when all Christians will hold onto their unity in Christ as one people. It may however be done in different ways though with the same goal. I hope that you live to see that day."

It was the grandfather who lauded the Archdeacon's dream for Christianity but was also practical in facing the reality of the 19th Century.

"A noble goal to be sure, Reverend, but right now if any of us are caught in condoning this marriage that may very well put back the achievement of all faiths coming to accept one another hundred years."

"Quite right Mr. McMahon. Please follow me. We'll cut through the gardens."

"For he's a jolly good fellow, for he's a jolly good fellow which nobody can deny…" the voices of Friars and O'Flaherty's shook the Friary as Adam and Aedan took hold of James and lifted him up on their shoulders.

Father Anthony came out with a loaf of brown bread. Stuck in it was a candle. "They say the Americanos put candles into a cake to celebrate the birthday."

"We are sorry that we don't have a cake but hope that bread and jam will be to your liking James," added Father Francis.

And so a very early tea was served and the departure was not discussed. Rather the conversation was of how James had become the hero of Inishbofin by saving the Captain and his sons who were blown off course by a storm. The Friars were duly impressed by the tale. It was only the ringing of the Church bell to announce the Angelus which brought their tales of lessons and exploration of Inishbofin to an end. It was time to leave for the docks.

The Friars rose at the ringing of the bell.

"The Angel of the Lord declared unto Mary,
And she conceived of the Holy Spirit."

All were invited to pray an "Ave."

"Behold the handmaid of the Lord…"

At the conclusion of the prayer, Father Anthony went into the kitchen and brought out a small crate. It contained lemons and oranges from Italy. He went on to explain that in the British Royal Navy some decades ago a Scottish surgeon named James Lind had written a treatise proposing that scurvy, a terrible disease affecting muscle tissue and organs was due to a lack of vitamin "C." The surgeon proposed that the eating of citrus fruit would stave off the disease.

"Our Prior had read the report and thought that we should gift you with these lemons and oranges."

"We wouldn't want our newest Augustinian to catch scurvy now, would we?" added Father Francis trying to add humor but not quite making it funny.

Nevertheless Father O'Malley and James were quite grateful for the gesture. James had no clue what the disease was but then again he had never seen a lemon or orange let alone eaten one. So a new taste once again would lie ahead of him.

Hundreds of people were swarming around the harbor area as a jaunty cart arrived pulled by a single horse. On it were the new Mr. and Mrs. Logan and Dennis and Catherine McMahon. Following them was another jaunty cart with Sean and Colleen O'Grady and Meghan along with baggage. The three mast square-rigged "Cushla Machree" was anchored alongside the pier. Products and livestock were being loaded before the humans were allowed on board. Up the gang planks the sheep and pigs were driven and then lowered into the livestock hold which was next to the steerage class for passengers who paid the least for their tickets. Hundreds upon hundreds wanted to get on that ship but only a fraction of that amount had the paperwork which would allow them to do so. These were the lucky ones, for that particular ship did not have the curse of being a "coffin ship" or so they thought.

"Oh Momai, look at all these people. What if they won't let me go?"

Now this was a difficult question for Colleen to answer as in the deepest place within her heart, she wanted her to stay with her and Sean. At the same time they wanted to offer Meghan a chance which they knew would never be possible in Ireland and that is to attend the best of schools and never have to worry about where her next meal would be coming from. Her reply reflected that torn heart.

"Mi darling girl, there is nothing more than I would desire than having you stay with us in Enniskillen. But a new world is about to open for you. Surely your new uncle has everything arranged."

This brief experience of fear was soon forgotten when Colin and Maggie came up to them with Meghan's grandparents. The time had come for them to say good-bye. Hearts began to thump and tears began to flow before a word was spoken. Colin had but to pull out the papers needed for boarding and the reality of what was about to happen hit them all.

"We need to get in line if we'll have any chance to get what is promised to us on these papers," Colin announced.

Sean was concerned about what his brother-in-law meant by "chance." The gossip that had reached Colin and which he had kept to himself so not to create emotional distress for his new family now had to be shared. He began with what was passed on to him regarding the boarding process. That was easy to see as everyone was held back from the ship until the livestock was boarded. What he wanted to insure was that wherever they were to be placed it would be away from the livestock hold. It didn't take much of an imagination to understand why distance would be best when it came to sheep and pigs locked up in a poorly ventilated hold.

The second part referred to their accommodations on ship. McBirney and Co. had indeed paid for first class passage but it became known that shipping lines were overbooking and cramming in as many people as was possible in order to make more money. When the cabins ran out, the people would have to go to second class and even steerage. It was for that reason that Colin wanted to be in the front of the line for boarding.

"I think you're right Colin. Would it be all right to stand in line with you? It might even be advantageous to hold away gate crashers."

Sean lifted several bags. With bags in hand, they made their way through the throngs of people milling about and not quite knowing what they should do next. They looked for people finely dressed or at least in traveling clothes which indicated that they could afford to book a cabin. The family surrounded Meghan so as not to have her exposed to any strangers, especially young men, who seeing her beauty might try to approach her improperly.

The crush of the crowd was becoming more intense as two wagons being pulled by a donkey approached the outer edge of the dock area. Father O'Malley and the Friars were seated on the luggage sacks and the crate of lemons and oranges in the wagon itself. Father Henry was actually at the reins. On the second wagon, Liam O'Flaherty held the reins with Nancy and the Captain on the seat as well. In the wagon bed sat Aedan, Adam, Aengus and James, who clutched the small sack containing the Family Bible and his journal so tightly that his knuckles were white. As soon as the wagon came to a stop, the O'Flaherty brothers bounded off the wagon, Adam to take hold of the donkey so he didn't get spooked. The Captain and his brother, Liam, then helped Nancy to climb down from the elevated seat in a fashion which still maintained the demeanor of a lady rather than a farm hand.

Their position at the outer edge of the docks was slightly elevated thus giving them a view over the crowds of people and out to the harbor, where the Cushla Machree, its three masts with lowered sails almost appeared to be majestic at first glance. Aedan, holding his arm over the shoulders of James and the other over those of his younger brother, Aengus, created quite the stir among the Friars and his family by his statement.

"So mi boys, there it is, in all its glory. Its name *Cushla Machree* means *Joy of my heart*. May it live up to its name as she sails you to a land of freedom where ye may pray the Rosary or go to Mass openly and where such opportunity exists that you will go to school and hold jobs which bring great wealth."

The Friars, who had kept all rumors of what they were hearing about anti-Catholic and immigrant activities in America close to the vest, forced a reserved smile. Their fear was that such glowing and poetic views were encouraging Aengus and James to develop an unrealistic romantic notion of what they would find in America. Therefore, even the slightest experience of those who didn't want them or their religion in the United States would prove quite devastating to them.

"Thank you Aedan, may God grant those we hold dear a safe voyage."

"Father Anthony, nicely put," said the Captain. "And now, how shall we get Father O'Malley and the lads through all those people?"

Of all the learned men present and those with the practical experience of life in a harsh world, it was James who put forth a plan which addressed the Captain's question. It was based on his lessons of ancient history, specifically that of Ancient Rome.

"I think that we should do what the ancient Romans did."

All eyes turned to the lad. He stood next to the donkey, petting it."

"James, exactly what did they do which would help us get on board that ship?" asked Father Anthony, who being from Rome, Italy was rather intrigued by the suggestion.

Now he had done it, or so he thought. *All these adults expect some brilliant idea and if what I am about to suggest isn't?*

Then they would just laugh, that is almost everyone. Certainly, Father O'Malley, who taught me about the ancient Romans wouldn't and my new friend, Aengus, well he might giggle but wouldn't make fun of me. All the others…well they would just see me as a little boy with crazy ideas. Okay here goes…

"Remember Father O'Malley when we studied how the Romans won battles?"

The priest nodded affirmatively, but without a clue as to where the lad was going with his thought.

"Now look at all those people down there. It's like the Romans going into a crowd of…of rioters or even another army of sorts. In any case, our goal is to get to the pier."

"Lad, we know that, so what's your plan? Spit it out. Begging your pardon Fathers…"said Aedan.

"Just this…the Romans used to create a square of army men with shields, just like my name, well inside the formation were other warriors or government leaders who were being protected from the enemy. They would slowly move into the mass of people and make their way to their fortress or whatever. We need to be like the Romans."

"Bravo!" exclaimed Father Anthony. "But we do not face an enemy… just a difficulty to reach the pier in time to get on the ship."

"Exactly Father, we just have to rearrange ourselves and stick together. So if we change the square to a triangle, like an arrow point, and lock arms keeping Mrs.O'Flaherty in the center, we would be able to move as one unit. People will move aside as we wedge our way to the pier."

"God almighty… isn't he the smart one," Aengus yelled out while taking the lad into a bear hug and lifting him up unto the shoulders of Aedan. "And this is how you will ride into that crowd James, as the hero of Inishbofin once again."

The Friars let the use of the Lord's name in vain go unaddressed as they cheered along with the O'Flaherty clan. Father O'Malley took the lead and began to create the arrow point. Aegnus would be the tip of the point. Aedan was placed directly behind him with James aloft on his shoulders to be the look-out as it were. Mrs. O'Flaherty stood next to Aedan. At an angle to form the arrow's shape were the Captain, Liam, and Father Anthony on one side and Father O'Malley, Father Henry and Father Francis on the other side of Aengus. It was done and they began to move down into the crowd. Rather than shields they held the baggage sacks, a rolled up mattress from one of the Friary cells and the fruit crate in front of them. James kept hold of the Bible sack. Slowly they inched their way along the stone path leading to the Evan and Co. check-in make-shift desk.

The people through whom they made their way didn't know how to respond to the formidable arrow point made up of people, especially with the Friars constantly thanking them for allowing them to pass and God Blessing them when they did move aside. Just as they made it to the check-in desk, a representative of Evan and Co., who owned the Cushla Machree, announced that First and Second Class passengers could now board. The gate was lifted and a large group of people hastily walked onto the pier toward the gang plank. Among them were Maggie and Colin Logan and Meghan

O'Grady. Off to the side were Meghan's parents and grandparents. All were in tears and waved their handkerchief after dabbing their eyes.

"Good afternoon sir," Father O'Malley said as he laid the paperwork before the clerk. "We just happen to have second class tickets."

"I see." The clerk was very business-like and didn't even bother to look up at who he was talking to. "So then it's a Thomas O'Malley, teacher, and his ward one lad named James Richard Shields who will be departing this day?"

He stamped the papers and handed them back, briefly looking up at them, James being on Aedan's shoulders attracting his attention. "Who are all these other people?"

"Oh my God, Da…where is my ticket?" an almost hysterical Aengus screamed out.

"Right here mi boy, don't fret. Uncle Liam and I picked it up this morning while you and the lad were packing."

"Here sir is my ticket."

"So then, it's an Aengus O'Flaherty, fisherman, who would be leaving this day, is it? You may move along to the gate."

"But Second class is being boarded. We heard the announcement."

"Aye so you did, but we're full up. You'll have to go steerage or not at all. No refunds however…but I'll let ye enter the pier first, is that acceptable for we have many others to check in."

The Friars were devastated for they knew how horrible conditions in steerage could be, given Father Anthony's voyage to Ireland from Italy and those passengers were not poor immigrants. Father O'Malley accepted the conditions.

"Now you other people need to move aside." And with a wave of his hand he called forth others in line.

The people arrow made its way to the pole now lowered to block entrance to the pier once again. The time had come for the final farewell. Aengus, Father O'Malley and James knelt on the stones to receive the blessing of Father Francis on behalf of the Prior of the Order of St. Augustine. Those surrounding them were horrified and joyous at the same time that such a public display of Catholic ritual was taking place. Soon dozens of others knelt and asked to be blessed as well. The Friars did so graciously and quickly so as not to create too great a commotion.

Nancy O'Flaherty took her youngest son into her arms, he being so much taller than she that he had to bend over quite a bit to accept the embrace. The Captain did so to James. Then a switch took place and soon all were hugging their farewells, Nancy tearing up along with all the others. The guards at the gate then told them to move to the edge of the dock away from the pier.

"Look for us lads, we'll be right up there by the wagons," called out Uncle Liam. "'Tis lucky that ye thought of the mattress good Fathers now that they must be in steerage."

"Indeed, only it was to give them extra padding in second class. Now they will all have to share the one mattress," a saddened Father Henry answered.

The pole was lifted as the announcement was made for final boarding. Soon the three found themselves without the formidable arrow point formation and being shoved and crushed in a crowd of people swarming onto the pier. On the deck of the bow, first and second class passengers watched as chaos erupted on the pier. So great was the rush that some people were literally shoved off the pier. They fell into the cold water of the harbor. Screams of distress and curses of anger could be heard throughout the harbor area. Rowboats with a one man crew patrolled the harbor to pick up such victims before they drowned for none knew how to swim.

With crate and sacks the three began to run as well to avoid a similar fate. People were now throwing their sacks of belongings up over the rail of the ship from the dock so that they could move unencumbered. Some didn't make it and these were not fished out of the harbor until the people were, thus many sank and all was lost.

Father O'Malley and Aengus kept James between them for protection. His scrawny frame would have no chance against the force of the crowd surging forward with yells ranging from "To America" to "Let me through" to "Go to hell Brits." Running up the gang plank was not easy as they balanced their belongings, fruit crate and mattress so as not to have their weight cause imbalance and their falling off the plank. This concern paled with the minds of the two teens reeling from trying to cope with such a scene they found themselves in. Both coming from such proper and rural areas as to never have seen more than a dozen or two of people gathered at one time save for Christmas or Easter celebrations.

The three stumbled over the last obstacle of the lip of the side of the ship as from the bow the second class passengers cheered them aboard while the first class passengers stood in shock at the scene. They were hurried to the rear deck, under which were the livestock and steerage passenger holds. No one was allowed to enter the hold until out to sea. No one wanted to for all was calming down once on board, at least for the moment. They wanted that last view of their homeland and as with Aengus, James and Father O'Malley to wave good-bye to their friends and family.

The three stood on the wooden deck at the rear railing, their belongings in hand. These slipped from their grasp as they spotted the Friars and O'Flaherty clan and began to wave wildly to them. Whether they could be seen or not didn't matter. It was that final wave as the ship was being towed to the harbor's mouth that mattered most.

"Do you really think they can see us, Father?"

"Now that's a good question James. We can see them so it is quite possible that they are seeing us at this very moment as well, so let's give them a grand wave."

The three resumed waving, Aengus most wildly as tears streamed down his smooth cheeks which reflected the wind-blown redness of being a fisherman out on the waters off the coast of Ireland on many a day. The cheering and shouts of those who didn't get on board or who had come to bid their loved ones farewell were fading as was a Church bell which announced the two o'clock hour sounded.

Crew members were now scurrying about climbing ropes up the masts and lowering the sails on a day of fine winds and blue skies. The Cushla Machree was now sailing on its own. The Aran Islands could be seen off the port side. It was now Father O'Malley who wiped tears away as Aengus pointed the islands out to him. Had he been able, he would have seen his parishioners had climbed to the top of the Dun Aengus prehistoric fortress ruin to say their good-byes to him with prayer and song.

As if Father O'Malley felt that song of farewell, he asked James and Aengus to join him in an ancient Catholic hymn, which now could be sung openly in his mind as they were at sea. No sooner had he begun the Salve Regina than dozens people about them joined in the hymn.

Hail holy Queen, mother of mercy,
Our life, our sweetness, and our hope.
To thee do we cry, poor banished children of Eve.
To thee do we send up our sighs,
Mourning and weeping in this vale of tears.
Turn then, o most gracious Advocate,
Thine eyes of mercy towards us.
And after this, our exile,
Show unto us the blessed fruit of thy womb, Jesus.

O clement, O loving!
O Sweet Virgin Mary!

Spanish Arch at Galway Harbor

Chapter Twelve: Wind At Your Back

The hymn had become infectious as all classes of passengers, most of whom were Catholic, joined in its singing. At its conclusion quite a number of people realized that this man dressed in a black suit as any walking the streets of Galway or Dublin might was no ordinary teacher. His manner, his knowledge of ancient ritual and song made it quite evident that they had a priest amongst them. To most this was a blessing, for they could now pray as they wished in International waters. Up on the deck of the bow, the First and Second Class passengers were being allowed to go to their cabin, if First Class, or the hold located right below the forward deck.

Maggie, Colin and Meghan, with their pieces of luggage in hand were being told that First Class was overbooked and that they would be in Second Class. Colin's protest availed them nothing but scorn as there was little they could do at that point. Maggie, seeing the anger erupting, encouraged Colin to move along to the Second Class hold entrance. They were slightly elevated on the bow deck and could look down on the steerage passengers. They too had joined in the hymn… that is two of them. Colin didn't know the hymn. During its singing Meghan scanned the ship with its giant masts with crew members hanging over the beams and lowering sails, its wheel cabin where the Captain and steersman were at the wheel, the barrels of water and food products strapped to the masts and each other and the people in steerage. Most of those people were dressed quite poorly, some in rags more than clothes. There was one however, who was leading the hymn and he wore a suit just like Colin did. Beside him were two lads in knitted sweaters like those she often saw in Doolin.

When the hymn ended as the last view of Ireland faded out of sight those three had turned to pick up their bags. Meghan gasped. "Could it be?" She thought aloud. She caught herself as Aunt Maggie asked if anything was wrong.

"Oh no, just thought I saw someone I knew."

"Well dear, this will be a long voyage. Perhaps you might come across many who are travelling from Doolin to America."

"Perhaps Aunty," Meghan responded then picked up her leather bag in which was held the leather portfolio which contained her family's legacy, the title to Doonagore Castle.

The second class area was somewhat better than steerage in that it had three tiered bunks, but each person had their own bunk. There was also a toilet area of sorts. Still men and women and children were mixed and there was little privacy. This was particularly upsetting to the new groom and why he had protested so vehemently. Still they had some ventilation and they were away from the livestock hold. Maggie had the forethought to bring extra blankets which could be attached to the wooden bunk frame thus creating a curtain to bring some privacy to them. And so they went about placing their things onto their bunks one above the other. Meghan was given the top bunk. The six-foot long bunk also served as the luggage rack. This wasn't terribly uncomfortable for either Meghan, who at 5'2" and still growing, and Maggie, at 5' 4" who had long since had stopped growing. But for the 5' 10" Colin it would present somewhat of a problem given he had most of the luggage on his bunk.

Father O'Malley, Aengus and James stood with dozens of other steerage passengers at the closed hold leading to steerage. A rather big burly crew member dressed in a filthy shirt revealing his hairy chest and torn pants showing that he did not wear long johns stood before them. He had a barrel of a chest and arms like a cannon. A scruffy beard and unkempt bushy brown hair gave him the appearance of a Hun from James' study of ancient history. The look would serve to give pause to those in steerage should they complain about the accommodations which they were about to enter.

"My name is Paul, it's my job to tell ye when you may go to your quarters. This hatch will be closed whenever a storm approaches. You are to remain below should we hit a storm. Come up at your own risk, but stay out of the way of the crew. Everybody got that?" His eyes burned into the lads who stood next to Father O'Malley.

All answered "yes" or nodded their understanding.

"Good, now you there," Paul pointed to Aengus. "You go down first. There will be no pushing. You'll each get a place on the bunk. At least three to a bunk, is that clear?"

Again, silent nods of understanding.

Paul unlatched the hatch and opened it. Immediately an odor was emitted which gave notice that there was indeed livestock on board. It wasn't as yet overpowering but it was distinct. Aengus began his climb down to the lowest part of the ship. As he descended he called up to Father O'Malley to toss down the bags before he and James climbed down. This example was to be followed by all the others who were to follow.

Aengus turned to look about the hold. On each side were tiers of wooden bunks with loose straw spread over them. They were built into the timbers of the hull of the ship. On one side they were three tiers high and on the other two tiers high. He quickly chose the top bunk on the two tier side, the one closest to the hatch entrance. As Father O'Malley and James climbed down, Aengus opened the mattress and spread it across the straw. Then he threw the sacks upon the bunk as now a steady stream of people were entering and throwing down their sacks, if they had one. The fruit crate he placed at the foot of the bunk.

"So what do you think? Smells like sh...I mean rotten fish don't it?"

"Indeed Aengus, the scent is rather pungent. But then again it's not as bad as prison."

The priest fell silent when the look on the lads' faces turned grim. It was his first mentioning of his time in prison to the lads. He dropped the reference and went on to speak of seeking out the facilities and food arrangements.

As dozens of fellow steerage passengers claimed a bunk which had to be shared with strangers if they had no family, the three explored the cramped quarters. They found several buckets. These would be used to carry water and two were for the purpose of eliminating waste. These would be carried out and its contents would be thrown overboard. There was no privacy to do one's business, to wash, to change clothes...that is if one had a change of clothes which many didn't have.

"Father," James began. "How are we to sleep in this place? I bet the bunk isn't two feet wide at best."

The priest gave some thought and suggested that he'd try to organize a steerage class meeting of some kind to discuss such matters. Now most in the hold knew that the man who led the hymn was not just a teacher but a priest. This gave O'Malley some authority and respect as he was considered educated. So when he stepped into the center of the room and called for attention, a respectful attitude was given.

He presented James' concern first. Sleeping three or four in the bunk at one time he observed would be quite difficult.

"Unless you are able to sleep in a sitting up position," he added. "May I suggest that some of us go up on deck at different times of the day, given good weather conditions, so that others may recline and rest. It seems two might fit at one time if we don't toss about too much. Alternating this way would afford us time to get fresh air and perhaps wash our clothes on deck."

The passengers received the suggestion as workable. Then he went on to a more serious issue in his mind, that of privacy, especially for the women and young girls.

"It seems that the only toilet facilities in steerage are these two buckets. The lads and I have three blankets between us. I would be willing to give up mine to create a curtain...let's

347

say here in the corner. This would afford some privacy for our ladies present as well as for the men and boys."

There was overwhelming gratitude offered to him for the sacrifice of his blanket as many hadn't one nor did they have a mattress for that matter. Not that the two or three inch thick mattress offered such great comfort anyway. Aengus offered his blanket as well as did James. However the priest thought two blankets would be sufficient to create the curtain of privacy. Aengus was sent up to seek out crewman Paul and ask for the use of a hammer and some nails so that the "Privy" curtain hanging could be created.

The next topic on the first day of the voyage was that of food preparation. As yet no one knew what the food promised by Evan and Co. would be. If it did require cooking then that would have to be done on the open deck to insure the safety of the ship.

Up on the rear deck Aengus caught a view of the open ocean. He was mesmerized by its expanse and no matter where he looked he saw nothing but water. The huge white sails billowed above him so as to remind him of angels' wings. Would they watch over them was his thought? Just as he asked the rhetorical question, the very person he sought out approached him.

"What are you doing up here?" asked the burly seaman, Paul, as he looked Aengus up and down in the manner in which the lad termed eyeballing when explaining such an act to James.

The intensity of the stare made Aengus ill at ease, so much so that he backed away several steps to keep a distance between Paul and him.

"Mi teacher would like to use a hammer and a few nails if that was possible."

"What for?"

"Oh, nothing special, just to hang up a blanket for privacy."

Paul laughed with a cynical sneer. "Afraid someone might see your little pecker, are we?"

Now despite the attempt to act quite worldly and all-knowing of manly things, Aengus hadn't a clue as to what the seaman meant by the term "pecker." That is until he pointedly jabbed toward the lad's groin. He had heard of such men, who became so crazed at sea so as to search to take advantage of both boys and girls for their satisfaction. He wasn't about to become one of them.

He stood his ground, gave back the same sneering laugh saying words to the effect that he was a full grown man, "if you get my meaning."

The seaman took on a threatening stance with his huge hands on his hips which he rotated in a circular motion. He sneered back with a heckling laugh.

"So you say…prove it."

"Now what can I do?" Aengus asked himself, stalling for time. *"I need to stop this guy in his tracks. I guess I'll have to fight fire with fire."*

Aengus loosened his belt and began to unbutton his pants very slowly. He gave every impression that he was going to show the seaman proof in the flesh. He could hardly breathe as he went through the action.

"What's going on here?" The harsh sounding voice came from across the deck. It belonged to the First Mate who had been circulating around the boat making sure all crew members were on task. Unlike Paul, he was dressed in a blue and white striped shirt which was clean and tight fitting pants which came to the ankle.

Paul jumped to attention stating that the lad had asked to use a hammer. He cast a quick glare to the young fisherman as the First Mate then walked up to the lad.

"That's right, I need to use a hammer," Aengus stuttered out.

"And what's this state of undress all about?" asked the First Mate.

"I was just about to relieve myself as this rocking of the ship and the sight of all this water gave me an urge to go."

The First Mate softened and took pity. "Well then you go right ahead. We wouldn't want you to burst now would we Paul?"

Aengus stood flush up to the railing and lowered his pants just enough to enable him to add water to the sea. Grateful that he could even go, he smiled over his shoulder and made sure the seamen saw the stream of water coming forth but nothing else. The wind shifted and suddenly he felt the spray of his own water.

The First Mate had been instructing Paul to find a hammer and nails for the lad when he heard the yelp when the spray hit. Both he and Paul let out a full laugh.

"Lad, 'tis with the wind at your back that ye must stand to relieve yourself in the future," advised the First Mate with a hand on his shoulder and sucking a finger of his other and holding it up to test the wind direction.

Quick as a bunny being hunted by a fox, the lad buttoned up and followed suit by sucking his finger and holding it up likewise.

"Thanks sir."

In the steerage hold several people were already becoming seasick. The constant rocking of the ship, even as gentle as it was on the smooth sea, had gotten to them. Father O'Malley suggested that they go topside and lean over the railing rather than using one of the buckets. What they didn't need in their quarters was several people vomiting at the same time. Two men and a woman climbed up. As they crawled out holding their mouths they encountered Aengus ready to go down. Seeing how green they were, he suggested that they go to the opposite railing from where he stood to keep the wind at their backs. He then climbed down with hammer and nails.

The three of them, Aengus, James and Father O'Malley sat on their bunk side by side after having nailed up the blankets thus creating a Privy Curtain.

"Father, what do you think about making a counting of the days we are at sea?"

"I rather like that idea Aengus."

"I know how we can do it. "I'll keep track in my journal." He took his journal out from the Bible sack. "Oh, oh…I doubt that there is ink on this ship for my use."

"Then it would be fortunate that Father Francis gave me bottles of ink for our use." The priest rummaged in his bag and pulled out a jar of dark liquid. Giving it to James, he excused himself to go topside for prayer.

Aengus and James did offer to accompany him, but he thought it best for them to get used to the roll of the ship. They were left alone, well not completely alone as there were at least two dozen people sitting on their bunks or the floor. But they were without their mentor and priest. James dipped the pen into the jar and began to write. He wrote:

July 29, 1849 My Birthday

at the top of the page.

"What should I write?"

Aengus grunted as he thought hard, then he giggled.

"What's so funny?" asked James.

"Just this, I took a pee off the side of the ship using no bucket, just right into the wind which in turn brought mi water back to me."

James laughed from deep within his stomach. "Even I know that you have to keep the wind at your back when doing that. There were many times on the top of the wall of the fortress on Inishbofin that I had to go, but had the sense to adjust my position."

"So…okay, you're clever. Everyone knows that but I still think you should write mi story in your Journal. It's funny." He had left out what had caused him to do such a thing in the first place.

"Yes, it is." James wrote the following.

After we said our farewell to the Friars and O'Flaherty clan we boarded the Cushla Machree with a crushing hoard of people at our back.
The steerage quarters are very small with bunks on each side.
Our first order of business was to create a "Privy" area with blankets. It was Father O'Malley's idea. But Aengus went topside and proudly relieved himself over the railing directly into the sea, only to have his water spray back on him.

James read aloud what he had written. The two lads howled as he finished the last sentence.

Topside, Father O'Malley watched steerage passengers sitting around the deck. Some were having a hard time of getting their sea legs. Most just talked about what they would be getting for their first meal. Paul, the seaman who had given them their directions, was climbing up the mast to adjust a sail attachment. The priest held the book of the Divine Liturgy which he had just used to pray. Not knowing of the confrontation between Paul and Aengus he was lulled into thinking that the voyage would be as uneventful as the first day.

The second class passengers were also milling about the deck at the bow of the ship. Among them was Meghan. Aunt Maggie was with her. Colin, exhausted from the emotional turmoil of breaking Church laws, getting married but not having a wedding night let alone a honeymoon, hauling bags and arguing about their accommodations needed some alone time. He needed to put things into perspective, he had told them. Stretched across his bunk, he had fallen asleep dreaming of a wedding night that wouldn't be possible for another month.

The Union Jack flag of the United Kingdom flew from a pole attached to the far rear of the ship. At the bow there was very little ornamentation save for some carved wooden trim. Meghan leaned over the railing pointing at some Dolphins following the ship.

"Aunty, look at those fish. Aren't they beautiful?"

"Yes dear, but they're Dolphins and not fish. You will learn the difference when you go to school in America."

The ship bounced over the waves, the salt water spray shooting up and into their faces.

"Yuck," shouted Meghan.

Maggie wiped off her face while agreeing with the lass' opinion.

In the steerage quarters, Aengus and James leaned back onto their bags still giggling over what James had written.

"Aengus, you don't think I committed a sin by writing about you peeing over the side of the boat do you?" It was asked in all seriousness, for this came from a lad set upon being "Pure of Heart."

"James, you worry too much. It's funny and we need to laugh a little on this long voyage."

"I guess you're right."

They were both quiet for a time as they attempted to get in touch with the rocking of the ship to and fro so as not to make them sick. Aengus broke the silence. He was already a seafarer of sorts as a fisherman who went out to sea often. What he was distressed over was the event which played itself out when he had been topside. It was both embarrassing and threatening to him.

"James, I must share something with you," he whispered. "But you must promise not to tell Father O'Malley."

The lad looked over toward the young fisherman sitting at his side. He was aghast worrying that his friend had done more than just peeing overboard.

"I...I don't know what to say. It's not bad is it?"

"Well, kind of bad but not too bad."

"Oh, a venial sin then, is it?"

"Yeah, that's it, but then again…"

James gave into friendship and decided to support Aengus.

"I promise. What happened?"

Aengus took a deep breath and went on to tell how Paul made fun of his being a man and in response he was going to prove his manliness by showing him that he was a full grown man.

"Oh is that all. You mean like what happened to me in the waterfall on Inishbofin, when you all saw that I was becoming a man."

The young fisherman blushed not only for what the lad said but for his own misguided plan.

"Well it's not quite like that. You see you weren't showing it off. I was going to do just the opposite."

"Ohhh! Well in that case I'd just say a Pater Noster for that."

"Really, so you're Father James now is that it?"

The lad was mortified. He didn't mean to come off as the all-knowing one. He only wanted to say that what Aengus almost did was not a grave sin.

"I'm sorry…I didn't mean…"

"I know. It's just that this bloke Paul needs to be watched. You should never be alone with him, promise me."

"Sure, I promise. But why would I want to be, he's rather mean-spirited."

"That's it James. He's mean, so stay away."

Another period of silence fell over the two friends, both satisfied that they had bared their soul to the other. Soon they dozed off with the rocking of the ship acting as a cradle of sorts.

And so it went over the next few days. The lads talked of silly things, Father O'Malley prayed his office never knowing of the Paul incident. Sometimes the lads would join him. He never knew that it was a penance of sorts for them and their talk of manly things. The ship flew over the ocean waves as if on angels' wings.

**Typical 19th Century Ocean Crossing Ship,
as painted by the author's grandfather:
Louis Stella**

Chapter Thirteen: The Sixth Day

On the evening of the sixth day the stars shone in the heavens like diamonds under candlelight. Not a cloud hindered their glorious light. The moon added to the starry night with its glow from reflecting the sun's rays off its surface. It appeared as a giant white disc. In that moonlight Meghan decided to explore the ship once again in the hope of finding someone she knew, particularly the boy who bit the cookie for her. She was so sure that he was on board that she had walked stem to stern every day hoping that he too might be topside. Each day came and went without meeting anyone she knew.

Now under the bright moon and diamonds in the sky she just gazed out over the ocean from the tip of the bow. Aunt Maggie and Uncle Colin were having some alone time having been given assurance that she would stay near adults on deck and not go near the crew. She dutifully obeyed. The winds were picking up and blowing that red hair so admired by a certain boy like a flag on the mast. People about her were talking of a change in the weather. It was August but still the North Atlantic had a chill to it at night. The days had been warm but not unbearable. So she was enjoying the wind in her face as she imagined how life would be in that place called New York City. She would be a true lady when her schooling concluded. One day she might even be smitten with someone like that boy holding the cookie. However it would have to be that boy with that cookie which she had given him.

As she dreamed on another youthful explorer roamed the ship. Only James wasn't looking for anyone in particular. He just needed some solitude. How he expected that in the overcrowded ship hadn't occurred to him. He was thinking about his nightly Journal entry. Aengus was never without an escapade which could add humor to the passage. In fact just the previous night he had inadvertently done to an unsuspecting woman what he threatened to do to Paul. He ended up embarrassing himself and the lady by not calling out that the Privy was in use and when she entered, there he was with his pants down. That very night Father O'Malley found a plank of wood and some paint and wrote "occupied" on one side and "vacant" on the other so that such an incident would not happen again.

James enjoyed Aengus' company. He kept him laughing and not always thinking about home. They had their serious moments as well. After prayer with Father O'Malley, they would often talk about God and what the Lord was calling them to do. Girls, of course, were always a topic which brought on wild tales that young men create to prove themselves. Sometimes, they would explore the ship together so that Father could have a time of solitude. They realized all too well that his burden of teaching and guiding them was great indeed. Especially since one had no intention of becoming a priest.

Staying "Pure of Heart" continued to be his goal, but on ship with so many people coming from such varied backgrounds often made that quite the challenge. What happened to Aengus in the Privy might be funny now, but for him it was also horrifying. Men and women would sleep together and he would hear moaning and terms of endearment which in his mind were meant to be said only between a husband and wife. Entering manhood was difficult enough without that type of carrying on. His battle with the swelling continued. Aengus didn't miss a chance to point it out but in a funny manner. The same thing was happening to him as well but it was also a way for him to deal with the same issue being an older teen in Victorian society in which such discussions would not be addressed openly. And yet these two friends were teenagers caught between being a child and a man. They were also from rural Ireland where such restrictive conversations and prim and proper decorum were more relaxed. So they found themselves thrust into a new world smack dab in the middle of maturation with only a holy man to be their guide. Thus their mutual sharing of what they thought, how they felt about their experiences helped them get through each day. James even got to a point at which he could jest about Aengus' condition when it presented itself.

For Meghan, there was no one near her age with whom she could share stories and dreams, no one with whom to speak of private things, like boys and becoming a full grown woman. She couldn't and wouldn't do so with Aunt Maggie, after all she was a new bride and adapting to that role in a difficult situation aboard a ship with little privacy. So she strolled along the port side of the ship trying to figure out what she was called to do in America when Colin went about his business and Aunt Maggie entered society in New York City.

On the starboard side of the ship, James was mulling about such issues as well. He had paused at mid-ship to lean over the railing and just look at the reflections of the stars on the dark water of the Atlantic Ocean. Meghan had done the same thing on the port side. Both were pondering the beauty of God's creation, then dreaming of what life would be like in America where all things were possible.

The thud of a sail being lowered too fast drew their attention high up the mast. A crew member was calling out that clouds were visible at the horizon. This was possible because of the bright night sky. A lantern hung from the lower beam of the jib. It rocked back and forth casting its light on James' face and then Meghan's face. Both looked to the opposite side of the ship to see the clouds just as that lantern swayed back and forth.

"It's you," Meghan called out, while not moving an inch.

"It's you!" James said simultaneously. He leapt across the deck and Meghan finally had the nerve to take a few steps toward him. They stopped within an arm's reach of each other.

"I never thought I'd see you again," James quietly said.

"Nor I you," she replied.

"So you're going to America, I see."

"Well yes as is quite evident."

They began to laugh at their own silliness, both dreaming of a day when this meeting would take place and then just being able to state the obvious.

"Would you like to sit down with me?" asked James.

"That would be nice, but not for long. I promised Aunt Maggie."

They walked side by side to the barrels. He helped her up onto one and jumped up on the adjoining one. She adjusted the floor length skirt of her dress to insure that her petticoat wasn't showing. As this was being done he turned his head on the pretense of looking for those clouds spotted earlier by a member of the crew. The swells of the waves were getting larger as the ship was no longer gliding across them but plowing through them. This observation gave the lad fodder to begin a conversation.

"It seems that the sea is getting rougher, don't you think?"

"Oh yes, I'd say so."

"I hope that I don't get seasick. A lot of people do you know."

"Indeed, I see many at our end of the boat hanging over the side…" she abruptly stopped in mid-sentence thinking that she was getting too unladylike with her description of the seasick people.

"Yes indeed, many folks in steerage are very ill all ready."

"That's too awful for them, isn't it?"

The ship took a deep roll compared to what they had experienced in all the days since leaving Galway. Meghan grabbed hold of James to steady herself and then immediately let go.

"My, it is getting rough isn't it?"

James sat rigidly upright with a tingle in his belly which was quite different from being seasick. He had never been held onto by a girl in all his life except for his mother and Mrs. O'Flaherty but then they weren't girls, they were moms. He rather liked it, as brief that it was. He pulled at the ribbed collar of his sweater.

"You know we have never been properly introduced?"

Now that did it. He virtually called her a hussy of a girl for the second time.

"Well now, I suppose that's true. I suppose you think that I'm rather forward then?" she asked through tightly held lips which she thought gave her an appearance of superiority.

"That's not what I meant at all. I just don't remember if I ever gave you my name and I know that I know yours because of you being called by it in St. Nicholas Church."

She relaxed and stopped holding her mouth tightly shut.

"Oh, then perhaps you are correct and we should properly introduce ourselves; after all we have met twice."

"That's quite true isn't it? We are practically old friends."

"Yes indeed, so what is your name boy with the cookie?"

He looked at her askance and she looked back quite embarrassed that she had referred to him as she dreamed of him. He didn't know what to do for fear if he said anything about that cookie thing she would get upset again. So he simply told her his name.

364

"My name is James Richard Shields and I come from the island of Inishbofin off the west coast of Ireland. I am most pleased to meet you officially, that is."

"My pleasure to be sure. And my name is Meghan Catherine O'Grady of Doolin, which is in County Clare."

"I am most pleased to make your acquaintance." He held out his hand and she took it and shook it vigorously.

Then they laughed at themselves. It was a hearty laugh from James and a little giggle type from Meghan.

"Well then, now that's over."

"Yes indeed, so now we may talk to each other any time, right?"

"Well I suppose so. Now then I want to hear all about this place called Inishbofin."

"There isn't much to tell really. It's a lovely island, that is, when the weather is fine. Quite small so it's easy to explore all around it. The sheep roam about grazing on what little there is that grows for the soil is mostly rocks so even before the potato blight we had a hard time growing something people could eat."

"That must have made your life quite miserable." She expected his look to reflect that misery but it didn't. He glowed even in the dark as he spoke of his island home and his eyes sparkled.

"Oh no, not at all…I had a wonderful life and mi mom and dad are the most wonderful parents in the world. You'd be surprised what mi mom could do with a bit of carrot and a touch of barley when the potatoes gave out."

"She sounds like a wonderful cook and mother too."

"Aye, she's grand to be sure." He drifted off to Inishbofin and his family cottage in his thoughts.

After a few minutes of his being off to Inishbofin, she spoke again. He snapped right back giving her his full attention once again.

"Tell me James Richard Shields, did you have any friends?"

"Oh, I had mi pirates' spirits in the ruins of Cromwell's fortress. What adventures I had climbing those walls. Then one day a fishing boat was thrown off course in a storm and I guided the Captain and his crew of his sons to safety in our harbor. From then on I had real friends. There's Captain O'Flaherty, his eldest son Aedan, his son-in-law Adam and my best friend, his youngest son Aengus. But most of all that's when I met Father Thomas O'Malley, he's a real hero, even went to prison for his faith just like the ancient martyrs."

"Really? You're not giving me the blarney are you?"

"Indeed not as God is my witness." He held up his right hand as if taking an oath.

"But these friends they were older people weren't they?"

"Well yes, but Aengus is seventeen so he's around mi own age. He's like a big brother to me who never had a sister or brother."

"Then you must miss him…and the others terribly."

"Indeed I do, but not Aengus or Father O'Malley."

"But I thought you said…"

"I see where you're going Meghan, but Aengus and Father O'Malley are with me on this very ship. So you see I will have friends even in America."

The ship began to rock more violently as the swells increased in size. People across the deck who were hanging over the railing fell backwards being quite ill at the same time.

"Oh James, look at those poor people. Maybe we should go offer our help."

"Right you are Meghan." He then helped her get off the barrel.

At that moment the ship crashed down off a large swell causing Meghan to fall into James' arms and both crashing to the now wet deck.

"Well I'll be. 'Tis us who will be needing the help I'd say."

James was looking directly into Meghan's face as he was on top of her. Realizing that he was in such a compromising position caused him to panic. He lifted himself up by placing his hands on the deck on either side of her. His hands slipped and he crashed back down on her. She let out a scream just as one of the crew members, Paul, came down from the mast having tied a sail up as the winds were getting too strong for full sail. In an instant he had grabbed James by the collar of his sweater and back of his breeches and pulled him up. Meghan continued to scream, the sick people about could hardly move let alone offer help. James was now screaming as well, demanding to be let go.

In one swooping motion, the burly seaman slid his hand down between James' legs and grabbed hold of his family jewels. Then he lifted James over his head, squeezing his man parts as he did so. The pain was excruciating but James refused to yell in pain. He groaned and grimaced and tried in vain to get out of Paul's vice like grasp.

While this was taking place at mid-ship, Father O'Malley was preparing to pray his office in the steerage quarters. He too had felt the ship rocking more violently and had sent Aengus to seek out James. He knew that the lad would want to take part in the night prayers. Aengus was just climbing out of the hold as the rocking of the ship intensified. Waves now splashed over its side just like on his father's fishing boat in the storm outside of Galway. Keeping his balance was quite difficult but he was a fisherman and determined to do so and search for his friend whom he now feared could have been swept into the sea.

He began to shout, "James, where are you?"

Meghan lay on the deck, now drenched from the sea water splashing on the deck. She grabbed hold of the barrel behind her and got to her feet. Struggling valiantly she stood and ran with fists flying to and fro toward Paul. Pounding on his chest, she yelled over and over again for him to let James go. The six-foot tall seaman with the barrel of a chest and cannons for arms barely noticed the discomfort of her fists pounding on his chest. He glared down at her while still holding James above his head and tightening his grasp on the lad's private parts. Just as James couldn't stand it any longer and let out a yell, Paul in a flash of fury tossed the lad and grabbed hold of Meghan.

James crashed on the deck with a scream of pain as he slid into a stack of crates. He was heard by Aengus who had gotten to mid-ship. The lad curled into a ball holding himself and writhing in pain. At the same time he tried to yell for help as Paul took hold of Meghan by her shoulders.

"So then, you are nothing more than an Irish tart. You wanted him to have his way with you." Paul was enraged now and had lost all control of his reason.

"No, no…we were just talking that's all. Let me go."

Paul grabbed for her skirt and began to lift it up. Meghan struggled and screamed but the sound of the waves crashing aboard washed out her pleas for help. James began to crawl toward her and Paul, who now had her in an embrace and lowering his head to kiss her. Out from behind the mast Aengus appeared, saw James in pain on the deck and Meghan in the embrace of that seaman who had once before given them grief. He lunged for Paul and though not his size was of a challenging build to confront the burly seaman.

Aengus grabbed hold of Paul's neck. "Pick on someone your own size, asshole."

369

The seaman pushed Meghan away. She made a dash for James still crawling toward her. Kneeling beside him she took his head and held it in her lap while screaming for help. His body went limp.

The young fisherman and the bully seaman were at it big time now. Rolling across the deck there were fists swinging and curses being yelled.

Paul rolled on top of Aengus and grabbed hold of his manhood. Aengus gave a yelp and then kicked up his knee into Paul's groin.

"Why you Irish scum," with those words he took Aengus by his sweater pulling it so hard that its weave was pulled out and a gaping hole was left.

Now Aengus was really out for the kill. A jab into Paul's stomach followed by an upper cut to his jaw sent the seaman reeling backwards and crashing into the barrels. Shaking his head he breathed deeply and puffed up his chest so that it was a giant of a man who came for the young fisherman who had his fists raised and the stance of a Celtic Warrior ready for battle.

"I'll show you who's the man here and when I'm done that runt will feel mi manhood in his arse."

"Not if I have anything to say about it," and with that Aengus grabbed hold of a loose rope dangling from the mast pole tugged on it and then ran in a flying leap horizontally feet first crashing into that massive chest of the seaman.

Paul went crashing across the deck and sliding into the base of the ship's side with a bellowing of curses. Waves continued to crash over the side of the ship when Father O'Malley being worried as to why it was taking Aengus so long to find the lad came upon the scene. On the deck of the bow Aunt Maggie and Colin had appeared looking for Meghan and hearing the commotion and men swearing came running toward mid-ship.

Aengus was now pounding his fists into the dazed Paul's face. Blood splattered out from the seaman's mouth after each punch and dripped from a cut on Aengus' head into his eyes. Blurred vision or not the young fisherman would not let up the pounding. Paul got him off with a kick between the legs but Aengus even though doubled over for a time came back with fists flying again. Only Father O'Malley coming between the two stopped Aengus. Paul however took hold of the priest and violently pushed him aside. With that the priest grabbed hold of the ship's railing, turned and in a swift move laid a punch into the seaman's stomach followed by a blow to his jaw. Paul crashed down onto the deck at the feet of Maggie and Colin who had just come running toward Meghan, who was still holding James in her arms.

A blood curdling scream came from Maggie as Colin had to jump over Paul's body and pull up Maggie to do likewise lest they tumble down over him.

The First Mate and several other crew members were right behind the newlyweds. They took hold of Paul and pulled him off to the other side of the ship. There was a ship doctor on board and he was sent for. Paul was still yelling curses at Aengus as he was being dragged away.

"Stop your cursing or it's the brig for ye," a stern First Mate demanded. The seaman finally quieted down. "Tell me what happened here."

Maggie was now holding Meghan, who was hysterically trying to tell what had happened. Tears not from her pain but from her concern for James steamed down her face. Colin stood helplessly watching the scene.

"Colin, see to this lad."

The businessman lifted James, who could hardly speak. He curled into a ball when Colin gently lowered him to the deck boards. He touched the lad's arm and asked where it hurt. At the barrels Father O'Malley was seeing to Aengus who was insisting that he go to James.

"We shall both see to James. Can you walk?"

"I think so Father. Can you? You don't look too good right now." Aengus tried to give out a smile as with one hand he held his head and with the other he reached out for the priest.

With that they held onto each other to steady themselves as the waves continued to crash up on the deck. People from all the classes had now heard of the fight and were coming to watch the scene unfold. As for the crew they were taking Paul to the crew's quarters before the passengers took their anger out on him, for in their mind two lads and a lass had been brutalized by him.

Colin had returned to Maggie and Meghan and was suggesting that they take the lass back to their quarters after the doctor spoke to her.

Father O'Malley was seated on the deck cradling James whom he and Aengus had managed to uncurl. It was evident where the pain was located but the priest asked if he had pain elsewhere.

"My head hurts too," a weak voice replied.

"Father, let me take him, if you don't mind."

"Are you able my son? As you noted, you don't look too good either."

"I'll be able to do it Father." Aengus placed his arm under the legs of James and another under the lad's back. He gently lifted him up. That's when blood was seen to have covered Father O'Malley's hand which had held the lad's head.

At that precise time a scream was let out by Maggie as she saw blood on Meghan's skirt. At first she thought it was that of her niece, but the lass assured her that she wasn't injured.

"James is bleeding Aunty, I must go to him."

"Colin see how the boy is doing. Meghan, right now the doctor must tend to him." She took the lass into her arms as they watched the arrival of the doctor.

The doctor arrived with a small black bag and a blanket. Aengus was still holding James in his arms while Father

O'Malley was placing his handkerchief onto the back of the lad's head where the blood was oozing out. The First Mate had remained to report to the Captain of the Cushla Machree.

"This boy cannot be lowered into the steerage hold, not with a head wound and whatever else seems to be the problem," the doctor told the First Mate. "The sea is rough but nonetheless we must create a tent here on deck."

"Aye, Doctor McMillan, I'll see to it." With that the First Mate left to report to the Captain and give orders to the crew to build a tent like structure at mid-ship.

"Now as for all of you standing about, it's best that you return to your quarters, a storm is brewing." The Doctor then asked Aengus to lower James onto the blanket that he had spread out on the deck.

As James was gently placed on the blanket, Father O'Malley never removed his hand from holding the lad's head. The lad was barely conscious and this seemed to worry the Doctor. "Does anyone know what happened here?"

Aengus told the story of what he found when he came to look for James. Father O'Malley explained that he saw a fight going on between a crew member and his student, Aengus. He attempted to stop it.

"But what started it in the first place?"

The priest and young fisherman couldn't answer the Doctor's question. Meghan had refused to return to the second class quarters until she knew James would recover.

"Doctor, I think that I can answer that question," Meghan said softly.

Father O'Malley and Aengus looked up from their position at James' side on the floor of the deck. Neither could fathom how a girl would be privileged to know such information. Meghan smiled at them for she knew from how James spoke of his friends on board that these were them. She then began to set the scene for what took place. It was some time later that the Doctor then thanked her, asked if she was in need of attention and then suggested that her family take her back to their quarters. This time Meghan agreed to go with them.

"And you are his Father, I presume sir." The doctor spoke to Father O'Malley.

"I'm his guardian, yes. Thomas O'Malley is my name."

"And this lad, who seems to need my attention as well, how are you related to this lad?"

"I'm kind of his big brother," answered Aengus smiling at James as he spoke.

"I see, then where are his parents?"

"They live on Inishbofin, a small island off the west coast of Ireland," answered the priest.

James' eyes flickered as Aengus told the doctor that he was the lad's older brother. But he hadn't spoken coherently as yet.

Then in a tone so low that the Doctor had to bend near his mouth he did so.

"I need to speak to mi brother," James said weakly.

"Of course lad. Mr. O'Malley, perhaps the older lad might get something out of him that I haven't been able."

The two men stepped to the side railing and rehashed what they knew so far. Aengus knelt next to James, then laid flat down face to face with him so that he could catch every word.

"It hurts bad."

"I know little brother, I know."

James tried to smile. "I mean more than just my head. It really hurts you know where. He squeezed me pretty rough."

"Aye that he did to me as well. But don't you fret, the doctor will see to it."

James was getting exhausted, his head throbbed and he felt dizzy.

"Please Aengus, make sure Meghan doesn't know about this part of the pain."

"Oh, the girl with the cookie is here is she. Well don't you worry about that bit of news. She'll know only about the head wound."

"Thanks big brother…" and with that James turned his head and closed his eyes.

"Doctor, doctor come quickly. He's gone out. Father O'Malley he's gone out," Aengus was now shouting and crying hysterically. "He's gone out I tell you. He's gone…"

Father O'Malley took hold of Aengus. "We don't know that lad. Come with me. Praying is all we can do now."

Aengus sank into the priest's arms thinking that he had lost his "brother." The guardian, called father of the lads by the doctor, consoled the young fisherman as he throbbed with pain and sorrow.

The doctor hovered over James. He placed a tube on his chest and listened. Then he smiled. "He's still with us…is it Father O'Malley then sir?"

"Yes, I'm a priest and the lads here are my wards."

"I see. I won't say a word sir. Now then the lad is only unconscious. While he's out I must tend to his head wound and his…am I correct in thinking that his male parts are injured young man?"

"Aye, sir 'tis true but no one is to know about it see."

"The secret is safe with me lad. And when I'm done here, we'll see to you.

"Aye, doctor, the bloke was pretty rough with us, if you get my meaning."

"I understand. No one will know about you either. Father perhaps you would like to say that prayer now."

Aengus and Father O'Malley knelt at the ship's railing and prayed. The crew returned to construct a tent. The Doctor called for watered down rum for James as he would have to sew his head up. The praying ceased on Aengus' part.

"Wow did you hear that Father? James gets to drink rum. I wonder if I'll get some because of mi injuries?"

The priest smiled, made the Sign of the Cross, and prayed the Lord's Prayer for the lads.

When the make-shift tent was ready, Aengus carried James to it and placed him on a dry blanket. By then he was somewhat conscious as he was moaning. The doctor then entered with a lantern for Aengus to hold while Father O'Malley looked on. There was barely room for all to be in the tent but the doctor made due. After a patch of the lad's hair was cut away and the wound washed, the doctor proceeded to stitch it up. There were a few moans of pain uttered but for the most part the rum had done its job both externally on the wound and internally inebriating James.

"We will examine the other source of pain now. Perhaps, Father, you would feel more comfortable outside the tent."

"Yes, of course. I'll be right outside."

"As for you lad, hold the lantern steady, the ship is rocking quite roughly and we wouldn't want to be poking around and causing any more discomfort."

"Yes doctor…do you think he'll be all right everywhere?"

"We'll soon see. You'll be next by the way. That's a nasty cut on your head."

Aengus held the lantern in two hands. He would eventually have to tell the doctor that it was more than a cut on the head which was bothering him.

The seaman who caused this bodily injury sat in the putrid smelling brig as it was located next to the livestock hold. Captain Stephen Waterstone was a seasoned veteran of ocean crossing and normally considered quite the gentleman by the owners of the ship. All that veneer of Victorian etiquette was gone as he was furious over the altercation which now had the entire ship buzzing about the brutality of a crew member to innocent lads seeking to defend a girl's honor.

"Irish or not," the Captain Waterstone yelled into the seaman's face. "They were children in the eyes of all aboard this ship. You leave me no choice but to send you to the brig. And be grateful that there isn't more to the sentence."

What he meant in that last part of his tirade was in reference to Paul's argument that he had actually interrupted what he thought to be a young man trying to take advantage of the girl in question. The Captain had bought it and thus the seaman was saved from a flogging. In any case the Captain felt he not only needed to cool that wicked temper of his but also keep him hidden from the passengers who were now so angry that the mere sight of Paul might be a cause for a riot.

"You're an idiot," said the Captain as Paul was taken from the wheelhouse to the brig by the First Mate and two crew members. He was in chains. "It wasn't bad enough that all I hear is that our food is fit only for the pigs in livestock."

That reprimand was constantly being replayed in Paul's mind and each time he began to curse and scream that he had wished he had finished them off.

"At least they will not be adding any more Irish scum to the world population," he yelled to the First Mate who fastened his chains to the iron ring on the floor of the brig.

"Keep your mouth shut," responded the First Mate. "You're lucky you weren't thrown overboard by that mob when they saw your handiwork on those lads."

"Again I say they are papist scum. Their intent was to defile one of their own true but nonetheless an innocent lass."

"So you say. But how many heard you threaten to rape the young lad when you were done taking care of the older one? Now shut up and maybe I can get you out before we get to America."

Paul pulled on the chains and began to pace as the cage door was locked. "You think I'm an animal that you chain me like one?"

There was no response forthcoming. Paul's actions were far worse than an animal seeking out food or protecting its young. He tried to destroy the lads' ability to bring new life of their line into the world. No wild animal would approach that level of savagery.

While this drama unfolded, in the second class quarters Meghan lay sobbing on her bunk. No effort from Maggie could console her.

"He was only trying to protect me Aunty, that's all it was." This she stated over and over again.

Maggie was concerned that there might be more to the hysteria than this boy being hurt.

"Colin, would you find the doctor and also check on the condition of the lads."

"Of course love, should I send the doctor to you?"

"If he thinks it is needed, by all means."

The new groom made his way amongst throngs of people who being thrown about in their quarters because of the increasingly rougher sea, many came topside with the hope that fresh air might ease their queasiness. The topic of conversation however was not the weather but the brutality of the seaman towards the lads who saved a lass' honor. Making his way to mid-ship was not an easy task because so many people were now asking him what he knew of the incident. Colin played it dumb and said little so as not to fuel their anger.

The tent structure stood out at mid-ship. Standing next to it was Father O'Malley.

"Father O'Malley, it is you isn't it?" asked Colin.

"Yes…weren't you with the lass my lads tried to protect?"

"Yes Father, I am married to her Aunt. My name is Colin Logan."

"I regret to have to meet you like this. How goes it with the lass? I am told that she did not sustain any injury, praise God."

"Well Father, not physical ones but she won't stop crying. I think she's blaming herself for what happened."

"I understand. Would you like me to speak with her? I might be able to calm her with the news that the lads will recover. The doctor is just finishing up as we speak."

"If you think it will help, Maggie and I would be most grateful."

At that point the doctor emerged from the tent.

"Ah, Father, I am pleased that you're still here. Would you have someone fetch nightshirts or some other garment for the lads to wear? I'm afraid the blood on these should be washed off before their clothes become useless to them."

With that he held out two pairs of trousers, two pairs of long johns and two Aran knit sweaters. All were splattered with blood.

"I'll be honest Father, I had a dickens of a time getting those undergarments off them as they didn't cooperate willingly given how they would be to one another, if you understand what I'm trying to say gently."

"Of course Doctor McMillan, I'll get them myself." The priest took the clothes from him and turned to Colin. "Mr. Logan I shall come to your niece as soon as I get my lads settled properly."

"I'll be happy to help you. In fact Maggie is a weaver and seamstress by trade. She might be able to help repair the rips in these clothes, as for the knit, I don't know. But I'll ask about that skill as well."

Father O'Malley peeked inside the tent, not knowing what he would find. James was still in a rum stupor and groggy. That was good given his state of pain and his all togetherness. Aengus, in the same state of undress, was sitting upright. A blanket was pulled over both of them. He held a wet cloth to his head. Seeing a head peeking inside the tent he slid under the blanket holding it at his neck.

"Oh it's you Father. James is still out of it but the doctor says he'll heal in a couple of weeks. Lucky aren't we?"

"God be praised. And what about you, how are you getting along? I mean…well you know what I mean don't you?"

"Aye, that I do. We'll both be able to have children, though I guess for James that's not such an important thing given that he'll be one of you in a few years."

With a kind smile the priest noted that was some time away. "I'll be right back with your nightshirts. Stay covered so that you don't catch a chill."

"That won't be a problem, trust me." Aengus held the blanket tightly. Just glad none of mi mates will hear about how I spent this night. James is the lucky one being as he is."

"Well if it's any consolation to you lad, when he awakes he'll probably be feeling just as you do now. I'll see that your clothes are washed and mended. Just rest now with the angels watching over you."

"Well I hope that it's Michael the Archangel given my state."

Father O'Malley was laughing softly as he exited. Colin noted that the lads must be in good spirits given the laughter. "Oh, well now that remains to be seen. Let's just say that by morning we shall have two very red faced lads greeting the day when they awake.

When the two men returned with the nightshirts, Father O'Malley found Aengus dozing off. James was already soundly asleep. He gently placed the nightshirts at their feet which stuck out of the blanket and quickly left. By morning Aengus would have taken great care to put the nightshirt he found on James, but first he made sure he was covered with his own.

When the priest and Colin entered the Second Class quarters, it was crowded with fellow passengers all concerned over Meghan's condition.

"Oh, Father, she still sobs. I don't know what to do," Maggie gravely said.

384

"I'll try to talk with her if you wish."

"Yes please do so. Colin and I will stand out of the way." Maggie went to take Colin's arm and saw the bloodied clothes in his hands. "Heavens what are these?"

Colin went on to explain that they belonged to the lads who defended Maggie's honor and that they needed repairing and washing.

The task would give Maggie a diversion while Father O'Malley spoke with Meghan. He placed his hand on her throbbing shoulder.

"Meghan... it's Father O'Malley here. I'm a friend of James and Aengus, the lads who fought for you."

The lass lifted her head buried as it was in her arms and a rolled up blanket.

"You are one of us Father, I mean Catholic?"

"Yes child that I am. I've come to bring news."

"Thank God someone knows something. How is James? I want to see him."

"James is recovering nicely as is Aengus, I might add. Now as for the latter request, I'm afraid that a visit at this time would not be possible."

"Then he's really bad off isn't he? Tell me the truth, Father."

"Child, he is recovering but it shall take time and he needs rest and privacy right now. Can you understand that?"

The lass was filled with emotions she had never experienced before. She yearned to see for herself that the lad was in good condition. She was embarrassed that she had forgotten about Aengus' role in protecting her. She was angry at the seaman who hurt the lad. She looked at the priest with watery eyes and threw her arms around his neck.

"Bless me Father, for I have sinned."

Father O'Malley looked at her with pity and concern. He couldn't believe that she had chosen that moment to confess. Now his emotions were coming into play as he had entered the fight not only to protect the lads but also her and now it seemed she was about to confess that what the seaman claimed might be true.

Meghan gave no time for him to follow the usual ritual of Confession.

"I thought about James while taking my bath. I held his hand just before the fight and I liked it."

A relieved priest noted that those were not grave sins and absolved her with a penance of obeying the doctor's orders and wait until the lad was healed. She accepted the penance readily.

"You will tell me about his recovery though won't you?"

"Yes child that I will do. Rest now… this has been a frightful day not only for you but also for your Aunt and

Uncle. Be kind to them and share with your Aunt in particular your feelings about James. She will be able to help you, of this I'm confident."

After thanking the priest, Meghan called for her Aunt. As she went to her, she stopped to say that she would mend the clothes and reknit the pulled fibers of the sweater.

The sea once again became calm which was beneficial for the lads as each rock and roll of the ship sent sharp pains through their bodies. The sunrise was breathtaking with not a cloud in the sky. James and Aengus slept soundly side by side as the O'Flaherty brothers did back in the family cottage. Aengus rose first. He took the bucket the doctor had left for their use. Then he opened the flap of the tent to take the bucket to the railing to dispose of its contents. He found Father O'Malley kneeling at the entrance praying his Divine Office. Placing the bucket down, he knelt next to the priest and asked if he could pray with him.

"Of course lad, but do sit down. I think pressure on your knees isn't the best thing for you right now."

"I get it."

They weren't quite finished with "Lauds" when they heard moaning coming from inside the tent. James looked about him and called out in confusion.

"Aengus, Father O'Malley where are you?"

Priest and fisherman entered with relief written all over their faces.

"Look Father, 'tis himself speaking as if nothing at all happened."

Kneeling beside the lad, who still laid prostrate on the blanket-covered floor, they both said that they were right there for him. The lad rubbed his head and let out a yelp of pain.

"Careful there James. Ye have a bit of a gash on your head. But it's all right now, or will be, right Father?"

"So did we win at least? I mean how does that bully fare?"

"Well you'll be pleased to hear that he's been placed in the brig," answered Father O'Malley.

"What's a brig?"

"It's like a jail cell. He won't be hurting anyone any time soon."

James looked about again. Asked what it was. Father explained that the doctor ordered a tent to be built so that recovery would be private and in the fresh air. "Aengus here, shares it with you. He's a bit bruised as well."

James looked under the blanket and for the first time realized how he was dressed and also being reminded by a twinge of pain that more than his head had been injured. He looked up at his protector with a sheepish grin. Aengus returned a half smile not wanting to address the obvious in front of a man of the cloth who lived under the vow of chastity.

The attempt at this silent communication of raised eyebrows and crooked smiles did not escape the priest, who may be chaste but was also a man in good health and one who had lived in Italy. There, love and romance were looked upon quite differently than in Victorian Britain and Ireland. He took this need for them to speak as an opportunity to leave the lads alone.

"Well now that you're on the way to recovery, you may wish to resume your Journal writing. I'll fetch it for you. How does that sound?"

"I would be most grateful, Father."

The priest turned to leave. "Watch over him Aengus."

The young fisherman nodded and watched the priest go off toward the rear of the ship.

"He's gone. Now what's your problem that you couldn't speak in front of him?"

"Glad you caught on," James tried to sit up, but it hurt. "Ow, this isn't easy. It hurts down there and up here." He pointed to his injured areas.

"It's no fun to be sure. I got it over mi eye and down there too, but not as bad as you that's for sure. That jerk threatened to rip mi you know what out of mi sack so that I couldn't add more Irish children to the world."

"Mother of God, he has to be so cruel as to be off his rocker. He told me that he'd show me how it felt to be filled with a true man." Then the lad became very quiet. He squirmed. It hurt again, so he lay back down.

"Good Lord James, he is a bit off."

"Aengus, I need to know the truth. Did he…I mean you know…do it to me?

"God no, James. I got there just when he threw you into the shipping crates. You were quite out of it until this moment. 'Tis only your front parts which were injured. But the doctor said that you should heal. Let's see, he put it like this. 'The younger lad will be able to have children one day of that I am confident.' I told him that didn't matter since you were becoming a priest but that it was nice that you would be in good working order, just in case."

"I thank you for the good wishes. But there is one more thing I need to know. Is Meghan well?"

"Well now, I guess that you are in good working order."

"'Tis a bold one ye are Aengus O'Flaherty to suggest such a thing about such a kind and gentle person."

The older lad now became quite agitated and red-faced. He protested that he didn't mean anything like what James suggested. "Anyway, she's quite well indeed. The only reason she's not standing here right now is that Father and the doctor directed her not to bother you. After all ye are in nothing but a nightshirt, I might add."

"I'm sorry Aengus. I love you like a brother and wouldn't hurt you for any reason, but the last thing I saw after being tossed aside like a sack of potatoes was that bully grabbing hold of Meghan who came to defend me as you did at that same time."

Aengus softened and knelt at his side. He dipped a cloth into the water bucket and wiped James' brow. "And I love you too as if you were mi little brother. So now what's the plan?"

"Plan? I don't understand."

"James Shields are ye telling me that you have no plan to get back at that bully and to see this girl again?"

"That's exactly right. I just came back into this world but five minutes ago. But now that you mention it…I think we need to talk of what to do. How long must we be in this tent?"

"Until your head heals and stops oozing blood and stuff. The swelling of your parts should go away on its own. We've been placing cold water on them every hour."

The younger lad's eyes popped open as not done since before the fight. "We! Who's we?"

"Just the doctor and sometimes me, I didn't want to say anything. It's not the most manly thing to do to another bloke. But what was worse is that I had to hold such a wet rag on myself and it was cold. At least you were out of it and felt nothing."

James let out a laugh and then a groan. "Fear not brother, I shall say nothing to anyone ever."

As the two giggled over such delicate issues, Father O'Malley returned with the Journal and oranges. Daybreak was about to make a show of it. The ordeal had brought them through the night.

"Now then, isn't it nice to see laughter from you two once more? I brought each of you an orange. We wouldn't want you to get sick. It's been several days at sea already without taking in some citrus fruit. And now tell me all about your private talk. I may be of help to resolve your concerns."

The two lads looked at each other wide-eyed and thinking that this man of the cloth doesn't miss a thing. But they told him that he needn't worry, everything was under control.

"Well then, I shall tell Meghan and her family that you are awake and well. Would you like a visit from her?"

"Good grief not yet Father. I need mi pants on first at least."

"Me too," added Aengus.

"Oh that is a grand thought. I shall ask her Aunt when the mending and the cleaning would be achieved." He then peeled an orange and fed James lifting his head slightly so as not to have pressure on his stitched wound. It would be his first nourishment since he was knocked out, save for water, since the fight.

"Who is this priest who endured imprisonment, suffered a flogging and ministered to his flock with a passion, fought with raging fists against the giant seaman and yet found time to take a lad whose life had no future and a fisherman

who had dreams which would lift him out of future uncertainty?" would have been the thoughts of the lads if they could have left their bodies and looked at what had happened to them all due to their Father O'Malley. On his part he humbly left the tent and headed for second class at the bow of the ship, rubbing his ribs which had slammed into the ship's railing during his encounter with Paul.

That walk to see Maggie and Meghan in particular would have him thinking that perhaps not only should James attend St. Augustine Academy but perhaps Aengus should rethink his plan to be a fisherman out of Boston and come to Philadelphia. "No seventeen-year-old in our restrictive society which exists in these days would do what that young fisherman has done. First he saved the life of his friend and then nursed him back to health in a discreet and compassionate manner." He spoke this aloud to the ocean beyond as if hoping that an angelic reply might come to confirm his theory that this youngest of the O'Flaherty clan may have something within him quite similar to that of young James. "Perhaps, 'tis two future Augustinian priests that I am watching grow in faith."

On the bow the very people whom he sought were busily taking down the wash which Maggie had hung earlier. Meghan carefully folded the pieces which her Aunt handed to her but when they came upon the long-johns Aunt Maggie suddenly stopped.

"My dear, perhaps you should go to bed now. The tent looks rather quiet. The lads must be sleeping." This of course she suggested so as not to shake the lass' senses when she would fold the boys' undergarments. Such an act would only be done by a spouse or servant.

"Please Aunt Maggie just a minute more. I saw Father O'Malley at the tent earlier."

Before her Aunt could respond, a familiar voice intervened.

"How right you are lass."

"Ah, Father O'Malley how nice to see you again," greeted Maggie. "We've just now taken the clothes of the lads off the line."

"And they will be most grateful as I am. They just retired, but look forward to thanking you in person."

Meghan couldn't hold it in any longer. She had to know if James' injury really would heal.

"It's been so long Father and no word if James will…oh my God I can't even say it."

Father O'Malley took the lass into his arms. "My dear child he is awake as I indicated. He will heal, please believe that. And so will Aengus."

"Oh yes, I am pleased about him too. But James, that man, he just threw him like trash. He didn't care what happened to him."

"And for that he sits in a cell. Now lass your Aunt had a good suggestion. Take some rest and I shall bring you to the lads tomorrow, I promise."

The sea rolled the ship so as to lull most to sleep, even on wooden bunks filled with dirty straw for bedding. Like her new Uncle, some of them who had the seasickness would get some rest. But that night Meghan O'Grady could only look up at the wooden beams above her bunk. Tomorrow she would finally see that boy with the cookie again. She would have to look her best, but how could she do that if she couldn't sleep. So she took the Rosary out from under her mattress as she had done after the fight. Before she had reached the second Joyful mystery she had dozed off into a dream of that day when they would be together in America.

If dreams could reach out to each other and blend into one, then that would have been the night for that union to take place. For in that tent James rolled over very carefully so as not to disturb his friend who was sleeping with the look of angels on his face. *"So at peace you are Aengus,"* reflected James. *"You are the one who is really Pure of Heart not me. I lie here with thoughts of that Doolin girl instead of my desire to be a priest."*

"Oh Lord, look on me and give me your grace that I may know your will for me," he prayed aloud.

"Huh…" Aengus twisted to his side to find himself face to face with James. "Are you feeling well? I heard you calling out…was I dreaming?"

"No, I was just praying. Sorry to have disturbed you. But now that I have… would you mind praying with me Aengus? I need your courage in the coming days and the strength of your faith as well. Maybe if you're right there with me in prayer, the Lord will listen."

"James, I think your head wound is worse than you think. I'm no prayer. I swear and curse and fight and spit and do all sorts of evil."

Only a laugh came forth. "Maybe, but you do so for others with the purest of hearts my friend." Thus did the fourteen-year-old think and thus did he believe that he was protected by an earthly angel from Inishmor.

"All right then, my head is swelling with being made a saint or something like that. I'll pray with ye."

And so they began. "Our Father who art in heaven, hallowed be thy name..." Before the prayer had finished the two, exhausted from such philosophical thinking, joined the lass in a dream-world in which the three of them would face any danger to walk those streets paved with gold in America.

**Celtic High Cross Depicting Redemption
Clonmacnoise, Ireland**
397

Chapter Fourteen: Reunion, Revenge and Redemption

The praying of "Lauds" had long since passed as Father O'Malley walked the deck of the ship on a morning which for the first time since sailing brought warm breezes across the Atlantic. He paused momentarily to take in the majesty of the billowing sails and take out his Divine Office for it was time for "Terce" the mid-morning prayer. Not a stir was coming forth from the tent next to which he now stood. Malachy Kilkelly was standing looking over the railing, rather being sick over the railing, and that when the seas were relatively calm. Only three or four foot waves and a steady wind which carried the ship onward met the new day. The twenty-year-old turned having wiped his mouth and taken a palm full of water from the water barrel. He spit it out as soon as it entered his mouth.

"This tastes like shit." He then took a metal cup hanging on the side of the barrel and filled it with water. He smelled it, stuck his finger into it and tasted it again. It wasn't his seasickness that altered his taste. The water was foul. He decided to seek out the Frist Mate, with the cup of water in hand. Not ten steps later he ran into Father O'Malley just finishing his Morning Prayer. He had heard the young man's expletive but said nothing, rather he inquired as to what was in the cup.

"Good morning to ye, Father. Oh this is but putrid water. I'd be on my way to seek out the First Mate to complain."

"Well lad perhaps seeking out the doctor might bring about better results. I'm beginning to think that much of what ails our shipmates is not the rolling of the ship. For each time they begin to feel better, they take water to wash out their mouths and become sick again."

"Would ye help me find the doctor, Father?"

"I would indeed. Let me just peek in on the lads."

Malachy opened the flap of the tent for the priest who stooped in. Both lads were so soundly sleeping that not even snoring issued forth. Aengus had kicked off the covers and James was curled in the blanket like a butterfly in a cocoon not yet freed to fly. Aengus grabbed for the blanket that was not there. He took hold of the priest's jacket instead pulling the man to the deck floor. *The lad is gaining his strength back,* thought the priest who wiggled out of the grasp and slipped the edge of the blanket into the older lad's hand. Taking two oranges from his pocket, he placed one at the head of each lad. At their feet he had already placed the washed and mended clothes which he had picked up from Maggie Logan the previous evening. Seeing them, he was reminded that a promise was made to Meghan. He would keep it…that is if the lads ever stirred from their slumber.

"The lads look like angels don't they?"

"Ah, I guess so. Tough ones like Michael the Archangel, I'd say Father, from what I hear tell," Malachy answered.

"Indeed, the sword of righteousness in their hand so to speak. But sometimes lad the word can be mightier than the sword."

"I don't get it."

"Well let me explain my meaning as we go and find the good doctor."

Below the deck of the bow in the Second Class quarters, Meghan sat in her bunk brushing her hair. Maggie and Colin had gone to fetch the meal for mid-day which like the others was a concoction of barley, rye, peas and water. "Pantiles" also called water biscuits were also part of the meal allotment.

"This is an outrage. First we're kicked out of First Class by some arse who booked too many. Now this slop they call food is all we get. Look at these biscuits." Colin pounded one on the railing of the ship. It thumped and didn't flake in the least. "They're hard as rocks."

"Now love, we're not the only ones being fed so. Every soul on board, even the crew, is given the same type of food. Now just give me those biscuits. I'll soak them in water and hold them over a fire to warm them up."

"Well, I'll be. It's a saintly woman that I married to be sure."

With a wink and twirl of her skirt to show her petticoat, Maggie went off to fetch a pan and seek a crew member to start a fire in a metal barrel. "We'll just see about that when we finally have our own room in New York."

Colin blushed beet red, pulled at his collar and said he'd better get some food to the lass before he did something un-gentleman-like.

Doctor McMillan was just leaving the Captain's quarters when Malachy and Father O'Malley approached him. The young man shoved the cup of water into his face much to the priest's surprise. The doctor backed off as the priest took the cup from Malachy.

"Do pardon the enthusiasm of Malachy, Doctor McMillan. We've come to present this sample of the water to you for examination."

"Sir...I mean Father, I am well aware of the state of the water on this ship. I have just brought the news of its condition to the Captain. At this very moment the crew is adding rum to the water. The alcohol will cure its ills."

Malachy licked his lips in anticipation.

"And it will produce a ship full of drunks up to no good, I'd say as well."

He pointed to the young man with a big grin and wet lips.

"Need I say more?"

"I see your point. But what else can I do? We have no way to get good water out here in mid-ocean."

The priest asked the Doctor to accompany Malachy and him to find some clean barrels and also burning barrels in which a fire could be built. He told McMillan of something he learned in Italy. Scientists were experimenting with boiling water to give it renewed purity, as in boiling water to make tea.

"Does this ship have a shipment of tea aboard?" Father O'Malley asked.

"I will check with the steward in charge."

And so the three men went to seek out the steward and a possible shipment of tea. Malachy was a bit disappointed but needn't have been for the crew had already poured the rum into the water barrels. By night fall scores of passengers would be wild in their cups and worse. Malachy, by the grace of God, was a kind drunk and just sat on deck talking to the stars. Those however were beginning to be covered over by clouds. The kind inebriated twenty-year-old ran for the priest and found him outside the tent getting ready to pray "Vespers."

"Father, it's getting cloudy."

"So it seems lad."

Dozens of people were now spilling out from below deck seeking fresh air. Sick from rum and bad water some flung themselves over the railing and several had to be pulled back or they would have fallen into the sea itself. Others vomited wherever they stood with no shame and no memory of what they had done.

The sight of women pulling up their dresses and men pulling down their pants shocked the young man into sobriety and the priest into action.

Inside the tent, Aengus and James were awake. They had found the clothes and happily removed their nightshirts, splashed water on their bodies and began to dress. Aengus having to help James who was still weak and dizzy, took him by the arm, stooped down and placed his arm under his legs.

"Now just sit James. I'll carry ye outside for some fresh air."

"That's kind of you, but I want to walk on my own two legs."

"I know, but one step at a time little brother. First let's get you out onto the deck."

"Right big brother." And with that he allowed himself to be carried.

James pulled back the flap of the tent as Aengus stooped with the lad in his arms and stepped out onto the deck. They took a deep breath and sighed. It was a good feeling to be able to breathe God's good air. Their euphoric reaction to being under the now dull stars because of the cloud movement didn't last but a few seconds for right before their eyes two men had come up to a staggering lady and lifted her dress so high that more than her petticoat was seen. Her bloomers were there for all to see. She squealed with delight at first until one of them crawled under her and tried to pull the bloomers down. Then she screamed with fright.

The lads didn't know what to do. Aengus carefully placed James on a barrel and wasn't in running condition as yet but walked briskly to the men. He pulled the one on the deck out from under the woman who then ran quickly to another lady who was not far away from the scene. The two men, Aengus knew well from steerage. Lawrence McHugo and Martin Morris were their names.

"Larry, Martin…are ye mad this night?"

The two raised their fists ready to attack Aengus. Coming up from behind the young fisherman was a slow moving James. In his hand he held a club found along the railings of the ship, used to pound in nails or tighten fittings, or on occasion to bash the heads of crew members who were derelict in their duties. He was immediately recognized by the drunken young men.
Then they took a better look at who stood before them with his fists raised.

"Aengus, James ye are alive, praise God," yelled out Martin. His long brown hair fell into his eyes as the swaying of the boat caused him to stagger into Lawrence. They held onto each other fearing that they would be swept over the railing and into the sea. It was but a mild rolling the ship was doing but to them it might as well have been a hurricane.

"We thought you were dead. Everyone had heard different tales," a remorseful Lawrence added.

James held onto Aengus' arm and dropped the club. "We live, didn't Father O'Malley tell ye that?"

"He did, but no one saw you and we thought…well we just thought the worse."

The two fell to their knees and began to beg forgiveness. They crawled on all fours to the lads and kissed their feet as if they were holy saints. The lads jumped back as best they could for James was still rather unstable in his footing.

"Stop it lads," Aengus called out.

"We're so sorry…we're so sorry. We meant no harm honest."

"Ye are rascals and that's that," a self-righteous James responded. "But ye might have a chance at redemption."

"What's that?" asked both drunks.

"It means ye can be saved from hell, idiots."

"Thank you Aengus, we are truly idiots to be sure," a now sobbing Martin said as he clung on Lawrence and fell backwards onto the side of the ship.

"Anything, we'll do anything lads. Just tell us," pleaded Lawrence.

Now Aengus was just as much in the dark as were the drunken lads about this redemptive plan James offered. He with a quizzical look turned to James holding onto him, as did Martin to Lawrence, but for a proper reason and asked what his thought was.

James slid down to the floor to be eye level with the other two, Aengus followed suit. The fourteen-year-old announced that he wished to go and see the seaman who hurt him and Aengus.

"No way James…it's out of the question."

"Hear me out Aengus. I need to get this out before I can't speak any more."

The excitement, the confrontation with the drunks had exhausted the lad. Aengus placed his arm around the lad. "All right then spit it out."

James laid out his plan which was to be enacted the next night after "Vespers" when Father O'Malley would retire to the steerage deck. Under the cloak of darkness Martin and Lawrence would meet them at the tent. From there they would go to the livestock hold. Next to it was the brig. In that cell was Paul the seaman, who had beaten him and Aengus to a bloody pulp.

"Now that's where you two come in," James continued. "Somehow we must get into that cell and then since you two are strong and unhurt, you shall give to that bully what he did to us. How's that sound lads?"

Martin and Lawrence were all for it. Then they were being saved from hell so they thought by helping with James' plan. Aengus however, sat in total silence and looked at James as he never had before. *"Can this be the lad who cried that he wasn't Pure of Heart because he thought of a girl instead of his call to the priesthood?"*

"What's the matter Aengus? Why are you looking at me that way?"

"I…I just don't know James. This sounds pretty dangerous. What if we're caught? What will Father O'Malley say?"

"Don't worry Father won't know about a thing."

"What won't Father know about lads?"

The four virtually succumbed in their own spit as they choked upon seeing Father O'Malley standing over them. Each began to offer a lame excuse for their behavior. Finally, they told a half truth. That is Martin and Lawrence were not quite themselves because of the rum water forced upon them. The latter part of the explanation was to add a bit of drama to their tale. They went on to explain how Aengus helped James to get out of the tent.

"That's when we saw these two and not wanting them to sin we came to them and called them to their senses." James beamed with the success of his half-truth which was also a half-lie. Suddenly he felt a twinge of pain not from his wounds but in his heart. He grabbed his chest and collapsed on the deck.

"James," Father O'Malley was now on his knees was lifting the lad into his arms. "Are you in pain?"

The drunken lads began to cry again from worry that they had caused James pain from their misdeeds. A tear fell from Aengus' eye too, but not for the same reason. He had never seen this side of James and hoped that once this plot of his was fulfilled he would never have to see it again.

"No Father, I think this first outing was just a bit much for me. Maybe I should go back to the tent."

"Perhaps that's best. I'll tell Meghan that I'll arrange for her to see you tomorrow night." The priest began his exit, but slowly hoping that the lad would recant the lie, for he was sure that the tale told him was not all together true.

Now the lad was in quite a tizzy and not only from his unstableness because of the head wound. His plan was to be enacted the next night.

"Meghan wants to see me?" James asked.

Father O'Malley turned to face James. He explained that she had not stopped asking about his health since the fight night and that she was anxious to see for herself that he was healing. There was disappointment in his voice in that it was not what he had hoped to hear.

"But if it's too much for you, then another night can be arranged."

"No Father, I can do it. Where is she?"

"She's standing on the bow deck. I can bring her here if you'd like."

"I want to go to her. It will show her that I'm well." James stood and took a couple of steps. He staggered and began to fall. Aengus ran up behind him and steadied him. "Maybe, if you'd be so kind...I need a little help."

"I'll carry you there," offered Martin.

"No way, I'm stronger. I'll take him there," insisted Lawrence.

"You are most kind lads, but I need your help. You know Malachy Kilkelly I'm sure. Go with me to help him strap clean barrels to the mast so that we may catch rain water."

The somewhat sobered up lads grabbed hold of each other and climbed up each other to their feet. "We're ready to serve Father."

"Aengus, will you be able to handle James?"

"Sure Father."

"That's a good lad." And off went the priest, his ducklings following him beating their chests in a "Mea Culpa" asking forgiveness.

Disillusioned though he was, Aengus swept up James and held him gently in his arms and carried his bird bone self toward the bow deck. As soon as they could see Meghan standing with her Aunt and Uncle, he lowered James to his feet. Aengus called out to her. She began to wave excitedly.

"Aunty, he's here, he's here."

"Yes dear, we'll just go below for a bit and tidy up the bunks. Call us if you need us."

"Thanks ever so much Aunty, Uncle Colin." Meghan turned around so that the lads would be in view again. "Hi there, I'll be right there."

"Aengus, I want to see her on my own power."

"Right, I'll be right here just in case."

James hugged the fisherman turned nurse for him. It was not returned. This lack of affection didn't impact him for his thoughts were elsewhere. He called out. "Meghan I'm coming right up."

Slowly but surely and grabbing hold of the staircase railing he pulled himself up the five stairs to the bow deck. The ship bounced over the waves and the wind lifted her hair from her shoulders. Yet it was a warm night, dull because of the increasing clouds and yet a moonbeam managed to peek through the clouds and illuminate Meghan as if she was the Madonna herself in an apparition. James reached the top and stood as straight as he could still holding onto the railing to steady himself.

"Good evening Meghan. I'm so glad to see you."

"Hello James." She stopped and ran to him to throw her arms about his neck. Suddenly that moonbeam shifted and shined on James. His gaunt wretched appearance froze her in her steps. "James, you look…"

"I know. It hurts but I'm doing much better. That doctor did a good job on my head. Hardly any blood came out today."

"Oh goodness, but Father said that you're well."

"I am really. It just takes time to heal I'm told. One day I think I'd like to learn more about this healing of people."

"I never heard of a doctor priest before James. Maybe you can be the first one."

James forced out a smile. For the first time in quite a while, he had been reminded that the reason he was even on the

Cushla Machree was to go to America to study to be a priest. He decided to not dwell on the topic.

"Who knows. So how are your quarters…I mean are they nice…I mean…I don't know what I mean."

He was mortified that he was asking her about her bedchamber. He was just as bad as Martin and Lawrence lifting the girl's skirt. Meghan smiled and talked of the "Pantiles" and how hard they were but that Aunt Maggie was able to soften them up with a pounding of one of those clubs over there and cooking them in a kettle. James just sat there thinking that he could listen to her going on and on about the food and the water forever. Finally he spoke.

"Oh yes the water is making people sick. And then today they added rum to it and people got wild. Aengus almost got into another fight to save this girl. Her dress was lifted up by these drunken lads and…."

Now he had done it again. He is nothing more than a pervert and scum like Paul said he was. Talking to a girl of proper background of such things just wasn't done. Meghan however laughed.

"James have you ever heard of the story of King Arthur and the Knights of the Round Table?"

"Yes, loved that tale when Father O'Malley first had me read it."

"Well then, remember what those knights did?"

411

"Of course, they saved damsels in distress and fought off bad people and courted lovely ladies and searched for the Holy Grail…that's the cup of Christ which he used at the last supper."

"Well that's how I think of you James…and Aengus too. You may ask him to join us. I see him down there waiting to make sure that you are all right."

James couldn't be more pleased than to invite his best friend to be with them and make their meeting proper. Aengus bounded up the stairs.

"What's the matter? Are you all right?"

"Oh James is quite well Aengus. I just wanted to tell you both that I am most grateful that you came to my rescue. You are my Knights of the Round Table as far as I'm concerned."

Aengus hadn't a clue as to what these Round Table Knights were but he did understand the concept of being a Knight. And so James, Meghan and Aengus sat on the deck rocking up and down into the night and discussed the tale of King Arthur, his knights and the search for the Holy Grail. Time passed without notice until Aunt Maggie came out of the hold.

"Well now, it's pleased that I am to see you. But it's quite late and I think Father O'Malley might be worried as to your whereabouts."

The lads stood as soon as she appeared. "Yes ma'am."

"Fare thee well my sweet knights. I shall see thee on the morrow."

Meghan in poetic fashion tried to elevate their conversation about knights and battles to a lofty level. James virtually swooned as she spoke in Shakespearean fashion. Then he came to his senses.

"Oh, the morrow, right, that would be tomorrow. Well we're pretty busy tomorrow, what with the water barrels and such. Maybe the day after would be better."

Meghan suddenly saw a change in James and in Aengus which she hadn't seen before. Aengus seemed nervous and James was definitely attempting to cover up something, even lying about his day. Of this she was sure. Her knight on the shining white horse appeared tarnished as he limped off holding onto the arm of Aengus.

The lads had little to say to each other that night. James thought that washing their nightshirts might be warranted in the morning. It was idle chatter just to get Aengus to speak. A terse "yes," was all he got in return. Not a word was spoken of James' plan for revenge on the seaman or the time with Meghan which ended in a lie.

Aengus spent a restless night tossing and turning and full of guilt over what they planned to do. James spent most of his night staring up at the top of the tent canvas. Neither let it be known that the other knew he was awake. For vastly different reasons they struggled with their conscience and moral fortitude. Finally the sea air and rocking of the ship swayed them into slumber. That night there were no dreams of themselves and Meghan walking the golden streets of America.

Aengus rose first, removed his nightshirt, splashed some water on his face and under his arms and then used the nightshirt as a towel. He was buttoning up his pants when James made it known that he was awake.

"Good morning Aengus."

"Yea, good morning… I'll be on deck doing the wash. If you want me to wash your nightshirt, hand it over."

The tone and coldness of the request stabbed James in his not so pure heart. He took off his nightshirt without the slightest joke of the bones of his body showing or manly things. He threw it at Aengus, who caught it without a word. James pulled on his pants.

"So what's the matter? You sound different today."

"You're not serious are you James?"

"That's just it, I don't get you. Last night you hardly spoke a word to me. We didn't even pray together like usual."

James pulled his sweater over his head very carefully so as not to rub the wound. He then took the cloth from the bucket of water and dabbed his head, grimacing as he did so. Usually, it would have been Aengus who did that for him. He looked at the cloth and then at Aengus, who was just standing there watching him. There was blood on the cloth.

"Here, let me have a look."

Dropping the nightshirts, Aengus knelt down behind James.

"Oh Christ, your head is bleeding again. Give me the cloth."

With light dabs he cleaned the wound not saying a word but thinking all the while that James wasn't healing because his heart had turned to cold rigid stone because of his desire for revenge. With each dab James moaned softly but said nothing. The silence was deafening and neither could stand it any longer. Both spoke at once.

"As Jesus is my witness, I can't not talk to ye James."

"Forgive me Aengus if I hurt you."

"Ye didn't hurt me. You disappointed me. I'm the elder brother type here yet I look to you for example. It's just that simple."

Instantly, the lad knew what he meant. Yet he didn't know how to address it. Tears welled up in his eyes. *Thank God Aengus can't see my face,"* he thought as the water overflowed with sea like water streaming down his smooth cheeks touching the corner of his mouth. He sniffled. Aengus realized what was going on. He dropped the rag in the bucket. Crawling from behind James, it was too late for the younger lad to do anything to hide his emotions. Tears silently made their way down those still baby-like cheeks. Aengus choked up, but he had to stand his ground and be truthful to James no matter what.

"Don't look at me that way. I can't stand it. Isn't it enough that I'm acting like a little girl?"

"I can't help it. You're breaking mi heart and there's nothing to be done about it."

Aengus wiped his eyes gruffly with the sleeve of his sweater. James grabbed his nightshirt from the laundry pile and did the same to his eyes until they were red with irritation.

"That won't help you know."

"What won't help?"

Aengus grabbed hold of James' shoulders. His strong but hurting arms took hold and he shook the lad very gently.

"No matter how hard you rub, the sin we are about to commit won't be rubbed off our hearts."

Now James understood what the silent treatment was all about. He comprehended the message sent in that cold tone of voice. He knew that what he proposed to do to Paul had cracked the bond of friendship and brotherly love which existed between them. He placed his hands on each arm holding his shoulders and pushed them off. Aengus was devastated by the act of severing but remained silent. He just leaned back on his legs and looked into the eyes of his closest friend, closer than even his own real brother. James felt that silent agony and tried to address it.

"I need to do this Aengus. Don't you understand that I must do this."

"I don't understand you at all anymore. Why?"

The sin which blackened his soul and destroyed the purity of his heart (or so James thought) was about to be revealed.

"Because…because I was in sin when Paul came upon Meghan and me."

"What! That's not possible for you."

"It is and was that night. We held hands and I became swollen. Then the ship rocked and I fell on her and wanted her to know that I wasn't a boy anymore."

"Good God almighty James, you didn't…I mean you couldn't."

"That's just it, I don't know if I could or couldn't for that's when Paul came and grabbed me. I was still rigid and that's why it hurt so much. Now are you satisfied. I am not Pure of Heart. I am not worthy to be a priest. I am a sinner. Only bringing justice on this bully might cleanse me of my sinfulness."

It was as if the wind had been knocked out of Aengus. He could hardly breathe. He couldn't accept what he just heard. He slumped into a heap, deep in thought. James was now sobbing so loudly that he feared those on deck might hear. From the heap of crushed human a head rose and words came out so softly that his words could hardly be heard by James.

"Ye can't cleanse a sin with another sin."

"I can and I must. Are ye with me or not?" asked James.

"Aye, I shall stand by you." Aengus pushed himself up on his knees, eyes as red as beets burned into James' very soul. "But then I'm done. I go to Boston to fish with people that I can understand."

James wanted to say more. He wanted to embrace Aengus for standing by him. He could not bring himself to do either. So they just knelt facing each other until no more tears could form and their hearts returned to normal patterns of beating. And none too soon for a familiar voice penetrated their wall of silence.

"Lads are ye decent? I've brought you an orange."

"Yes, Father, we're decent," they said in unison. Neither felt that they could ever be decent human beings again after what was to take place later in the day.

The three enjoyed a feast of Father Anthony's oranges once again in virtual silence. Night couldn't come fast enough for the lads. They went through the motion of praying "Vespers" with Father O'Malley. He knew that their hearts weren't in it. Afterwards they excused themselves to go and visit Meghan or so they said. They had, for the first time, lied to one whom they loved as their own flesh and blood "dadai" back in Ireland. But the plan was made and it needed to be followed.

Martin and Lawrence staying true to their word met the lads at the tent and then the four made their way to the livestock hold as planned. At its entrance sat a sailor. It was his job to check on Paul and keep people out of the livestock hold.

"Sir," began Aengus. "Mi little brother would like to visit the sheep below."

"Out of the question, now get out of here."

James began to weep crocodile tears for effect.

"Oh sir, look at the wee lad. His heart is broken. He misses his home. He has no family aboard ship."

"True as can be sir, the sheep remind him of his flock back home," added Martin.

Now Frank Doody the tough skinned sailor was actually Irish. He remembered his days tending his dad's flock at the same tender age which James appeared to be before he went off to sea. He relented and allowed them to pass.

"But no shenanigans, if those beasts get excited ye shall all pay the price."

"Aye sir," Lawrence saluted as he passed Frank.

Down the four climbed with hearts pounding and nerves on edge. Pigs and sheep did their business in their pens and the smell was pungent. They nevertheless couldn't help but to pause to gaze upon the sheep which did remind them of their home. They crept up to the corner of the pen beyond which stood the Brig. It was nothing more than a large cage of metal bars. Paul was just rising from the stool in its center. Behind him was a hammock hanging from the beams of the hull. A shirt hung over one of the metal bars. He was bare-chested thus giving an appearance of a big bear. Mumbling to himself it almost seemed that he was repeating a prayer

419

but the sounds were too crude to be so. The sounds were angry tones.

The four lads stayed behind the corner waiting, for what they hadn't decided as yet.

"How do we get in?" asked Martin.

"Look for keys," directed James. "Someone has to bring him food and empty his waste bucket."

A porthole behind the hammock let in some moonlight which still managed to get through the darkening clouds outside. There was a lantern hanging from the top of the cage but it wasn't lit. Paul stretched then pulled on his chain as he moved toward the hammock. Flipping himself into it he sunk down. The swaying ship rocked the net like bed back and forth as the waves swelled. Rain drops began to fall. The drip-drip sound of water splattering on the deck was audible below.

"There's something shiny hanging across from the cage." Lawrence pointed to a round metal object. It was a key ring.

"Stay here, I'll get them." Aengus crawled along the floor in front of the cage well below Paul's line of vision should he turn toward them.

Kneeling directly under the key ring he reached up to grab it. Paul snorted. Aengus quickly retracted his hand and waited. The other three held their breath. All became still save for the occasional bleat of a sheep. In a flash the keys were in his hand. The others scooted across the floor to him. He placed the key in the lock on the gate to the cage and paused to look at James. The hope burning within him was that the lad would come to his senses and abandon this act of revenge and cruelty. Instead James took hold of Aengus' hand and turned the key in the lock. It clicked and fell open. The four crawled into the cage. Martin and Lawrence went under the hammock. They signaled that they were ready using a thumbs-up gesture. Aengus took the loose chain and began to tighten up on it. James took the shirt off the metal bar and nodded ready.

Martin and Lawrence pounced on Paul while Aengus pulled on the chain and pulled it so roughly that Paul had no flexibility either at his feet or his arms. James wrapped the shirt around his mouth to gag him. Paul though groggy from slipping into sleep came to with the strength to knock Martin and Lawrence to the ground. But they didn't let go of his arms. The two were of a good size so as to give the hulk of a sailor competition. The restriction of the chain by Aengus gave his leg no movement at all. In one sweeping motion they dragged Paul to the stool. Aengus then wrapped the chain around his neck. James stood in front of him, his hands were on his hips but there was no rotation, his still reddened eyes met those of Paul. His large hazel eyes peeked above the gag glaring at the lad.

"Will you stop the struggling? I want to talk with you." James spoke boldly.

Paul's response was to lunge forward but Aengus held that chain tightly causing the seaman to gasp for air. He tried to pull his arms in and dislodge Martin and Lawrence from their hold on them. The young men responded by untying the rope on their pants. They tied the rope to each of Paul's wrists and stretched out the rope held arm tying the other end to a metal bar. James gulped hard as the image of Christ on the cross came to mind.

"Now will you allow me to speak to you?"

The seaman had little recourse. He nodded yes.

"Then we have an understanding. Aengus remove the chain from his neck."

The chain clanked as it was lowered to the straw strewn cage floor. The hazel eyes still bulged out above the gag in his mouth. Through them he took in every feature of his captors so as to find them when he was freed.

"Now if you remain calm, I shall remove the gag."

Paul nodded. Martin and Lawrence checked the ropes to insure that they couldn't be loosened. James untied the shirt gag and tossed it aside.

"You little asshole, when I get out of here you'll pay for this."

"Tell me Paul, are you an honorable man?"

The seaman was not alone in looking at James as if he was a nut case.

"Well are you?"

"More than papist scum like you could ever hope to be, that's for sure."

"Excellent, then may I speak to you as one human being to another?"

"Get it over with, so that I might get to mi bed. Where's the whip?"

James smiled and looked about the cage and at each of the lads with him. "There is no whip."

"Then what the hell do you want of me?" Paul's mind flashed to his own threats against both Aengus and James. He shuddered with fear of being violated.

"I want your understanding and just maybe your forgiveness." James was quite sincere.

"You are mad. Get this boy to an asylum you pea brains."

The three lads stood like statues in a church. Two couldn't believe what they just heard, but one could. His eyes lighted up with renewed admiration for his "little brother." He smiled that kind of grin that all would be well to his partners in crime and then to Paul.

"Paul just listen to him. Just listen," Aengus requested.

"Go on then, say your piece."

James sat on the floor. The ordeal was weakening him but he would not relent and give up. "First let me say that I am sorry for having to sneak up on you in the dead of night. It's the only way I could get in here. You see, I've never been beaten before. Nor have I ever met someone who hated another because of one's faith with such sincerity as you. I

423

had to do this for I knew that at a Court Martial, emotions would run high and anger would fill the room."

"Aye and mi pecker would go right up your arse too."

"Vividly put and trust me when I say that the thought struck me, didn't it Aegnus? But such threats are not why I'm here. I don't want you court marshalled or even to stay in this cage. I want you as I said before to forgive me for giving you the reason to act as you did. I am as you say attracted to that girl I was with but not in the way you thought. True I was swollen but it just happened I didn't mean to be that way, the way you threatened to use on me and my best friend here. I am in sin, yes, but not of the kind you thought. I didn't want to hurt anyone, but I had to save that girl. You can understand that can't you?"

Such outpouring of one's feelings was an experience this sailor never had. No one had ever just sat down to talk with him and pour out his heartfelt feelings. No one treated him as an equal. Paul couldn't grasp all that was happening. He didn't trust it and lashed out as the other lads took a stance to protect James.

"Then I was right. You are a pervert."

"No, I'm just a sinner as we all are in our imperfect lives."

This not only began to touch the seemingly heartless sailor but also those who stood with James. Paul asked what Martin and Lawrence thought.

"How old are you?"

"Fourteen," James quietly answered.

"You just don't sound like a young lad."

"Thank you, I'm trying to adjust and be a grown-up, but it's awfully hard to do."

The big bear of a man began to soften to James and even toward the others. Not that they would ever be true friends. But just maybe an understanding might be achieved. James saw the change in Paul's eyes and in his threatening posture, so he asked again for forgiveness.

"I am truly sorry that what I did created a situation which provoked you to act as you did. I also hope that the friend I love above all others will come to forgive you as well."

The tension of the moment tugged at everyone's heart. Martin and Lawrence began to understand what was going on. Aengus would not let himself become emotional in front of them or Paul. He did, however, step forward and placed his arm around the now shaking James.

"I stand with mi friend. I forgive you. Will you take pity on me and do likewise?"

A wave of reconciliation flooded the cage as Martin and Lawrence then stepped forward. They asked for forgiveness for being drunk the night before which caused all present grief. Then they spoke to Paul directly.

"And to you, sir…we beg forgiveness for having to tie you up."

Topside a sudden flurry of activity had erupted when Meghan came to steerage with her Aunt and Uncle seeking out Father O'Malley. She knew in her bones that James had lied to her about his duties. She just didn't know what it was about. What she did know was that he had to be found before something more dreadful happened and he got himself really hurt. Instinctively she knew that he was out to protect her again.

The four of them were now searching the ship. When they came upon the sailor guarding the livestock hold entrance, they questioned him. They were told that four lads had requested to visit the sheep. The priest knew that it was indeed an animal which they wished to visit, but of the human kind.

"We need to get down there and quickly. These lads are in trouble."

"I knew they were up to no good. Go ahead in. I'll get the First Mate. Ladies, you will have to stay topside I'm afraid."

Reluctantly, Maggie and Meghan agreed.

When Father O'Malley and Colin approached the cage with its open door they couldn't believe their eyes. James and Aengus were kneeling before the sailor with locked arms as did Martin and Lawrence. Paul sat on a stool. Tears rolled down his bearded cheeks.

"I forgive ye, I forgive ye. Can you forgive me?" The giant of a man blubbered unashamedly.

"Aye," said Aengus as he tightened his grip on his best friend.

"I do forgive you Paul." An emotional James spoke with conviction in his voice.

The four lads rose as the men outside the cage watched in awe.

"Untie his arms," ordered James.

Martin and Lawrence did so immediately. His arms dropped to his side. All Paul had to do now was reach out and grab hold of them and thrash them with his chain. Instead he knelt in front of them and all five prayed the Lord's Prayer while Colin and Father O'Malley fell to their knees to do likewise.

"And forgive us our trespasses as we forgive those who trespass against us…" they prayed and never had those words meant so much to those who uttered them than on that night when the rain began to fall and the ship was cleansed, the water barrels filled and the hearts of four lads and three men were filled with the Lord's grace.

Meghan and Aunt Maggie paced back and forth waiting to hear something from below, a scream even a yell…something. The rain was coming down steadily now and they were soaked. That flaming red hair which took wind like a sail sagged in ringlets of dullness as Meghan pulled her shawl over her head. Maggie's bonnet was but a limp mass of linen and straw. They stood at the entrance to the "livestock hold" watching. James emerged first. They screamed for joy and both hugged him. He was followed by

427

Aengus and another round of hugs ensued and so it went for each of the lads and men who came back onto the deck.

Back in the cell Paul sat on the stool. The lads had to lock the cage door. But he understood that they had no authority to free him. Aengus and James would go to the Captain to explain the events of that night when things got out of control.

The rain had kept all but the crew below deck. The First Mate came running to the group with Frank behind him. He was assured that all was well and that the sheep were just fine.

"However," added Father O'Malley. "We would like to visit with the Captain tomorrow."

The little procession moved on. Only the rain pitter pattering on the wooden deck broke their joyous silence. There would be many questions which would need to be answered but that night none would be asked. All returned to their quarters giving a wave and a smile when they went their separate ways.

As all settled in the lass returned to her dreams of America and the lads would join her once again in those dreams. Before that embarkation however James and Aengus had to renew a friendship and a brotherly bond. Drops of rain made their way through a tiny hole in the canvas above them in the tent. Both saw this as a sign of being washed clean of their sins. They held out their hands until water collected in their palms. Then taking the water they traced the sign of the cross on each other's forehead.

Nightshirts back on, they crawled under the blankets exhausted yet renewed. Aengus had one final request.

"Next time little brother, place your trust in me and tell me the truth of your plans."

"I promise big brother, to do that no matter where we are in life."

Totally exhausted they rolled over so that once again they might meet Meghan on the golden streets of their dream-world America.

Chapter Fifteen: Seafarer Lads

It was another week before the pleas of all four lads finally moved the Captain to release Paul and place him back on the crew. His position was that he still did bodily harm to young people and that required punishment. It was the day of his release and the 15th day of sailing. James and Aengus were excited to be the first to greet Paul as he was freed. However Martin and Lawrence wanted to go as well, so the joyful group grew to four.

It was early morning and the seas were a bit choppy but otherwise the weather was fine, even warm. The four lads made their way to the livestock hold. Frank was on duty again and waved them in with a smile.

"Picking up the big bloke are ye?"

"Right you are Frank," began Aengus.

"We wanted to be the first to greet him," added James.

This time they were not quiet and when they passed the sheep pen they stopped and talked to them as if they knew them personally. Laughing that the sheep seemed to talk back to them they turned the corner of the pen and stood in front of the cage. Paul was standing totally nude and pouring a bucket of water over himself. The lads couldn't speak. He not only had the appearance of a bear but perhaps that of a stallion would be best to describe what they saw.

"Ahh…I think I'm quite glad that he's on our side now," James gulped out.

"Mi arse hurts just looking at him." A red faced Aengus then rubbed his posterior.

As for Martin and Lawrence, they didn't understand the references being made by the others but they certainly were impressed by this giant of a man. Just as they held their mouths as well as a gasping laugh, Paul noticed them and called out to them.

"Ahoy lads, is it really the time already?"

The sailor wasn't a bit inhibited nor embarrassed that virtual strangers were seeing him in his all togetherness. He just kept on chatting about being a free man once again and how it was all due to the lads' words to the Captain. It wasn't until the lads couldn't hold in their giggles any longer that he realized what had attracted such attention.

"So what's the surprise? I told you that I was quite the man.' Then Paul laughed heartily and took his pants from a metal bar and pulled them up. "There, now we can talk. One day maybe you'll be as mature as me."

"I…I don't think so sir, I'm already twenty-four and well…it's just not to be," noted Martin.

With his pants on Paul wasn't quite as intimidating to their maturation as men. Well at least to Aengus and James who were still teens and with proper food would fill out. As for the other issue, well that would be left to nature and genetics; both of which none of the lads had much knowledge.

In short order the lock was removed and Paul, clean shaven and hair cut quite short stepped out of the cage. He just stood there and looked each lad in the eye. Without the slightest hint his arms opened and in one sweeping motion gathered all four to form a group hug. With everyone virtually in his face he made a request.

"I need to see that girl of yours James. Would she meet with me?" Paul released his arms and the lads fell out staggering into the crates behind them.

James didn't know what to say. It wasn't that he would refuse to ask her, indeed he certainly would. It's how Paul presented the question, calling Meghan his girl. It never occurred to him that people would think that. They were just friends and now Aengus was part of that friendship. His mouth dropped open and the other lads looked at him and winked. Aengus gave him a light jab in the ribs urging him to say something. James couldn't speak. All these last three years it was all about the faith, then about his becoming a priest. *How can I get involved with a lass now?* He thought.

He began to think quickly of the road which led him to this ship and what he would find in America. *"Maybe God is testing me? That's it. I'm sure of it."* As these thoughts filled his head, he relaxed. Confidence rose within him again. He knew what he was called to do and do it he would, come any obstacle or test. He was able to put that confidence in words unrelated to the real issue of his vocation.

"I will be pleased to ask Meghan to meet with you. And I'll do it this very day."

Paul shook his hand vigorously and the lads clapped him on that boney back of his.

Emerging from the hold and walking toward the bow of the ship was suddenly a new experience for Paul. He had walked the deck thousands of times but on this day of freedom he did so with no malice in his heart, no hatred for the Irish, no need to put down the Catholic faith. Dozens of passengers watched the procession-like movement. There were few who didn't know at least one or two of the lads and certainly the seaman who herded them into steerage.

On the bow deck Meghan and Aunt Maggie were doing the wash. Only this time it belonged to them. Colin had just handed Maggie his undergarments with a grin. His beard covered most of his blushing cheeks. The chatter which came from some of the passengers caught their attention.

"Aunty, look there, it's James and Aengus and those drunken boys…and that sailor."

Meghan was well aware of how the lads went to the Captain to seek freedom for Paul. She however never expected that she would ever have to see him again.

"Aunty, I don't think I can get close to that man. Tell James that I'm sick or something."

"Now my dear child, they can see you as well as you can see them. Do you want me to lie for you?"

433

She looked to her new Uncle. He took a position to stand between her and the lads and sailor. "Perhaps we should see why the lads have brought him here."

Meghan took a step in front of her Uncle. She untied strings at her waist and let the apron covering her skirt fall to the deck. In her heart there had been no reconciliation, no miracle of truth which brought down barriers of prejudice and hatred. And certainly there was no cleansing of her soul as James and Aengus experienced and shared in their story of that night of forgiveness.

Colin picked up the apron and Maggie gathered the wash in her arms as the lads and Paul reached the steps leading up to the bow deck.

"Hi Meghan," all the lads called out in unison.

"Good Morning to ye." She curtsied. It would be a formal encounter as far as she was concerned.

James raised his foot, grabbed hold of the railing and lifted himself very carefully up to the first step. He knew how difficult this was for her. He could see it on her face. The lines on her forehead, the crinkled eyes, and the taut lips all spoke of apprehension and controlled emotions.

"Meghan O'Grady may I present to you Paul Noon."

Meghan stood without emotion and said nothing but did crack a smile and curtsied again. Aunt Maggie desperately wanted to say something but felt that it wasn't her decision to speak to the seaman if her niece wouldn't. Other passengers milling about the deck area paused to watch the scene unfold. Still no one moved or said anything. The ship then rose up on a good sized swell and crashed down. As if the ship said, "get a move on," Paul skipped up two steps toward Meghan. The lads thought to grab hold of him, James reached out in fact to pull on his shirt but thought better of it.

Paul then fell to his knees on the third step and eloquently offered his plea.

"Miss O'Grady, I beg your forgiveness before all present here. I don't deserve it that is well known. Your James has taught me to open my heart. Aengus has helped me to take a leap of faith with others who don't believe as I do. Those two have given me an example as to why I should give up the rum. And I have, I really have. Jesus said, 'Father forgive them for they know not what they do.' You might say that I didn't know what I was doing because of the rum. But I'm not here to hide behind the drinking of the rum. I knew full well what I was doing. I wanted to see what I thought I saw. I wanted to hurt the lads and even you. I don't know if Jesus will forgive me but I hope that you will. I shall protect you always while you're on this ship and the lads too. That's all I can promise."

A heart melted that morning in a lass who swore never to forgive the brute that threatened her and injured James and Aengus. She moved toward Paul. Sweat beaded on his forehead. His hands were folded as if in prayer and trembled as the little lass moved and took one step down. She stood just above his elevated clasped hands. She took his hands into her own as if in a scene of a drama on stage. Indeed she had an audience but was unaware of their presence.

"If our Lord can forgive from the cross and my friends with bleeding heads could forgive how can I not also forgive? I do forgive you and will pray each day for you."

For only a second time in his time at sea, the burly seaman shed tears. Only the appearance of Father O'Malley, who had been seeking them out, broke the spell.

"There you all are. I have brought oranges to salute our new friend. Perhaps Mrs. Logan, a bit of tea would be possible. The Captain sends his compliments and this tin of tea."

The "Cushla Machree" seemed to support the celebration as she bounced up and down over the swells and made her way to what all there thought to be the new "promised land."

Their day ended when all joined Father O'Malley to pray "Vespers." In a week's time two lads had indeed become men of mercy, two young men began to reflect their maturity responsibly and the lass began to understand the power of forgiveness and the Scripture passage which says, "Love one another as I have loved you."

That night Meghan lay on her bunk thinking of that boy with the cookie. *'Her James' that's what Paul had said,* she thought. *What did he mean by such talk? Didn't he know that James was called to serve God as a Priest?*

She turned onto her stomach and rested her head on her arms. Her dream that night would not be of America but of a certain lad who told her that he had no intention of being a priest. She was thrilled with the news heard in her dreams.

As for the one particular lad at the center of Meghan's dream, he sat on the floor of the deck at mid-ship as did his bosom buddy Aengus. Both sat crossed legged in their nightshirts which in itself was a sacrilege for the fisherman. It was however quite a warm day for these lads who came from a land of coolness, dampness and lush green. And it was their last night in the tent. The doctor had given the all clear to James and its function was no longer needed and was ordered to be dismantled. On the lap of James rested his now famous Journal which Martin and Lawrence had learned about and now wanted to be featured in it.

"I thought you'd never be caught dead like this on ship and here we sit well into a week of the wearing of this drafty thing," observed James.

"It's hot and besides, if you don't get yourself into another scrap with another sailor, no one will ever see us."

They laughed as Aengus tugged on his nightshirt to create wind and cool himself. Getting onto his knees he looked upside down onto the Journal page. It was blank.

"So tell me James, what shall be the start of your story?"

"I don't know, so much happened so as to make this entry quite a long one."

James picked up the pen and dipped it into the ink bottle. Aengus held the lantern over the Journal to give good light. James began to write.

Day 15: August 12, 1849

Our day began with the release of the seaman who had beaten us. It was a happy day for him and for us who pleaded with the Captain to free him.

"What the hell are you writing James?"

"I'm writing a summary of course."

"Are you crazy? After all that happened today this is all you can say. What about the funny part?"

"There was no funny part. First we felt like we had no you know what when we saw Paul and then we stood there like dead fish and stared at him on top of it all. The high point was when Meghan forgave him and we all ended up crying like the girls he thinks we were in the first place."

"Shit...is that how you saw today?"

"Well how did you see it?"

Aengus lay flat and placed his hands behind his head and said nothing for the longest time. Just as the silence became unbearable he bolted upright.

"Let me see, how's this sound? The four lads made their way to the livestock pen and greeted the sheep on the way to free the seaman who beat them to a bloody pulp over a week ago. When they came to the cage there stood Paul naked as a jay bird pouring water over himself and washing. The youngest lad felt that he looked more like a stallion than a bear as his best friend thought. In any case none of the four had what Paul has and that made them feel unmanly. Only Paul thought we had potential to be men…"

Aengus stopped speaking. He looked at James with his gapping mouth so widely open that his tongue fell out like a puppy dog.

"That was…I don't know the words to explain it. I think my dadai would call it sex."

"Saints preserve us, I hope not. We're all lads. My da would say that the words were sexual in nature."

"SEXUAL?" James questioned.

"Yeah, it means when something is said that makes someone think of sex."

"I still don't get it Aengus."

"Me either, but maybe Martin or Lawrence would know."

"Or Paul, he seems to know all about sex."

"Yeah with lads…I don't think we should ask him. It may bring up that night again."

They agreed to drop the whole topic for now and when confessing they would ask Father O'Malley who would then guide them and not be able to repeat to anyone what they had said. It was a good plan.

"Good, now tell me every word you said so that I can write it down."

And so the two filled in that blank page with laughter, joy, redemption and forgiveness and something which James remembered and added.

This day Paul called Meghan my girl and he told Meghan that I was her lad. I don't know what he meant, neither does Aengus but he won't admit it. I hope it means that she will be my girl-friend just like Aengus is my boy-friend. The three of us will always be the best of friends.

On that page the Purity of Heart which both now sought was seen in the indigo ink which illuminated their sincerity, innocence and loyalty.

It was done. The two knelt on the blanket and said their prayers, this time offering them for Paul.

Besides their return to the bunk in steerage the next several days saw the lads collaborating on the Journal at the end of each day. Aengus always saw the humor in a given situation and James the qualities of a person and the significance of the event.

Then on the 20th day of the voyage there occurred an experience for the lads, which was both hair raising and exhilarating at the same time. That day began with Father O'Malley addressing the increasing number of cases of fever illness being exhibited by many in steerage. All but he and the lads had straw in their bunk. The only reason they were an exception was due to the quick thinking of Father Francis back in Galway who took a mattress from the Friary at the last minute All others were sleeping on the same straw which had been placed on the bunks on day one.

The priest called for a steerage meeting and addressed the growing issue of sickness and filth in the straw not to mention the bugs. By the end of the meeting Martin, Lawrence, Aengus and James were hauling out bales of straw to the burn barrels. The days left for the voyage might be somewhat less comfortable but far safer.

The final bundle was turning to ash when Paul climbed down from the tallest mast under which the four lads stood. Watching him lower himself on the ropes and jumping to the deck left them in boyish awe though in their early twenties were Martin and Lawrence. The seaman greeted them with a clap of his hand on their backs.

"Up there the wind is like the breath of God. Would ye like to feel God's own wind?"

The two who once would do anything if they had the promise of rum as a reward were horrified at the thought. But there was one among the four who was not.

"Paul, show me how to climb and trim the sail."

Aengus glowed with excitement. James could feel the burning desire to be next to God within his friend. It became contagious.

"Me too, I can do it."

Paul took James in his arms as he had done on that awful night only this time it was with gentle hands and concern for his well-being.

"Lad, see how easily I can lift you without the slightest loss of breath. The winds would toss you into the sea once you were up there."

James pleaded. He wanted to be a man. He wanted to prove to himself that though slight in build he could be as brave and confident as men as big as Paul. The bond between him and Aengus had become a lifeline during those days in that tent together. Each began to feel the hurt or joy the other felt even if unexpressed. So it was at that moment. Aengus knew that James had to prove himself.

"Paul, I'll tie James to me. If James slips, I would be able to pull him back to safety. Besides he's a strong lad, he's the hero of Inishbofin who saved my life and that of my father and brothers."

The seaman was duly impressed though still skeptical of any success. There was a time that he wasn't big. It was when he was just a cabin boy on a ship. He too had to prove himself amongst grown men. This day he would help the two lads to do so as well without losing their honor. It was the loss of that honor which had made him the bully he was as he matured, for that became the way he could conceal his shame. What he was about to agree to was his attempt to redeem himself.

"Aye, I'll go for it. Take this rope and tie it about your waist. I'll tie this end to mine until we get mid-mast. After we trim the lower sail I will have to untie my end so that I can go on to the topsail and trim it. I'll come right back to you afterwards. Do nothing unless I do it first. Once balanced atop the sail hang on side by side."

"Aye sir," answered James.

"Lead on," bellowed Aengus.

The climb began as the ship rose up and down over the swells of the sea in August, a sea which was warming. Paul did lead the way, shouting orders with each hand over hand pull up the mast's climbing rope. Neither lad would look down; that was a good thing. They just followed as sheep to the shepherd. The wind whipped through their shirts creating a mini sail of sorts. This day they wore no long-johns, it was too hot. But up on the mast and easing over the sail which billowed out beneath their feet they had wished they were on. James was like a sparrow in a wind storm fighting to stay aloft. Aengus wrapped his arm around him but in a way so as not to embarrass him but to ask for his help so that he might not fall. Paul was within an arm's length away when he ordered them to pull up the sail.

Hand over hand the lads pulled on the ropes which controlled the level of the sail from full open to completely trimmed (rolled up). It was no easy task. The muscles in their arms ached but they kept pulling. The sail was a bit lopsided with Paul's section far up and the lads only half-way up. That unevenness was to challenge them as Paul climbed around them to even out the sail. Giving them a nod of encouragement, the three managed to even out most of the sail. Paul then went on to the mast and up to the topsail. While busily trimming the smaller topsail, a gust of wind caught an exposed bit of sail canvas. It blew with such force that Aengus lost his footing and hold of James. With a scream he slipped and rolled off the boom. He was dangling face down, held by the rope at his waist. James yelled to him to be calm, he would pull on the rope and get him back up.

His thin arms worked so hard to pull on the rope which held the now violently swaying 150 lb. 5'8" lad. With each pull up there began to develop a series of two slips down as James continued shouting that he'd get him back up as he held onto the rope which was tied to each of them. Paul struggled to finish the trimming of the top sail so that he could get to the struggling lads.

Aengus was shouting up to James but only so that he could hear him over the screams of the passengers below. "Untie the rope. There's no sense for both of us to fall."

"Never," James screamed back. Then he did the impossible. He grabbed hold of the bottom of the top sail which he told Paul not to pull up. Swinging himself out over the beam holding up the lower sail, he dropped his hold. His intent was to swing around the rig thus preventing Aengus or he from falling. For a brief moment he became like a bird in flight, able to glide over the main mast sail. The wind however turned nasty and did not cooperate. Its force came over him and forced the lad downward and then upward again.

"O God, O God…no, no," screamed out James.

Splat, the two bodies collided chest to chest, belly to belly.

They both let out a blood curdling scream which was echoed by the passengers below as James impacted Aengus' body. Among those watching was Father O'Malley who had gone topside from caring for sick passengers to seek the lads' help. He at first was upset when he came to mid-ship finding Martin and Lawrence cheering their climb up the mid-ship mast, which was the tallest of the three masts.

"And you two mature men never thought to advise the lads against such a folly as this?"

There was no rational explanation which could explain how they saw themselves as being too afraid to do such a thing while the two teens they allowed to do exactly what they could not. So they fell to their knees and beat their breasts repeating over and over, "Mea culpa, mea culpa" (through my fault).

The priest had no time to react as emotions quickly changed to that of concern and even horror as the lads followed Paul onto the beam which held the lower sail. Soon he had his Rosary out, for he felt helpless to do anything else. His rapidly pounding heart gave evidence to his concern that he might lose the lads before they even got to America. He stooped down to the distressed young men.

"There, there, all we can do now is pray that somehow Paul or another crew member might reach them."

On the bow of the ship a few passengers were watching a group of ominous dark clouds approach. The crashing waves and howling winds made the screams of both the lads and that of the mid-ship passengers watching the dangling boys impossible to hear as sounds of fear. Among those watching the clouds were Maggie, Colin and Meghan.

"And where might be that lad whose attention you are actually seeking?"

Meghan tried but failed to remain focused on the storm clouds. She just had to grin.

445

"Aunt Maggie, I have no idea what you're saying, ah...he's probably busy praying or something like that with Father O'Malley."

"No doubt child, no doubt," added Colin.

The three then locked arms and held firm as the wind swept over the bow and into their faces.

When the collision took place the lads instinctively grabbed hold of each other. Aengus wrapped his arms around James who did likewise around his friend. The younger lad being around 5'4" and maybe ninety pounds could barely get his arms around Aengus. When he finally did, both were out of breath and just dangled horizontally some forty feet above the deck. They looked down and saw Father O'Malley kneeling with Martin and Lawrence.

"Jesus, help us... I think Father thinks we're goners."

Aengus being face down on James clearly saw the deck below. James had to turn his head to catch any view of it at all.

Their eyes met only inches apart. Fear was evident in both of them.

"I'm so sorry Aengus. I thought that I could do a loop around the boom."

James grew silent as he looked up at the boom from which they hung.

"Well at least we won't slip. The rope lines on me and on you are twisted."

Aengus gave the lad a squeeze. "Indeed, it wasn't a complete failure."

"No, Paul was right. I should never have come up here. I'm just a lightweight not fit for climbing masts."

"James Shields, ye are braver than I ever was. You tried to save me."

"But here we hang. We may not be able to fall but what happens if these ropes loosen and Paul doesn't get here in time?"

Neither wanted to think about that prospect, especially then, as their swaying had become more pronounced. Each swing back and forth brought a gasp from those below at mid-ship. Crew members were scurrying to get their sail trims done for they could clearly see the lads dangling from the main mast. Paul had finished the top sail and was moving to the mast for the downward climb to the mid-sail boom.

Despite their bravado, the lads were getting more and more anxious as the ropes were now grinding into their now torn shirts and into their skin. Almost simultaneously they began to talk of anything except the pain around their waists from the ropes.

"So do you think Father will be angry with us?"

"I can't say James but even from up here he doesn't look pleased."

The idle chatter wasn't working. Both felt each other trembling. So Aengus did what he always did to deflect a grave situation and that was try to create a diversion.

"I have to pee."

The Inishbofin lad took him to be quite serious.

"Don't you dare do such a thing in front of all those people down there, not to mention that I am under you."

"Well do tell, don't want to get a bit damp lad?" Aengus crossed his ankles.
"There, I've cut it off."

"You're an idiot O'Flaherty. We're about to die up here."

"But you love me anyway, right?"

 James was exasperated. "We're still 'brothers' but shouldn't we pray and prepare to meet our maker?"

"Stop it. We're going to get out of this. Now think. You're the smart one hanging around here."

Their swaying continued and dizziness was their next fear. Paul was on the mid-boom; James could see him and the twisted rope as well. Their hold on each other became tighter each time a gust of wind pummeled them. Shouts from below were reaching their ears. They were cheers as Paul made his way on the boom. To and fro they swayed to the accompaniment of the gasps and cheers from below. Even Father O'Malley was shouting words of encouragement as he paused after each decade of the

Rosary. It was just after such words that James came up with a plan.

"Aengus, do you think we can give ourselves a twirl when the next gust of wind hits us?"

"You mean opposite to the twist in the rope, right?"

"For a fisherman, you are quite the clever one, eh?"

A smirk crossed the face of Aengus as he winked.

"You know that's what I mean. It will separate us to hang on two separate lines of rope. And that's important, right?"

Now it was James' turn to smirk.

"Quite, for then I shall climb up your rope line."

What the lad went on to explain was why it had to be the rope section from which Aengus hung and not his. Going up that line would enable him to climb over the boom from the opposite side from which his rope section hung thus in effect keeping the rope securely tightened on the boom and less likely to slip to one end or the other as the winds increased. At the same time it was pointed out that James' weight would once again present a problem for he could be blown off the rope causing Aengus' weight to pull the lad up and over the boom in the wrong direction. Both would then plunge to the deck below.

"So you say fisherman. But I say that my weight will allow me to climb that rope quickly as I did those rocky walls on the fortress ruins on Inishbofin."

"No, I can't let you do it. It's too dangerous. Father O'Malley will skin me alive if anything happened to you."

Both fell silent for a moment thinking of the priest's hopes for both of them. Onto the face of the younger lad drops of water gently fell. They were not rain drops as yet for the lightning and storm clouds were still off the bow some miles away.

"And he'll have neither of us if I don't do this. So will you twirl with me."

Aengus sniffed loudly not caring that James knew he had gotten emotional. Then he gave one of his famous seductive looks with raised eyebrows and crooked grin.

"I'd twirl with you anytime." They both gave the other a squeeze of encouragement and laughed.

On the next bounce of the ship as the bow hit back down onto the sea they would give it a try.

On the bow Meghan was no longer looking at the black clouds coming closer. Despite the fireworks display of lightning bolts she had finally heard from passengers running back to the bow that two lads were suspended from the sail rigging by ropes tied to them and that one of them was climbing up the rope. The lass gave out a scream of horror. Her Aunt and Uncle ran after her as she bolted down the stairs and plowed through the crowds of people now fearful to be below deck and curious as to what those lads were up to. Before she saw the lads above her, she ran into Father O'Malley with Martin and Lawrence at his side. One

450

look at their reddened eyes and she knew the lads being talked about were her boy with the cookie and his crazy fisherman friend.

"Oh my God, Father…it is them then?"

The priest took the lass into his arms, turned her and pointed upwards. She grew limp but refused to fall into a faint. Colin and Maggie watched with hearts breaking as she grew white with fear and without a sound wept.

The lads were now twirling counter-clockwise so as to untwist their lines of rope. So strong were the winds that they were virtually parallel to the boom to which James had to climb. They held onto each other, the ropes grinding into their skin. Blood now stained their shirts. But they twirled and as the wind gusts eased up they swung down still lucid though dizzy. Their rope lines were now separated as they hung as one unit All was quiet, neither wind nor screams of passengers could be heard.

"Now on the next uplift on the swell push me away from you. But keep hold of my hands."

The ship rose on a hefty swell and crashed down. The jolt gave force to their push against one another to release their embrace and slide into a hand hold. Their legs swung out away from each other but the lack of strong winds for that moment allowed them to return to a vertical position which James needed so that he could begin his climb. The bouncing of the ship and the intermittent winds were having its effect on James. His hold began to slip. Aengus in a quick move grabbed hold of his wrists.

"Don't you dare let go of me. We've done it."

Indeed they had to the now cheering crowds below, though in truth they had no idea why they were cheering other than for the fact that the lads survived whatever they were doing. Meghan, nestled in the priest's arms made no sound whatsoever. James appeared to be non-responsive hanging up above her. But he was now in deep thought.

"Oh God help us," called out Aengus. "You're all right now, eh James?"

Both were fearful and could have easily let themselves become paralyzed with that fear. They kept their focus on each other now. Not even a glance was given below. What they didn't need now was to get dizzier and more off balance. The ropes were taut with them acting as weights at each end. How long could that hold being that one of the weights did not equal that of the other could only be guessed. Action had to be taken quickly.

"Holy Mother of God, look upon us with favor," prayed James as he looked into his friend's eyes and saw panic growing in them.

That panic was not for himself however but for James as they now had to implement the next step of the plan. They were breathing quite heavily now yet trying to calm themselves. They began a mantra of prayer like petitions as St. Patrick had done in the hymn sung in the ruins of St. Colman's on Inishbofin.

"Christ be with us, Christ be near us, Christ…"

"Oh, Christ save us," Aengus blurted out ending their prayer. "What do you think you're going to do now?"

Though only an arms-length away from each other James had to shout as the winds were picking up again and thunder could now be heard in the distance.

"If I tell you, you'll panic for sure. Just trust me."

Aengus had not gone through storm and rescue on Inishbofin when James saved his father, he and his brothers and their vessel without being able to place his trust in a lad three years his junior.

"Well I do, you know that I do. But you'll have to trust me too so that I can be of help to ye."

The wind began to pick up again as James nodded and asked Aengus to pull him back to him slowly. His was the anchor to this plan he told the older lad. He being the featherweight would use his anchor as a stabilizer for what he intended to do. Inch by inch their vertical bodies came closer. There were flashes of misgivings but there was also commitment to what was to be done. With one final tug the two were as one again, flush against one another but with the ropes at their waists still separated. Once again the fisherman tried to lighten up the situation. Making a fish mouth he began to pucker up seeking to plant a kiss on the lad who was literally in his face.

"You ass, stop it. I need to focus."

"Focus on what? We're back how we started."

"Not quite, we're hanging separately now." James barely got the response out as he was losing his breath.

The humor which Aengus attempted now waned. James saw Aengus beginning to get too petrified and that would spell failure before the next step even started. So he did what the older lad usually did, which was not in his nature at all. He was however a quick learner and went into action.

"Now big boy, let me go just a little, like before you bring in a lass for a kiss."

The eyes glowed, a smirk came forth and the fish lips pucker began anew. Now all of what he was doing was for effect. It was truly unknown if Aengus ever was with a lass long enough to hold hands let alone plant a kiss on her.

"Good, now just relax. I'm going to climb up on you."

"Huh, that's a bit too much mate even for me. I'm not Paul."

"Hush your mouth Aengus O'Flaherty. I need to get on your shoulders and then shimmy up the rope to the rig's boom."

Both looked up to the trimmed sail and the rigging which held it up. Paul was now making his way from the mast placing his feet in the straps holding the sail in place.

"Paul should be at the rope when I get up. So don't worry. He'll pull me up."

"No way James, you've lost your senses. If you slip God knows what would happen to ye."

"And if I don't do this, those storm clouds and what they contain will be upon us and then what?"

Aengus smiled one of those beguiling kinds which he thought would be seductive even though he had no clue what the word would mean.

"Make your move mate," Aengus winked. "And watch where you step."

"Aye, aye…" And with that James wrapped his legs around Aengus and began to scoot up. When he got to his shoulders, his crotch was right in the fisherman's face. Aengus just had to make a crude comment about the lad's man parts.

"Oh big boy, will Father O'Malley have words for you in Confession this day."

"And for you as well for lusting over mi manliness."

The laughter which resulted from the exchange could be heard on the deck. Father O'Malley just shook his head and giving thanks that Meghan was too innocent to understand what two lads in puberty were laughing about. It was that bond of becoming a man which they could make light of for in their hearts they knew that they may never see that day when they would be truly called men.

"Ah ha, then you shun me, do ye?"

Perilously perched in a most awkward position, the humorous exchange gave James just enough time to rest before his attempt to stand on Aengus' shoulders and grabbing hold of his rope line. Using his friend's head as a rock like surface James push himself up, then kneeled on his shoulders.

"Mi heart will only be yours if this works. So here goes."

Aengus placed his hands under James' bum and pushed while at the same time James pulled himself up on his own rope to a standing position. Then he let go of his rope and leaned forward to grab the rope line which held Aengus. For a brief moment he was free standing and open to the whim of the winds.

To say that those who watched below were holding their tongues so as not to cause a distraction would be an understatement. Martin and Lawrence were now locked arm in arm with Father O'Malley, Meghan and her Aunt and Uncle. It was as if their silent prayer had more strength when joined one to the other. For it was a little miracle they all sought for the lads.

Who would have thought that the miracle they sought would come from the very one who had once been the cause of their pain. Paul now hung over the boom but from the side not facing the rope line from which James was attached as it now was quite loose not having any weight on it. He held onto the top of the rope holding Aengus to insure that it didn't slip. James made his way up hand over hand he pulled himself. His feet and legs, wrapped around the rope, worked in sequence with each of his pulls. The loose rope was now grabbed by Paul as well. He slipped the loose part through one of the sail straps and fastened it as a back-up should his grip on Aengus' rope slip. With his own feet now wedged into the sail strap he leaned over as far as he could. His huge hands reached out from those cannon like arms. Once he got hold of James there would be no letting go. He had to do all that he could to save these lads whose honor he had once sought to destroy.

Lightning was now crackling nearer and nearer to the ship. The winds became stronger and James was having difficulty staying his course as his anchor wasn't quite heavy enough to hold both of them steady. Aengus was calling up to him to hold tight, to keep going. Paul would get him, he shouted. The would-be priest saw in Paul's face a look of the angels. It was Michael the Archangel himself he thought. God had sent the warrior angel to fight the storm and rescue him. Only inches separated his hand from that of Paul's.

"Come on lad, only a few inches more."

With bleeding hands James pulled once more, his feet shoving up on the rope as he did so.

"I've got ye, I've got ye," yelled Paul. With the strength of Hercules he pulled the lad up and onto the boom.

"We've got to get Aengus up, Michael…" James looked into that familiar face once more. "I mean Paul."

Paul tugged on the rope which held Aengus. He was able to gain some slack in his hands so that he could get a firm hold on the rope and give some to James as well. The lad had insisted on helping to bring up his friend. The crowds below were now wildly cheering as Aengus was slowly but surely brought up to the boom. Grabbing hold of the sail canvas and then Paul and James, the Celtic warrior was brought onto the boom. Paul held both in his arm span which enfolded them like the wings of angels. The lads were

457

crying uncontrollably and yet self-consciously as they so wanted to be strong men of their era. Paul felt their trembling as they held onto each other as he held onto them.

"'Tis a brisk wind we're having this day. Makes the eyes water, it does indeed."

The lads with their watery eyes looked at each other and then at their protector. Paul's eyes glistened as theirs did.

"So what do you say about getting down the mast? That sky doesn't look like fair winds lie ahead of us."

"Right you are Paul…and thanks," began Aengus.

"Aye, thanks for everything, if you get our meaning," added James as Aengus nodded affirmatively.

Paul took a knife from his belt and cut the ropes fastened at their waists. The tugging, swaying and weight of their hanging for so long had made it difficult to untie and rain drops had begun to fall. When he sliced through them, the blood stained ropes fell from the boom and hung over Father O'Malley and Meaghan. Droplets from the ropes hit the deck in front of them as they stood in anguish. By the time the hurting lads began their climb down the main-mast the storm clouds were overhead. With each step closer to the deck a cheer arose from below them. Paul jumped to the deck first so that he might steady the weakened lads should they need it. They jumped down on their own power and were swept up by Father O'Malley.

"Paul, you have my enduring gratefulness for saving these lads from their own folly." This he said quietly so as not to destroy their moment as so many came to them to wish them well.

"'Twas no folly good Father, these lads are not youngsters anymore."

The rain was coming down steadily as they spoke and Meghan and her family came up to them. The lass wrapped her arms around each of the lads in a most unladylike manner in that she planted that kiss, of which they teased about knowing so well when aloft, onto each of their cheeks. Aunt Maggie's eyes widened but she said nothing.

"You could have been killed. What possessed you to do such a thing?" the lass both joyous and incredulous asked.

With all the fuss being made and the slight scolding they heard in the priest's words to Paul, the lads had been unable to say anything at all. And that was probably for the best as they were trying not to show that they were in pain. They just stood there, well they were being held up there by Paul and Father O'Malley. Their legs were rapidly becoming like jelly and their crimson waists and bloody hands were becoming a source of pain now that they had a chance to realize that they were injured. Yet they made no mention of it. Paul answered the lass' question for them as he turned Philosopher.

"Men must do what they must do lass. That is to prove themselves worthy of being called a man. This day James and Aengus have proved to be men of courage and wit as they met face to face the breath of God up there where few could or would venture."

Such words from the seaman who almost killed them both were praise indeed not only to them but to all who knew of how Paul first encountered the lads and lass. But to Father O'Malley there was a more pressing need. He had noticed the blood on their shirts and on their hands.

"You should be in Parliament sir. But before we make these lads saints perhaps we should go to Doctor McMillan and have them checked over."

Without hesitation, Paul called for the clearing of a path for the men of Inishmor and Inishbofin. Though many wanted to clap the lads on their backs Paul would have none of it, as he guided the lads and the priest through the crowd.

"We'll see you tonight," called out James to Meghan as he swung his arm over Aengus who had done the same to him.

She smiled. "I'll be on the bow deck."

The ship rocked and bounced across the waves while the lads with arms over each other's shoulders walked onward with sore shoulders, hands and waists and yet with heads held high and hearts thumping out a prayer of thanks and the hope of getting a taste of rum to ease the pain.

Statue of a Roman man in garden of Kilkenny Castle, Ireland

Chapter Sixteen: The Facts of Life

Lying on their bunk belly down in steerage both lads opened the Journal. It was a tight squeeze even for two slender lads as James and Aengus but they made do for they had to attend to their daily task. James was the author and Aengus the silent partner in the writing of each day's exploits, experiences, and their feelings and insights into the humor of the given event. This latter focus was a relatively new approach for two lads from rural Ireland who had virtually no opportunity to have ever shared their feelings with anyone and certainly with the hard times Ireland was suffering not many opportunities for laughter until Father O'Malley came upon the scene.

"So James what shall be written this night?"

"That's a bit of a problem. I can't see anything humorous about what happened up there on the rigging boom."

"You're not serious mate, at one point we almost kissed."

"That was embarrassing not funny Aengus."

"You're dead wrong, think of the fish face…remember this?"

Aengus turned his head slightly and was directly in his friend's face and making those now memorable puckering fish lips. This time there was no threat of falling to the death. James began to laugh and make a similar fish lips face in response.

"See it was funny. And what about those man parts of yours right in mi face, not too funny, eh?"

James gave in and admitted that the fish lips were funny. He looked at the blank page once again. There was a desire within him to tell Aengus how he truly felt about that climb, their impending disaster, and their friendship which saved them from doom on the boom. Words failed him however. Taking the pen in a hand wrapped with bandages, he tried to guide the pen into the ink jar. Aengus gently took his hand and guided it. Together they dipped the pen.

James wrote.

Day 23: August 20, 1849
Today we learned about true friendship and what it means
to be a man.

Aengus was reading over his shoulder.

"Not very funny so far, what's your plan?"

"Be patient. Humor doesn't come easy to me."

"My lips are sealed, write on."

James wrote on.

Aengus and I pleaded with Paul, the sailor who beat us but is now our friend. We wanted to climb up the mast and learn to trim the sail. We wanted to prove ourselves as real men. And we did learn about manly things such as how to pucker our lips like a fish kissing. Of course this was done while

463

hanging from a line of rope from the rigging above from which we fell off.

We also learned how to embrace so hard that it hurt. We had to in order not to swing violently away. But it was good practice for Aengus who isn't going to be a priest like me.

But most of all this day we learned how to place our complete trust in one another by allowing me to climb up the body of Aengus, who did see my manliness at close quarters as he made envious mention of it...

"Hold it right there. I was joking. You need to make that absolutely clear. And as for that 'practice embrace' I've had plenty of practice."

James grinned ear to ear. "Would you have me lie even in my writing?"

Aengus sulked briefly then laughed. "No, trust is trust. I know that you're trying to be funny. I asked for it."

"Aye you certainly did, but I'm not done."

James continued to write.

In our mutual revelation of our manliness, I promised to give Aengus my heart if we succeeded. We are indeed alive and well thanks to our angel, Paul Noon. So here I write that my heart belongs to Aengus O'Flaherty. We shall be friends for as long as we live no matter where that life takes us.

"That's not funny. You've written a pledge, a statement of a bond between us."

"Am I wrong? So you don't feel the same way about our friendship?"

"It's not that…it's just that Paul called us men in front of the whole crowd on deck, even Father O'Malley and your Meghan. Can men express themselves with words like you've written?"

The lads were now in a quandary. How should they as newly proclaimed men of courage and wit express themselves?

It was the very one who proposed the question in the first place that came up with a solution.

"Here's how I see it. Paul called us men of courage and wit. It's easy to see why the courage part was there. I don't think it needs further explanation. But he also called us men of wit. Wit means funny, right?"

"So it does. It also means quick thinking."

"So, real men joke about sexual things all the time. I've heard it on many a fishing boat and in the Kilronan Harbor."

"But Aengus, I'm not writing about sex, like what sheep do to make lambs."

"I know that, but it's funny to talk about sexual things. So why can't we speak honestly of our feelings but in humorous ways?"

"It's just not done Aengus."

"I know James. Everyone thinks men must hide their true feelings, like when Paul knew that we were crying but said it was caused by the wind, is that it?"

"I think so…but then again we did pledge to trust each other up there completely. That should mean in the sharing of our thoughts, hopes, dreams and faith too."

In the end these two would-be men of the 19th Century would come to understand their manly relationship to be one in which they could say what they felt truthfully and openly but only between themselves and on the pages of the Journal. To others they would present the face of a typical Victorian man but with a bit of wit and tongue-in-cheek especially when it came to matters of the heart. It was that mutual decision which brought the Journal entry to a close.

James closed the Journal and tucked it back into the Bible sack. The two lads flipped onto their backs. Stretching their arms behind their heads, they just starred at the wooden beams of the hull.

"What a day this had been, eh mate?"

"Quite a day," began James. "God bless ye my friend for trusting in me."

"I've got your back mate, always. And don't forget that."

"I won't and remember that I shall be there for you as well whether you may want me there or not."

Aengus didn't quite get what James was driving at but accepted it to mean that if he had too much rum, his friend would be there to get him home. In truth James was reflecting on a time when they as older men of the world may get themselves into a situation as with a woman…of course he was thinking of Aengus. As a priest he may have to intercede in a disastrous situation to save his friend from a broken heart or worse. He decided to change the subject.

"What kind of place is this New York, I wonder."

"Oh I'd say it's like that city set upon a hill as the Bible says."
Both lads nodded that would probably be so. They flipped bum to bum and sank into slumber.

Above them Father O'Malley stood on the deck. Next to him were two bodies wrapped in blankets. They were fellow passengers who had caught the fever which would come to be known as typhus. With him were Captain Waterstone, Doctor McMillan and several crew members including Paul and Frank. The two were travelling without family. On other ships they would have been thrown overboard as soon as they took their last breath. On the Cushla Machree however, the priest and the ship Captain had formed a bond of mutual respect. Thus Daniel Ward and Antony Corbett were being buried at sea with proper ceremony and blessing as their souls were commended to their Creator.

When the service ended, he returned to steerage to check on the lads after their harrowing day. Not wanting to disturb the obviously exhausted lads soundly asleep he took note of the bandages of cloth surrounding their shirtless waists. There was some blood discoloring them but it appeared that no new seepage of blood was taking place. Next he looked at the hands of James without touching them as they hung over the side of the bunk. He of course had no knowledge that a Journal entry had been made so he was concerned that fresh blood appeared on the bandages of his left hand. Aengus was facing the hull wall and James faced out toward the bunks across from them and where the priest stood.

"And so these are the men of courage and wit described by Paul," he thought. *"Yet they appear as babes with angel-like faces who sleep in innocence."*

He blessed them and worried that with the fever having taken two already could others including the lads be next. Taking a seat on the floor near the steerage entry, he took out his Divine Office just as a blanket dropped on him from above.

"Good-night Father," James flipped toward Aengus. "It's warm up here, we don't need it."

"May the angels watch over you."

The squall had been mercifully brief thus enabling the ship to sail on course with no significant delay. When morning of the 24th day broke it was hardly noticeable as the steerage hold had only one source of natural light and that was through the hold entryway. Aengus woke first and found James wrapped around him as if he was hanging on the rope. His bandaged hands rubbed against his fair skin but caused him no discomfort. They did however cause him to think about what had happened on that mast rigging and of the silliness and seriousness of the plan they formed to be saved. Not wanting to disturb his friend, he lay quietly as James

468

seemed to be experiencing the same type of thought as he clung tighter onto Aengus as he had on that rope.

James was mumbling something in the Irish language. He was calling out, "mamai, dadai." His words reminded Aengus of his own mother and father. Would they be back on Inishmor with Father Henry who was to replace Father O'Malley or on the fishing boat? Being morning he decided that his dadai and brothers would be out fishing.

Rising from his sleep on the floor the priest was folding the blanket tossed to him, then decided to place it over the lads. He was about to do so when it became apparent that Aengus was awake.

"So you're awake are ye?"

"Aye, Father, but I didn't want to disturb mi mate here."

"Very thoughtful indeed…I was just about to go topside to pray. When James awakes both of you may join me if you wish."

"Actually, I would like to say something to ye Father of a personal nature."

"Oh I see. Then 'tis a serious talk you'd be wishing to have."

"Aye it is. It's just this. James and me had made a plan to confess to ye so that you couldn't talk about what we would tell ye."

"My son, would that be a sincere confession?"

Aengus couldn't abide looking at the wall any longer. Very carefully he twisted within the embracing arms so that he could look the priest in the eyes, but he ended up with James in his face. With a turn of the head he at least caught sight of Father O'Malley.

"That's my point Father, I don't think it would be. But I want to tell ye man to man as it were."

"By all means lad, do so."

Aengus went on to explain that while hanging above the deck on those ropes the two of them had talked about wild things, like the differences between sex and sexuality. Yet neither of them quite understood what they were talking about as they weren't sure of their differences. Being a priest since he was twenty-four had not prepared him for such a dialogue. Nor had he expected to be talking of such things with a lad who was like a son to him as was James. He listened carefully to the description of the Journal entry. First he was concerned that James had written with raw skin hands. Then he focused on the topic of the writing. He heard of the nonsense while suspended on ropes from the rigging and the lads' mutual pledge of trust and truthfulness.

Just as Aengus was describing the puckering lips, James' eyes popped open and looked directly into the face of Aengus who was just then reenacting the puckering lips episode. The shock of the sight was only lessened by how he felt when he realized that his arms were around Aengus's naked chest. He tried to move, but in a bunk only 18" wide there was hardly room enough for one let alone two. He did manage to swing his arms back off Aengus. In the process he hit Father O'Malley who stood behind him. He twisted his head and saw the priest.

"Oh my Lord, Father…I mean good morning."

"Good morning James, Aengus and I were just having an interesting discussion about sex," explained the priest.

"Huh?" the lad became distraught. "Aengus you didn't tell him everything?"

"Yes James, I did. Are you upset?"

There was no pause for thought; rather there was a sigh of relief. He too had intended to share the Journal entry when the opportunity presented itself. Father could read that relief on both of their faces as they sat up next to each other, their legs now dangling off the side of the bed.

"Well then, it appears that we're all about to engage in a discussion. Now wash yourselves, get dressed and meet me on the deck."

With the priest gone, Aengus jumped from the bunk. Then he helped James down as his hands hurt and he couldn't brace himself on them to leap off.

"That Father O'Malley, he's quite the man isn't he James?"

"I'd say so. He always seems to know what to say and in a way to make us feel good even in the most awful times."

Later that day, the lads relieved themselves of their worry over sex. They received the explanation of love a la Church teachings as well as the particulars of procreation; that is the coming together of a man and woman to create a new life. To say that two lads were enlightened beyond their wildest dreams would be like lighting one candle in a darkened room. That little burning flame would enable them to see more clearly indeed. However for them it was as if a chandelier of candles had been lighted and they had so much information thrust upon their developing brains and bodies that they were hard pressed to absorb all the details, though they made a gallant effort to do so.

As for Father O'Malley who would never be a parent, he was quite proud of himself as he left the lads on the rear deck and headed down to steerage. Now that the sex talk was over it was time to return to the studying of the Declaration of Independence and the United States Constitution once again. Only a few days of sailing remained according to what Paul had told him. The lads knowledge of what this land of America stood for was essential in his mind.

The lads couldn't help it. They sat on the deck behind a stack of crates and pulled on their pants at their waists, looking downward.

"So that's why it swells up like that..." an amazed James said.

"And then you just shove it inside the lady part and wham you get a baby, just amazing isn't it James?"

Suddenly both lads held their pants waist area tightly against them.

"Oh my God, it's happening again. All I did was think of Meghan hearing about this talk," cried out James.

"Well I didn't and mine's growing too."

Both rolled onto their bellies with the hope that the pressure would stop the swelling. They were wrong. It only added to the issue. Only the appearance of Martin and Lawrence seemed to help distract them and allow nature to return them to normal as they thought of it.

"So lads, what's with the secret talk with Father?" asked Martin.

"Yeah, it seemed quite cozy here, we didn't want to disturb you," added Lawrence.

The lads blushed with brightly crimson faces and said not a word. The young men didn't need words. The red faces were quite enough. In a second they were all over the lads jostling them and teasing them about the facts of life. This they followed up with the talk of women. It turned out they knew not much more than the lads in that regard for neither had a serious woman in his life.

It was mid-morning and they were still in a deep discussion about life and being men when Father O'Malley appeared on the deck. Upright they stood at attention and pointing fingers over the side of the ship as if trying to point out a land formation to each other.

"Lads, would ye like to join me in prayer?" asked the priest with a smile, knowing full well from the condition of them all brushing up closely to the side of the ship's railing that more was afoot than the sighting of land. He however chose not to pursue another sex talk.

It was James who broke the awkward silent response of not responding at all.

"We'd love to Father, but can we?"

"I don't understand your meaning James."

"Well, after that talk we just had shouldn't we go to Confession first, for we are not Pure of Heart any longer."

The priest was truly shocked. What could they have done now in such a short time was more along his thinking. But the others were right in tune with James. No sooner had the words issued forth than they fell to their knees and began pounding their chests with a fist while repeating, "mea culpa, mea culpa." James followed suit as their action convinced him that he was right. He would never be Pure of Heart again.

Father stood over them now with a gentle smile and hands outstretched over them as if in a blessing. "Lads, the Lord is with you even in these most difficult times and circumstances, such as what you're experiencing right now. You are young men and soon to be full grown men. What happens to you is natural, it doesn't mean you've lost purity of heart for that means more than just innocence. It means approaching life with eyes filled with the Grace of God and a heart open to accept all people as they are, flaws and all."

The four sat back on their legs and looked at their priest with a new understanding of what the human condition was and how they must live in that humanness seeking to know, love and serve their Lord. They were ready to join the priest in prayer.

Just as Father was to begin Paul swung overhead from the mast and dropped down among them, while coming to the rear deck there appeared Meghan. Both asked to be forgiven for their interruption but asked if they could pray with them as well. When Father welcomed them, Aengus and James were particularly surprised. James because he found himself quite nervous as he had never prayed with a girl. As for Aengus, he knew that Paul was a different kind of man than a Father O'Malley or his own brothers and yet Father accepted him. Soon others on deck joined them and the "Te Deum" once again rang out across the sea and over the decks of the ship.

It was a sign of hope for the scores of people aboard to hear what had been banned for so many years once again. For the lads and a certain lass it was a time of bonding as well.

Their bonds grew ever stronger over the next few days as they prayed together and joined in the lessons James and Aengus were receiving. On the morning of the 25th day of the Voyage, Aengus, James and Meghan were sitting on the bow deck studying. The lads had immersed themselves in the founding documents of America since the beginning of the journey. It had been only since that night of prayer that James thought to invite Meghan into the study group as well.

Meghan was reading aloud the words of the Declaration of Independence.

"'We hold these truths to be self-evident, that all men are created equal and are endowed by their creator with certain inalienable rights that among these are life, liberty and the pursuit of happiness.'"

Meghan paused and looked about her. She had attracted the attention of several other passengers. They had circled them to hear those words written by Thomas Jefferson in 1776. She laid the book from which she read on the crate which served as their desk. James thought that they should memorize those words just read so that should people ask them about their knowledge of America, they would be able to recite the passage.

"The Americans will be quite impressed, I'm thinking," Meghan said.

"Aye they won't think we're just some dumb ducks after we start reciting such passages from their own Declaration and Constitution to them," added Aengus. "Right James?"

James agreed but he felt that more would be expected of them then just reciting passages. "We need to understand the meaning behind those words. I think we need to get Father O'Malley to help us to understand them and be able to explain their meaning."

The three decided that after the Liturgy of the Hours "Non" prayer they would ask the priest to explain the passage to them. In the meantime they would reflect on what they had just heard. It was Meghan who spoke first as she wondered whether such a nation actually existed where all people were equal.

I don't get your meaning," a confused Aengus noted. "It says so right here in this book."

"I know," she responded. "But they're just words. How do we know if the people believe them?"

James tried to address her question by sharing his time with Father O'Malley in the fortress ruins on Inishbofin. It was there that he had first been introduced to the founding documents of America. He told them about their Revolutionary War which he explained was fought to establish the ideas put down on paper as sacred principles for a government and a nation.

"For seven years they fought an empire far superior in might and wealth than they were," James continued. "Surely after all those years and 75 years since, their laws reflect what is written in these documents."

"There's one thing for sure," Aengus began. "All these people on this ship and others like it are going to there because they believe America is a land where we can be equal, where the people are happy and free, where life is blessed with wealth."

James looked at his friend with an admiration usually saved only for Father O'Malley. "Praise God, if you don't sound just like Father."

Aengus puffed out his chest while making a comment about he not being too ignorant.

"I just hope that you're right Aengus," concluded Meghan.

And so went the next couple of days as the three young philosophers proposed how such noble principles as equality and freedom of religion would be witnessed in America, the land of opportunity. Each evening the Journal entry would reflect their discussions. On the evening of the 26th day that entry gave witness to a growing concern as of late among the lads, in particular. They had found it more and more difficult to express their deepest feelings and hopes for what they would find in America in recent days. It wasn't that they didn't accept the Bill of Rights, the Declaration's principles of government or the Constitution's governing process. Quite the contrary they did whole heartedly accept what they expressed. Their difficulty came from Father O'Malley himself. He as of late had begun to caution them to curb their expectations. Why this sudden change, they couldn't figure out. James who had spent the most time with him saw how greatly that change was from their Inishbofin lessons. The lad at first thought of how the priest had been imprisoned and even whipped. But for James those scars on his back were badges of honor which should give witness to why such a nation as America was needed.

In the end the lads and lass attributed such cautionary remarks as a way to help them understand that no nation was perfect despite their lofty goals and statements of principles.

Had they seen Father O'Malley sitting under the lantern on the rear deck rereading that letter from the Prior in Rome, perhaps they would have a better understanding of why he was cautioning them about expecting too much in America. There was trouble afoot there for immigrants and Catholics, in particular.

**Old St. Patrick's Cathedral/Basilica, New York City
Mulberry and Prince Sts.**

Chapter Seventeen: New York, New York

The dawn of the 27th day broke with wild enthusiasm already spreading topside on the decks of the Cushla Machree. During that time just before daybreak Paul was atop the mid-mast working on the sails with Frank, his one-time jail guard. They were convinced that they saw lights and land form. As the August sun rose on a warm morning those below could then hear their calls of "land ho" throughout the ship as it spread from one to another of the crew and then as passengers hurried topside, they too added to the call. Father O'Malley, once again sleeping on the floor of the steerage hold was one of those roused by the early call. With Divine Office book in hand, he had joined those already topside to see for himself.

It was indeed a land mass and buildings could clearly be seen on rocky summits as well as sandy beach areas. He began to pray.

"O, God we praise You and acknowledge You to be the supreme Lord. Everlasting Father, all the earth worships You..."

Below deck James and Aengus, still in the throes of sleep, squirmed as the sounds of clatter and chatter filled the steerage hold. People scurried here and there trying to get up onto deck. Their eyes slowly opened to find themselves face to face. There was no time to react to their position as Martin and Lawrence had arrived and were tugging at them.

"Get yourself dressed lads, we're here," an excited Martin shouted.

The lads propped themselves up on their arms and pushed so as not to press on each other to a sitting position. No blanket was needed during the night, given the heat of so many crammed in such a small area and the weather being typical summertime temperatures for the northeast United States.

The broad shouldered Aengus dwarfed the frail James as he now knelt behind the younger lad thus creating a look of a flaming Celt with nothing on but a loin cloth behind the pale and wild black haired lad from Inishbofin with his rib cage still quite visible as he had only half of his long johns pulled up to his waist. Lawrence was now taking hold of James and lifting him off the bunk as Aengus jumped down with the prowess of a lion leaping to prey. He collided with Martin, who like James was a very thin young man with hardly a scruff of a beard though in his early twenties. Martin crashed to the floor but Aengus stood over him with outstretched hand to give him a lift up to his feet. Martin accepted, took hold of the hand.

"God be praised but if all the lasses on this ship could see you now."

Aengus blushed looked down at himself and turned to grab hold of the tossed off blanket to cover himself.

Lawrence and James howled with laughter as the Celtic fisherman who so strutted about his manliness became like a sheep caught alone without his flock about him, quite shy indeed.

"'Tis not my fault that ye are not…well like me." His face, in fact his entire body, now matched his hair on his head and that tuft of ginger color on his chest. "We grow them big on the Aran Islands."

More laughter ensued as the three lads were now doubled over with laughter.

"That's not what I meant. You know damn well it's not."

James became suddenly quite still. He looked about the hold and found that they were the only ones remaining. Not a soul was about to take an interest in their carrying on, as they had hastened topside. Only the two who were quite ill and not able to move themselves remained at the far end unaware of the nonsense such being their state of condition.

"Aengus O'Flaherty, watch your mouth. You'll have Father telling you a sin would be forming in that mouth of yours."

"Oh yes, indeed," began Lawrence. "And who wouldn't want to kiss those lovely lips so red and ripe?" He then made a move as if to plant a kiss.

Now Lawrence was every bit as tall as Aengus though not quite as broad and filled out, which was what the young fisherman had meant in the first place before the others took it to mean quite another thing. In a flash Aengus lifted up his hands and made fists.

"You'll do no such thing Paul…I mean Larry, so help me I'll deck ye."

Despite his frailty, it was James who stepped between the two, one ready for battle and the other just into nonsense. The slip of the tongue had done it for James. The lad now understood why Aengus couldn't be teased about how he appeared. Despite their reconciliation with Paul and it was indeed quite sincere when it happened, the young Celtic Warrior had never let go of what Paul had said he wanted to do to him. And now his understanding that it was all show to cover up his true nature hadn't helped Aengus to let go of how Paul felt about him.

James picked up the blanket which hit the deck as soon as Aengus raised his fists. He hung it over the raised fists. Turning he took hold of Lawrence's hands now beginning to form a fist.

"There will be no spilling of Irish blood on this ship, lads."

The three older and bigger young men couldn't believe what the puny lad was doing. No one in their right mind would step between two Irishmen ready to battle. And yet this lamb of a lad did just that between the two lions of their little band of friends. No one moved except for James. He pressed on the hands he held and pushed them down. Turning, he took the blanket and began to wrap it about Aengus, who had just begun to crack a smile as the lad tightened the wool blanket about his friend's waist.

"I was only fooling ye Aengus, honest," a contrite Lawrence said.

The crack of a smile became a broad one as Aengus opened his arms and grabbed Lawrence in a bear hug.

"Aye, I know that to be true. 'Tis only this hot blooded temper I have brought on by this curse of the Celtic hair that made mi boil a bit."

Caught between this embrace was James. "God be praised but could ye release now before I am crushed half to death?"

The two jumped back and let James fall to the floor. Aengus swept him up and gave him a hug too. "Ye are mi best friend James Shields forever and ever. Are ye hurt?"

"I'm just fine. It'll take more than the likes of you two to get the best of James Shields. Now if you're quite done with the hugging and kissing can we hear Martin's message?"

All laughed, then became quite silent. The three then froze their eyes on Martin.

"Well I was just saying that land has been sighted. That's why everyone went up on deck."

Now in an instant of time the others began to cheer. James jumped onto Aengus and planted that kiss right on his forehead.

"Mi momai's dream has come true. We're here Aengus, we're here and all of us are alive and well."

The joy became infectious and all were hugging and then dancing a jig and then stopped in wonderment.

"Meghan, we need to get her and celebrate the news." James made a run toward the ladder of the entrance.

"Hold on squirt, not so fast unless you don't mind her seeing your manliness."

"Don't you dare speak of her like that, Martin." The lad then realized that he was still in his long johns with an open back flap at that. "Oh, I'm sorry Martin, I hadn't realized. I guess we should get dressed first."

"Well we can't go get Meghan smelling like steerage. Where's the bucket of water, we won't be needing it for the drinking anymore now." Aengus looked about and found the bucket Father had insisted on being used only for drinking water. "Martin, would ye pour this over the lad and me while we wash?"

"Sure…"

James interceded and suggested that they do so in the private area. The suggestion was well taken. He and Aengus went behind the blankets, out came the long-johns and loin cloth undergarment and over the top was poured the water.

In short order they were dressed in pants and their Aran knit sweaters, despite the August heat, as they wanted to be reminded of home when they entered what was to become their new home.

"Now then," James instructed. "Take this lemon and slice it in four pieces if you please."

Aengus took the fruit and took out his fish knife. He then handed the pieces to James who then gave one to each of the lads and told them to suck on the fruit and then rub it on their teeth to clean them, as Father had told them was done in Italy.

"Good lads, now I'll go get Meghan. You find Father and tell him we'll be right there."

"Aye Captain," Aengus saluted. "But I'll go with ye Father James, just in case…"

There was more laughter.

"In case of what? She always prays with us and studies with us too."

"'Tis true, but I'll come along as well."

"Fine, you two go find Father."

It was agreed that all would meet at the mid-mast starboard side where James and Aengus had almost lost their lives.

On the deck of the bow, the first and second class passengers had already gathered as well. The excitement was overwhelming as the land mass became clearer. Small boats had come out to guide the ship to the docking area.

Colin, Maggie and Meghan were discussing the disembarking procedures. Unfortunately since they had been relegated to second class they would have to go to Castle Garden with the steerage passengers and be cleared to enter America. First class passengers did not have to go through that system of scrutiny and registration.

"This is an outrage. We were to be First Class passengers," an angry Colin boomed out as he paced the deck.

"Colin, love, you're upsetting Meghan. There's nothing to be done, it'll be over soon enough."

He placed his arm around his wife and apologized to Meghan for his crudeness. Her smile which would melt many a heart if she would be so inclined, forgave him, though for what she would be hard pressed to say. She had seen her father on many a day bellow about this law and that, taxes and the having of no priest permanently assigned to their Church of the Holy Rosary in Doolin. Her eyes then betrayed her thoughts as she drifted back to Doolin and her family. Maggie gave her a kiss on the cheek and told her of the grand city in which they would live.

"Oh mi lovely girl, how grand is this? New York lies out there waiting for us. Your Uncle has letters of introduction to present to the Bishop and business leaders. We'll live in a house with a proper roof and there will be grand shops and markets. You'll never be hungry again."

"Aunty, I am so grateful…it's just that I wish momai and dadai could be with us."

"I know child and one day, God willing, they will be with us. Now then as soon as we get settled we'll take a carriage ride and send out a post to them, how's that?"

Meghan's eyes sparkled as she thought that to be a wonderful idea. She lowered the shawl around her head and let the wind take her crimson locks and fling them about. Voices quite familiar to her sounded across the deck.

487

There was no mistaking the lass with the flowing hair and green woven shawl seen so often on the voyage. Her heart began to thump faster as the thoughts of home faded away.

"Meghan, it's us, we're here," cried out James.

"We've come to get ye," called out Aengus.

The now radiant Meghan swung around to face the lads bounding up those stairs on which she had forgiven Paul and thus began a bond of friendship between the lads, she and the seaman. She gave a glance to her Aunt and Uncle. Maggie gave her a pat to indicate that it was fine to meet up with the lads. She flung out her arms, the shawl took to being a sail and billowed out floating her toward the lads. Both now frozen in place as what some might call a vision of loveliness or others an angel from heaven came as if on wings to them.

The Celtic warrior fisherman could have easily passed for her brother given their skin tone and similar hair color. The innocent lamb with his coal-like locks and sea blue eyes wasn't thinking of her in such a manner as she came to him first and wrapped her arms around his neck and then did the same to Aengus, who stooped to allow it to be done.

"James, Aengus, isn't it all too grand? New York, we'll be so happy now, won't we?"

Maggie was about to call her back upon seeing the hugging, but Colin took hold of her and gave her a hug as he explained that one could easily see that their embrace was done in innocence and friendship.

The lads were all too pleased to agree with the observation of the lass and refrained from reminding her that their home was not to be New York.

"Now as for you Aengus O'Flaherty, have you given up on that notion to be a fisherman in that city called Boston?" She had brought up what the lads wouldn't, that of New York not being their final destination. She had however, only allowed herself to mention one city and leave out Philadelphia.

The Celt swayed with the ship and gave the impression of deep thought. Then he beamed and told her that it would not be to his liking to leave such good company. He then took James into their embrace.

The three plopped down on a crate and began to talk about what New York might hold in store for them. Meghan bubbled over with news of her Uncle and the letter to the Bishop. James couldn't be happier for they too had such a letter of introduction to Bishop Hughes.

"Maybe we could go together. Then we'd know where you lived and..."

James was getting ahead of himself. But Aengus wasn't. He finished his friend's thought.

"And we could go out together and explore the city before..." Now Aengus stopped himself. He had gone too far. There was to be no mention of their departing for Philadelphia. Meghan ignored the reference and replied.

"That's a grand idea. Uncle Colin tells me that there are great boulevards on which people stroll, just to walk and greet each other. And there're markets for food too."

They went on and on about what sights they would be seeing when James realized that they had sent a message to Father O'Malley that they would join him at mid-ship. He begrudgingly brought up that message.

"...and so that's why we came, to get you Meghan."

"Well why didn't you say so? Aunt Maggie, Uncle Colin we're supposed to meet Father at mid-ship."

"Run along, we'll meet you there," replied Aunt Maggie. "Uncle Colin and I will get the bags."

The ship was entering what was called the East River, slowly moving up the shoreline of Manhattan to the dock area near a fort-like structure known as Castle Garden then (Clinton Castle today) in the area known as The Battery. Dozens of ships lined the route, some were docked, others formed a line to wait for an open dock. The teens could see hundreds of people such as themselves hanging over the ship railings. Suddenly two young men not much older than themselves jumped overboard from the ship whose name on the bow read, Garthsnaid. Meghan screamed as the lads held onto her yelling at the lads as they crashed into the East River. Miraculously the boys survived and came up from their plunge. James yelled to them as Aengus took a rope being readied to be tossed to the dock-men when they were ready to be secured.

"Grab hold of this rope," yelled James.

The lads in the river floundered for a bit and then took to the water in long strokes which kept them afloat. Being confident they turned and yelled back to James that they would make it to the shore. Soon they disappeared around the bow of the ship never to be seen again. It would be some time later that the amazed passengers would hear why they took such a dangerous jump. On the Garthsnaid were many passengers with the fever (Typhus). A quarantine would certainly be placed on the ship as measures were taken to insure the dreaded fever was not brought ashore in New York. The lads who jumped were lucky not to have caught the fever and desperate to get to America and not die on the ship. It was all they could think of.

James shook his head as he watched them swim out of sight, Meghan hanging on his arm. Aengus rolled the rope as he found it and replaced it in its location. Church bells could be heard from on shore announcing the noon hour. They turned to each other and held hands to pray for the lads who jumped into the river. When they looked up there stood Father O'Malley, Martin and Lawrence and many of the steerage passengers they knew quite well after 27 days at sea. They too had watched the drama unfold. Ellen Sweeny was asking Father to lead them in a prayer of Thanksgiving for their safe arrival. The priest leaned into Meghan first and wiped her tears of distress away with a handkerchief taken from the breast pocket of this jacket.

"There, there my child, all is well. They looked like strong lads and if they survived that jump then they would certainly make it to shore."

"Thank you Father. I'm all right really I am." She tugged onto James' boney arm a bit tighter as she spoke.

The priest nodded and suggested that everyone join him in one of their favorite hymns but in English as they were now in America. He began with the Sign of the Cross over the waters which took them to this city set upon a hill called New York. Then he asked that they join him in the pledge of St. Patrick.

"I bind this today to me, forever. By power of faith, Christ's incarnation: His baptism in the Jordan River, His death on the cross for my salvation; His bursting from the spiced tomb, His riding up the heavenly way, His coming at the day of doom, I bind myself today."

The crew was now throwing the ropes to the men on the dock who secured them to giant iron pillars. The gang plank now hung over the ship's side ready to be lowered so that the passengers might disembark. There was no Statue of Liberty to greet them with those words of "…give me your tired, your poor, your huddled masses who yearn to breathe free." on that blazingly warm afternoon for Emma Lazarus had not written the poem which is now found on the pedestal of the statue. And that would not happen until after it was fully dedicated to America on October 28, 1886. Lady Liberty's arm however arrived in time for the Centennial of Independence in Philadelphia. But that was decades away. What they saw was a fort like structure on the southern tip of Manhattan, which as it would happen years later, would be the site from which tickets to view the Statue of Liberty and depart to her island home would be sold.

And yet the sight on that afternoon gave a vivid expression to those words yet to be formed in the poet's mind. For indeed had these immigrants from Ireland arrive as huddled masses crammed into ship holds, deprived of proper food and decent water to drink and yet filled with hope and a vision to be free.

Those upon the deck were singing Hail Holy Queen as all was made ready for disembarkation. As those final words sung, as if from a choir of angels, filled the harbor area, lines of those huddled masses were already filing down the dock toward Castle Garden were the Commissioners of Immigration had opened the Immigrant reception station in the fortress which also served as a theater. They turned their heads toward the *Cushla Machree* and many crossed themselves while others waved a greeting to fellow countrymen come to this land of golden opportunity.

Captain Waterstone came out of the wheel house and stood atop it to speak to the passengers. He announced that the First Class passengers would leave first, followed by the Second Class passengers and then steerage. The First Class passengers were allowed to enter New York without going through the Immigration Station. All others were to follow the lines as seen on shore into the fort.

Colin and Maggie had arrived with bags in hand just in time for the prayer but no blessing or hymn was to move Colin's anger as he realized that his family would have to go through the long, often degrading and tedious process of immigration registration.

"Maggie, I'm going to speak with that Captain. We should have been in Frist Class."

Maggie pulled on him. "No love, leave it be. Look there."

She was pointing to Meghan who still clung on James on one side and now Aengus on the other side of her.

"Let them have their time of farewell."

Colin acquiesced to her wishes, dropped the bags on the deck, while mentioning that their trunks would have to be picked up in the warehouse anyway. Maggie held onto him and placed a peck on his cheek.

Chaos was now sweeping across the deck as everyone scattered about securing their baggage if they had any at all. Father O'Malley also watched the three teens as they held onto each other knowing that soon the lass would be placed in the second class line and be gone from them. He asked Martin and Lawrence to help him gather their baggage and silently left without a word to the lads or lass.

"So I guess this is good-bye then, eh?" Aengus quietly said.

Meghan sniffled a bit and nodded. She stroked the youth's flaming scruffy beard which barely showed on his cheek and turned to James while never letting go of the young fisherman.

"Aengus is right James. We're here. We may never see each other again." She couldn't go on.

"No, no, don't say that," he emotionally begged as he grabbed hold of Aengus' other arm and brought them into a tight circle in which no one could see their faces. "We pledged to be friends forever. We'll find a way."

"Aye, James is right. But how?" Aengus looked directly into James' eyes. There was a look of despair that there really was no possible plan. After all they would be going on to Philadelphia and she would be staying in New York. He cracked a fake smile to hide his true feelings. It didn't fool James or Meghan.

Lines were being formed on the deck outside steerage and also on the bow deck for first and second class passengers. The gang plank made a loud noise as it hit the dock. Only the three teens stood at mid-ship, where the gangplank had been lowered. A crew man walked up to them with a broad smile.

"Hey, there, it's me," began Paul. "I'm afraid I've come to send you to your proper deck."

Three heads popped up from the tight circle. Seeing the seaman who had helped to save the lads from the debacle on the rigging, they dropped their arms and opened the circle while remaining arm in arm.

"Oh…it's you Paul." The greeting from Aengus was kind and yet it seemed that something was off about how it was delivered because it wasn't really a greeting at all. It was more of a recognition statement for the man who once threatened them, then became their friend.

James jumped in as he felt Aengus tense up. "Hello there Paul, what were you saying?"

"I'm sorry to be the one to have to split you up. But it's time to get in your line. Miss Meghan would have to go to the bow deck and you lads to the rear deck."

The realization that this was it, the time to separate, stunned the three. Their eyes watered up and their grip on each other tightened if that was at all possible given how firmly they were holding on to each other. Paul's heart skipped a beat and hurt as he saw those whom he now so admired in such a state.

"Don't look at me so, please. I can fix this for a while at least."

The three perked up. "How?" asked James.

"I'm in charge of the line formation. I'll place Aengus and James at the beginning of the steerage line and you Meghan and your family at the end of the second class line. Then you'll be able to walk together for a time at least."

Meghan jumped up and gave Paul a hug and kiss on the cheek. He blushed bright red and rubbed the spot where she planted the kiss.

"No one has ever done that to me, Miss Meghan. Thank you."

"No, it's us who are grateful to you," she responded.

"Indeed, Paul you're great," added James.

Aengus then released himself from the two and came face to face with Paul, his back toward his friends. He spoke quite quietly.

"Paul, you've become a friend to us. I too am grateful. May I hug you good-bye?"

Paul stepped back. He knew that Aengus was very uncomfortable around the seaman because of what happened and the threat it rendered to his manliness. He shook his head first right to left and then up and down.

Aengus took hold of him and squeezed. Paul hesitated keeping his arms to his side. "Are you not going to return the gesture of friendship Paul?"

"I can't. I don't want you to get the wrong idea. You really know my true nature."

"Yes, I do. And that's why I'm doing this. We can be friends and I want you to know that if my nature was like that of yours, then I would welcome more."

The seaman burst into tears and gave a hug back. Meghan and James realized something was up but also felt that the seaman and Aengus had had a moment of some kind, and a personal one at that. James understood but the lass did not. Paul released Aengus and walked away telling them he'd go find Father O'Malley and tell him the plan.

Aengus stood there watching Paul walk away so that fellow crew members wouldn't see his emotions. His friends slipped their arms under his and gave a squeeze.

"Well that went pretty well, I guess, right mates?"

"Then he really is your friend, even after all that has happened?" asked Meghan.

Both lads answered, "yes."

"This will make quite the entry into the Journal eh Aengus?"

"Clean it up a bit…one day that Journal of yours may get made into a book."

The lads laughed as Meghan looked bewildered as she wasn't aware of the Journal entries having such vivid details in it. Before she could question what this Journal was all about, James brought them back to their planning on how to meet before the lads left for Philadelphia. He recalled what Meghan had told him about her Uncle having letters of introduction to Bishop Hughes as did Father O'Malley. He suggested that they arrange to have both Father and her family go to St. Patrick's Cathedral Rectory in two days after the "Non" mid-day prayer.

"Brilliant idea James." Meghan kissed him on the cheek.

"Whoa, Father James, that's just not done."

Meghan turned scarlet in the face and began to apologize for being so forward. James on his part did as Paul had done and rubbed the kiss into his cheek. He then gave Aengus a light jab in the ribs and soon the two were rolling about the deck in a playful tussle which rolled them into the feet of Father O'Malley. Their collision caused the priest to drop the Bible and Journal sack on the lads at his feet. He quickly swooped it up.

"So lads, this is how you say good-bye to Meghan?"

"Ah no…we were…" Aengus tried to explain and became tongue tied.

"Right…we were just getting a feel for the wood of this ship so that we wouldn't forget this journey to America."

"And such Blarney from a future priest is to by accepted by me is that it?"

The lads became contrite and just laid there on the deck looking up at him upside down as it were. Father O'Malley grabbed hold of their arms and gave them a pull up to their feet. Once again the lads realized that their priest and mentor was a strong man with a gentle heart.

"Now then Martin and Lawrence have our bags with them over there on the rear deck. I thought you'd want to carry the Journal sack, James, thus I brought it to you."

The lad thanked him and pulled the strap over his head, gave a tap to the Bible inside. From the bow deck Maggie was now calling to Meghan, waving. She and Colin had left when the lines were being formed to allow a private farewell to be said. Frank was told by Paul as to where to place the Logan family in line. Paul placed Martin and Lawrence at the head of the line for steerage to hold the place for the lads and the priest.

"I need to go, but we'll be together in a few minutes." Off Meghan ran to her Aunt and Uncle.

The first class passengers were already walking down the gangplank onto the pier when Meghan arrived. Colin was complaining about their location in the line but when Meghan explained that Paul did that so they would be right in front of Father O'Malley, he was satisfied.

"Well then, that's that then." Colin picked up the bags. Maggie gave Meghan the sack which held the folder containing the title to Doonagore Castle.

All was ready and none too soon as the line began to move. When they reached the gangplank Father and the four lads were already there, off to the side, ready to step onto it when they passed. There was happy chatter, expressions of fear and hope that none of the passengers would be so ill as to have to be quarantined and sent back.

For Father O'Malley, it was a time of great joy as he watched the lads happily walk down the plank with pride and wide smiles. And yet it was also a time of distress for he was recalling the words of warning of what might be found in America as received from his Prior in Rome, his fellow priests at St. Augustine Church in Galway and from the father of Aengus. He began to chant a verse from the breastplate of St. Patrick, softly so as not to disturb the joy of the lads.

"I bind unto myself today the power of God to hold and to lead, His eye to watch, His might to stay, His ear to hearken to my need. The wisdom of my God to teach, His hand to guide, His shield to ward; The word of God to give me speech, His heavenly host to be my guard."

By the time he had completed the verse, he and the lads were on the pier and making their way slowly to the southern tip of Manhattan and onto American soil. The lads followed in wonderment as they saw the mighty ships lining up on the River, the throngs of people, in various stages of joy and distress, and lastly the fortress walls ahead on the island of Manhattan. As soon as Father O'Malley placed his feet onto the soil of New York in America, he dropped to his knees and kissed the ground. The lads thought that he had stumbled. Only when they stooped down to help him up did they realize what he was doing. The line momentarily stopped as the lads saw a trickle of tears falling from those eyes of joy and worry onto the ground.

"Father, it's all right. We're all together." James was right. The four lads had been joined by Meghan and her Aunt and Uncle and thus had formed a rather formidable wall of humanity surrounding the priest. He rose and smiled asking forgiveness for having delayed their progress.

"Not at all Father," Colin stated. "It's a grand moment for all of us. I am about to introduce a business to America which will help Ireland rise from its ruinous condition and you shall be bringing the Word of God freely in your Catholic tradition to all here already and those who stand in line with us."

"It appears then that I have a bit of work to do with God's grace. So let's be on our way." The priest moved along with James and Aengus taking hold of his arms and Meghan that of James. With her Aunt, Uncle, Martin and Lawrence behind them the procession continued to what is now Battery Park. Only Father O'Malley had any hint of what they may find once they were released from the Immigration Reception Station in Castle Garden.

As for the lads and lass, they were talking about their plan to meet two days hence at St. Patrick's Cathedral at the corner of streets named Prince and Mulberry. Then they would explore this city of wonder set upon a hill.

Epilogue:

Join James Shields, Aengus O'Flaherty, Meghan O'Grady and Father Thomas O'Malley OSA as they enter America and begin an adventure in a United States which was quite different than the one we know and love today. Look for Book Two of The Doonagore Theft Trilogy titled: **Wonder and Disillusionment in America.**

Below is an excerpt from Chapter One of **Wonder and Disillusionment in America.**

Chapter One: Three Pure Hearts in New York

Paul Noon hung over the mizzen sail of the mid-mast calling out, of all things, a blessing on the lad from Inishbofin whom he had once pummeled and humiliated, a lad from Inishmor of the Aran Islands, whose striking Celtic Warrior appearance drew him to be closer to him then friend and "brother" which resulted in his beating the seventeen-year-old lad and to a laughing lass, who held onto the arms of the Inishbofin fourteen-year-old lad with the wild coal like hair and piercing turquoise blue eyes and that Celtic Warrior with flaming red hair, broad shoulders and green cat-like eyes which, like those of his younger friend and "brother," was taking in the new world which lay before them as quick sand sucking under anything that came upon its surface.

The sight which the lads were drawing into their very being was once a fortress, then a theater and now part of it was turned into an immigrant receiving station. It stood at the tip of southern Manhattan in the area known as the Battery. Until Ellis Island was established as the permanent receiving station, Castle Garden would serve to filter out those who sought entry into the United States or to accept them by issuing the would-be immigrant a small piece of paper on which was written "loose" in the status box. This would indicate that the person was free to become a resident and strive for citizenship as well. Neither the lads nor the lass or for that matter the leader of their little entourage from the Cushla Machree, one whom the three admired with unconditional love, Father Thomas O'Malley OSA (Order of St. Augustine) had any notion of what was to be thrust upon them once they entered through the gates of the granite block fortress as part of a long line of weary, destitute and deprived immigrants.

Statue of St. Patrick in Old St. Patrick Cathedral, New York City

References:

"The Bowery" by Eric Ferrara

"New York's First Cathedral" by Joyce Mendelsohn

"No Easy Road. The Early Years of the Augustinians in the United States"
Arthur J. Ennis O.S.A.

http://en.wikipedia.org

www.yourirish.com

Msgr. John Ahern
Old St. Patrick's Cathedral
263 Mulberry St.
New York City, NY 10012
Http://www.oldcathedral.org

Villa Nova University, Philadelphia, PA
The Heritage Room of the Province of St. Thomas of Villanova

Rev. Michael Slattery OSA, Pastor
 St. Augustine Church
423 N. Lawrence St (4th and Vine St.)
 Philadelphia, PA 19106

Methodist Church of St. George
235 N. Fourth St.
Philadelphia, PA 19106

St. Nicholas Collegiate Church
Galway, Ireland
Archdeacon Gary Hasting
http://www.stnicholas.ie

St. Augustine Church
Galway, Ireland

Inishbofin Tourism
Inishbofin, Ireland

Aran Islands Tourism
Inishmor, Aran Islands, Ireland

Cathedral of Sts. Peter and Paul
18th St. and Benjamin Franklin Parkway
Philadelphia, PA 19103

Philadelphia Public Library
Philadelphia, PA

www.belleek.com
Company Information and History

http://www.qub.ac.uk/irishhistorylive

www.bing.com

Acknowledgements:

With a grateful heart to the following:

To my wife, Donna, and our children: Ron(Tricia), Jana (Chris Smith), Kathleen (Mark Timler), John(Elena), Richard and our grandchildren:
Olivia Colaianni, Arthur Colaianni V, Connor Smith, Riley Smith, Meghan Timler, and Mack Timler without whom this book and my other books would not have been created.

My sister-in-law, Nancy Shields for Editing services.

Special thanks to our son, John Colaianni, who served as Illustrator and creator of the book covers.

My mother-in-law, Ruth Dooley.

In memory of my mother, Wanda Colaianni.

To my sister, Janice and her family for their support of my work.

About the Author: Arthur Cola

Arthur Cola was born in Chicago in the "Little Italy" neighborhood of the near west side. His family moved to Oak Park, IL where he attended Oak Park-River Forest High School. While attending Loyola University, Chicago, he met his future wife Donna Shields. Together they have five adult children and six grandchildren. He, his wife and family now live in Wisconsin.

He has been an educator for 35 years. During that time he served as a teacher of history and as a school Principal. He received his Master's Degree from the University of Southern Mississippi and post graduate work at the University of St. Mary of the Lake, Archdiocese of Chicago and Archdiocese of Milwaukee.

His research for his novels has brought him to Italy, Ireland, England and Wales and throughout the United States. He conducts tours based on his novels to Ireland and Italy.

Besides his novels, he has a children's Christmas story book titled:

Papa and the Gingerbread Man. ISBN: 0-9789423-0-2

His novels may be divided into family friendly tales:

Papa and the Leprechaun King: ISBN: 978-1-78176-087-1
A magical tale of American tourists traveling in Ireland who get caught up in a 1500 year old mystery as they meet the King of the Leprechauns.

The Shamrock Crown: ISBN: 978-1-78299-196-0
A family in Wisconsin is summoned to Ireland and the United Kingdom by the Leprechaun King to save the most precious relics of Ancient Camelot. As they enter the quest they bring King Arthur and the Knights of the Round Table into the 21st Century.

Stolen Christmas: ISBN: 978-1-78299-439-8
A tale of different cultures coming together to experience a Christmas miracle. It's a David and Goliath story in which a boy tries to save his Church from demolition by trying to stop Christmas from coming and in the process involves his sister and her secret boyfriend. Into their lives comes a white bearded stranger who brings a pastor, their families and an entire city together to experience Christmas love.

His adult novels also suitable for older teens include:

The Stone Cutter Genius: ISBN: 978-1-78299-244-8
Set against the backdrop of the most famous artist of the
Renaissance era, the legend of the Magi Ring comes to life
in the 21st century as Professor Colonna and his two teen
sons accept a quest to solve the mystery of the Ring said to
possess supernatural powers.

The Brooch: ISBN: 978-1-78176-542-5
The lives of six sons collide in a tale of love and revenge
which takes them on an adventure which begins in Britain
and takes them to Italy. There they seek to find a 500 year
old jewelry piece designed by Michelangelo for the only
woman he ever loved.

New Series: **The Doonagore Theft Trilogy**

A tale of three teens sent to America to escape the
devastation of famine ravaged Ireland. There they mature as
they encounter prejudice and anti-Catholicism and are drawn
into the American Civil War. Their lives become entangled
in a triangle relationship of friendship which grows into love
as they cope with prejudice, loyalty, war and love which
binds friend to friend, man to woman and "brother" to
"brother."

Summer of 2014: Book One: **Journey of Three Pure
Hearts**
Spring of 2015: Book Two: **Wonder and Disillusionment
in America**
Christmastime of 2015: Book Three: **Civil War and
Rebirth**

Author's web site:
http://www.legendarytalesofarthurcola.com
Email: arthurcola@yahoo.com

Books may be ordered at www.feedaread.com and
www.amazon.com/kindle

Author's Note on **Book One: Journey of Three Pure Hearts**

Though this story is a work of fiction, many of the events and places mentioned are historically accurate.

The Cushla Machree was an actual ship which sailed from Galway to New York. However that voyage of record began on March 1, 1849. It's also historically accurate to mention that many of the ships with immigrants made several trips to Britain, Canada or the United States. I have chosen a summer voyage to better blend with the time frame that I sought.

Momai and *Dadai* are Irish language terms meaning: Mommy and Daddy
Da is also an Irish language term for Dad or Father.

Pog ma thon is an Irish language phrase meaning: "kiss my arse."

"mi" from the Old Irish and Old English meaning me or mine.

Doonagore Castle: The Doonagore Castle is an actual historical castle overlooking Doolin in County Clare. All historical references to it are true in the story. However it is legitimately privately owned by a family in the present day. Any references in the story other than the historical background are fictional and any similarities to persons or the castle itself are coincidental in nature.

LATIN TERMS:

In nomine Patris, et Fillii and Spiritu Sancti
(In the name of the Father and of the Son and of the Holy Spirit).

Hymn of St. Thomas Aquinas: Panis Angelicus (Bread of Angels)
Panis angelicus (Bread of Angels)
Fit panis hominum (Is made bread for mankind)
Dat panis coelicus (Gifted bread of Heaven)
Figuris terminum (Of all imaginings the end)

O res mirabilis (Oh, thing miraculous)
Manducat Dominum (The body of God will nourish)
Pauper,servus et humilis (the poor, the servile, the humble)

Pater Noster (Our Father)